NEWCOMER'S HANDBOOK®

FOR MOVING TO AND LIVING IN THE

USA

1ST EDITION

D1048574

FIRST BOOKS®
6750 SW FRANKLIN STREET
SUITE A
PORTLAND, OR 97223-2542
USA
WWW.FIRSTBOOKS.COM
503.968.6777

Author: Mike Livingston

Editor: Jeremy Solomon

Proofreading: Wendy Dunham, Louis Solomon, Linda Weinerman

Design and production: Masha Shubin

ISBN: 0-912301-57-0

Printed in the USA

Published by First Books, 6750 SW Franklin Street, Portland, OR 97223-2542, USA, tel 503 968 6777, www.firstbooks.com.

WHAT READERS ARE SAYING ABOUT NEWCOMER'S HANDBOOKS:

I recently got a copy of your Newcomer's Handbook for Chicago, and wanted to let you know how invaluable it was for my move. I must have consulted it a dozen times a day preparing for my move. It helped me find my way around town, find a place to live, and so many other things. My only suggestion is a more detailed map of the area. It's just a small gripe however, as your book helped me so much. Thanks.

—Mike L.
Chicago, Illinois

Excellent reading [Newcomer's Handbook for San Francisco and the Bay Area] ... it seems balanced and trustworthy. One of the very best guides if you are considering moving/relocation. Way above the usual tourist crap.

—Gunnar E.
Stockholm, Sweden

I was very impressed with the latest edition of the Newcomer's Handbook for Los Angeles. It is well organized, concise and up-to date. I would recommend this book to anyone considering a move to Los Angeles.

—Jannette L.
Attorney Recruiting Administrator for
a large Los Angeles law firm

I recently moved to Atlanta from San Francisco, and LOVE the Newcomer's Handbook for Atlanta. It has been an invaluable resource – it's helped me find everything from a neighborhood in which to live to the local hardware store. I look something up in it everyday, and know I will continue to use it to find things long after I'm no longer a newcomer. And if I ever decide to move again, your book will be the first thing I buy for my next destination.

—Courtney R.
Atlanta, Georgia

In looking to move to the Boston area, a potential employer in that area gave me a copy of the Newcomer's Handbook for Boston. It's a great book that's very comprehensive, outlining good and bad points about each neighborhood in the Boston area. Very helpful in helping me decide where to move.

—no name given
(online submit form)

My dog (Sandy) and I are in the (slow) process of moving from Santa Rosa, CA to Seattle. It [Newcomer's Handbook for Seattle] is *vastly* superior to all the other travel guides I was picking up at the library – this is a "living guide." Not only full of all the practical (phone service, cable, moving advice, etc.) and vital (doctors, crime, weather) but also the *fun!* It seems impossible to have included so much helpful information in such a well planned, readable book, but you did it.

—Lisa S. and Sandy
Santa Rosa, California

CONTENTS

CONTENTS

HOW TO USE THIS BOOK

Welcome to the United States. You've arrived in a nation of nearly 300 million people—people of every nationality and religion, rich and poor, friendly and unfriendly. It would be useful to have an instruction manual for living here; unfortunately, U.S. culture and society is far too complicated to explain in a single book. You should be wary of any generalizations, including those in this book.

But this book will help you know what to expect as you explore and adjust. It will not try to explain everything there is to know—even if any single book could do that, it would take all the fun out of exploring a new country. Instead, it will give you an overview of some important subjects and tell you where to get more detailed information, especially through the internet.

There are two resources that will make this book much more useful to you. When you move to a new home in the United States—and this is just as true for native-born U.S. citizens as for international newcomers—your most valuable resources (besides the local **Newcomer's Handbook®** city guide) are the local **telephone directories** and the local **public library**. Get acquainted with these as soon as you can—ideally, within your first few days in the United States.

TELEPHONE DIRECTORIES

In most cities, there are two separate directories (often simply called *phone books*) published by the main local telephone company: the **Yellow Pages**, listing businesses that pay to have their phone numbers published (and sometimes additional information about their products and services), and the **White Pages**, listing the phone numbers of residential and business subscribers in the area. The **Blue Pages**, a small section within one of the local phone books, list the phone numbers of local, state, and national government agencies.

YELLOW PAGES

The Yellow Pages list businesses by category, with businesses arranged in alphabetical order within each category. The categories themselves appear in alphabetical order, too—so, for example, you can find accountants listed alphabetically, then bakeries listed alphabetically, then candy stores listed alphabetically, and then (after you visit the bakeries and candy stores) dentists. There's also a **consumer information** section in front of the Yellow Pages that typically includes:

- **maps** of the area;
- phone numbers you can call to get **recorded information** such as weather reports, news updates, and advice about a wide variety of products and services;
- information about local **public transportation** and regional **airports, train stations,** and intercity **bus terminals**;
- a directory of **charitable organizations** that help people in crisis, such as depressed teens or drug addicts; and
- information about local **parks, museums, and cultural attractions**, including seating charts for local theaters and sports arenas.

WHITE PAGES

The White Pages are divided into *residential* and *business* listings, and the **business White Pages** are sometimes included in the same volume as the Yellow Pages—but you can spot them at a glance, because the pages themselves really are yellow and white. In the **residential White Pages,** every person who has a residential phone number is listed along with his or her phone number and sometimes his or her home address. (The address is included in case two or more people have the same name.) Names are arranged in alphabetical order by the first letter of the *family name* (last name)—for example:

BUSH, GEORGE W.

CLINTON, BILL

EISENHOWER, DWIGHT DAVID

LINCOLN, ABRAHAM

TRUMAN, HARRY S.

Note that a residential phone number means a number for a traditional landline phone hooked up to a wire; cellular and other wireless phone numbers are *not* listed in the phone book. Also, people who do not wish to be listed in the phone book can pay a small fee to have their names and numbers excluded.

In the business White Pages, every business with a phone number is listed in alphabetical order by name—not by category. (Nonprofit organizations, places of worship, private schools, and other institutions that are not really businesses *are* listed in the business White Pages. The only institutions that are listed separately are government agencies.)

In the front of the White Pages, you'll find a **consumer information** section that includes detailed instructions for setting up home phone service and getting faulty phone lines repaired. This section also includes:

- numbers for **emergency services**—police, fire department, ambulance, poison control, mental health crisis, and electrical, gas, and water utility emergencies;*
- a list of **zip codes** (postal codes) in the area;
- **international dialing codes**;
- a map of U.S. **time zones**; and
- information about **recycling** and **trash collection** in your jurisdiction.

BLUE PAGES

The Blue Pages, usually a small section found near the front of the phone book or in the middle, list the phone numbers of **government agencies**. Local government offices are listed in alphabetical order, followed by state government offices in alphabetical order, and then U.S. government offices in alphabetical order. Public schools and many parks, museums, and other cultural institutions are government property and can be found in the Blue Pages.

PUBLIC LIBRARIES

Every community in the United States has a local public library that *everybody can use for free*. These institutions are funded and operated by local governments and are considered an essential community resource. Once you have a fixed address, you can register for a free library card that allows you to borrow books for several weeks at a time. Many libraries also lend recorded music and movies. But even without a library card, you're welcome to visit any public library and use any of its materials on the premises. Libraries are especially important to newcomers because they provide **free access to the internet**

---

* In most areas, the all-purpose emergency number for police, fire, and ambulance service is **911**.

• • • • • • • • • • • • •

ABOUT IMMIGRATION

This book is intended to help you make sense of the country once you get here. An introduction to immigration policies and procedures would fill another whole book—and it does: *The Immigration Handbook* (3rd edition) by Henry Liebman, published by **First Books**. To order, call 503-968-6777 or visit www.firstbooks.com.

• • • • • • • • • • • • •

(though you may have to get on a waiting list for computer time, grab a good book, relax, and wait until your name is called).

Public libraries have thousands of fiction and nonfiction books that local residents may borrow for several weeks at a time—and, perhaps more important, an extensive collection of **reference books** that *cannot* be taken from the library, so they're always available when you need to look up some information in a dictionary, encyclopedia, almanac, atlas, law book, or government publication. Reference collections also include authoritative guides to dozens of topics: etiquette, business, home and auto repair, pets, world religions, art, music, sports, travel, and more. Most libraries have extensive collections of **local interest** materials—information about government services, consumer protection, schools, health services, recreation programs, public transportation, and local history. And there is usually a **reference librarian** on duty who can help you find the information you need, no matter how specific or obscure. Many libraries also offer a variety of short **classes and seminars** for people who want to learn more about buying a home, applying to college, investing money to save for retirement, and other *life skills*, as well as **children's programs** such as storytelling or book clubs.

GETTING LOCAL INFORMATION

This book is a general overview of customs, institutions, and society in the United States. Most of the information presented here is just general background information, because the details will vary from one state to another and from one local jurisdiction (city or county) to another. A lot of the brief overviews in this book, therefore, will refer you to the Blue Pages to find the agency that can give you the right specific information for the area where you live. You can also find detailed information about your own jurisdiction on the internet. On page 59, there's a list of the two-letter postal abbreviations for each state; to find state government sites on the World Wide Web, use this standard address form with the state's two-letter abbreviation in the blank:

www.state. __ .us.

You can also find federal and state government agencies by topic at **www.firstgov.gov**, the U.S. government's all-purpose web directory. To find local government web sites for your city, town, or county, visit **www.officialcitysites.org** or **www.citysearch.com**. Many state and local government web sites feature—in addition to detailed information about every government agency—information for newcomers to help you get acquainted with the area. Explore... and enjoy!

CHAPTER ONE

America is too rich in contradictions for any definition of it to be possible. For every attitude that is supposed to be distinctively American one can find an opposite stance that is no less so.

— *John Gray, economist, United Kingdom; from "What We Think of America," a collection of essays in the British magazine* Granta, *Spring 2002*

The 2000 Census of population counted more than 281 million people in the United States. About 31 million were born in other countries. Another 1.2 million immigrants arrive every year, and 5.5% of eligible voters are naturalized immigrants. Only about 2% of the population traces its ancestry to the indigenous people of North America; the rest of us are all descendants of fairly recent immigrants, each from a nation whose expatriates bring along their own traditions, customs, beliefs, arts, and stories. In fact, the one safe generalization to make about "the American people" is that we're diverse; our culture is one derived from many. On the $1 bill and the penny, you'll find the Latin words *e pluribus unum*—"out of many, one." U.S. culture is often described as a *melting pot* in which elements of many different cultures are blended into a new culture reflecting a multitude of influences and drawing strength and character from their diversity.

It's almost impossible to make any completely accurate statements about a population so big and so diverse. The United States is a prosperous nation by many standards, but there are far more poor Americans than rich ones. There's a greater variety of religious groups here than in any other nation. We *tend* to be motivated by money, but a majority of us give money to charity or do some kind of unpaid volunteer work for the benefit of our communities. We *tend* to be patriotic, but we often criticize our government and mistrust our elected leaders—and then roughly half of us don't bother to vote. If you travel around the United States or live in a cosmopolitan city, you will hear a dazzling variety of accents and manners of speech. It's fair to say that most American children, rich and poor, from all over the country, eat peanut butter and jelly sandwiches for lunch more often than anything else; but then, some people are allergic to peanuts. It's worth repeating: Be wary of generalizations.

Here are some common perceptions of the United States and its people—and a look at the grains of truth at the heart of each stereotype:

Americans are wealthy. When 8-year-old Victoria Kao came to the United States from Taiwan, she expected to find "a shining land where everyone had chandeliers and spiral staircases." Sorry, but that sounds more like a fancy hotel than a typical American home. Yes, there are an estimated 1.7 million millionaires and nearly 300 billionaires. But it is also estimated that there are more than half a million homeless people; 35 million classified by the government as poor; and 41 million who do not have any health insurance—including at least 10 million who cannot afford basic health care. Moreover, every year, the rich get richer (income of the wealthiest 20% of households has increased by 21% since 1970) and the poor get poorer (income of the poorest 20% of households has decreased by 30% since 1970). According to a 1998 report by the Levy Economics Institute at Barnard College, the richest 1% of the U.S. population owns 38% of the wealth and the richest 10% owns 71%, while the poorest 40% owns just 0.2%. And in 1970, the average corporate chief executive was paid 41 times as much as the average factory worker; by 1999, the executive's pay was 419 times the factory worker's.

So it is not a land of universal wealth, not by far. Arguably the United States is a land of universal *opportunity*—family background and national origin do not officially restrain anyone from getting a good education, working in a trade or profession of choice, and earning money. However, there are many people for whom "equal opportunity" is just a theory. An African-American child born to an unmarried mother in a neighborhood with low median income is not as likely to gain wealth or power in U.S. society as a white child born to a

• • • • • • • • • • • • • •

WHERE ARE ALL THESE IMMIGRANTS?

The Center for Immigration Studies reports that five metropolitan areas—Los Angeles, New York, San Francisco, Miami, and Chicago—each have more than a million foreign-born residents, and together with Washington and Baltimore, these areas are home to nearly 53% of the nation's immigrants. California and New York alone have more than 12 million immigrants; in California, more than 25% of the population is foreign-born, and in New York and Florida, nearly 20%. Immigrants also account for at least one in 10 residents of Hawaii, Nevada, New Jersey, Arizona, Massachusetts, Texas, and the District of Columbia.

• • • • • • • • • • • • • •

married couple in an affluent neighborhood; in fact, the African-American child from such a background is, if male, statistically more likely to end up in prison than in college. Anywhere in the world, if you grow up surrounded by poverty, it's hard to gain a foothold in any other way of life. It *can* be done here, but the so-called "Land of Opportunity" is still figuring out how to give everyone a level playing field.

Americans all own guns. A majority of us don't, but it's hard to get exact figures. Law-abiding people who own guns for hunting, sport, or personal protection obtain licenses from the state and buy firearms from licensed dealers who register each gun's unique markings with the government. Criminals, of course, do not. Statistics compiled by the Federal Bureau of Investigation suggest that 44% of the population owns at least one gun. (Many people who own guns have more than one. The Bureau of Alcohol, Tobacco, Firearms & Explosives estimates that there are nearly 202 million guns in the country—including 67 million handguns. At the rate of one per person, more than 2/3 of the people in the country would be armed.)

Americans are Christian. Well, many are. Researchers at the City University of New York did a study in 2001 of religious beliefs found in the United States and estimated that more than 159 million adults here (77%) profess some form of Christianity. But they also estimated that the country is home to 2.8 million Jews, 1.1 million Muslims, 1.1 million Buddhists, and 30 million adults who consider themselves nonreligious, atheist, or agnostic. The 10 largest faith communities in the United States also include Hindus; Unitarian Universalists; Wiccan and Pagan groups; spiritualists; followers of Native American (indigenous) religion; and Baha'is. And dozens of religious communities can be found in the United States in smaller numbers. Even Christianity is a diverse category—just over half of the U.S. Christian community is Protestant and just under a quarter is Roman Catholic, and other Christian groups include evangelical, Mormon, Orthodox, and nondenominational sects. (See Chapter 16 for more about the role of religion in American society.)

Americans are loud. Sometimes, sure. The 2000 Census found that 80% of us live in urban areas, amid the constant clatter of traffic and crowds. Most of us grew up in homes with television and amplified music. We talk over the background noise of our modern habitat. But you'll find that most people take their cues from their surroundings; in a quiet café, or a library, most Americans do not behave the same way they would on a crowded bus. Please don't mistake a handful of noisy tourists in your home country for appointed ambassadors of U.S. culture. For what it's worth, one of the most influential American philosophers, Henry David Thoreau, wrote about the value of quiet reflection and meditation after deliberately spending a year alone in a cabin in the woods by Walden Pond in Massachusetts. "The winds which passed over my dwelling," he wrote, "were such as sweep over the ridges of mountains, bearing the broken strains, or celestial parts only, of terrestrial music. The morning wind forever blows, the poem of creation is uninterrupted; but few are the ears that hear it." (Of course, that sentiment might not be very comforting when some loudmouth is talking on a cellular phone in a fine restaurant—but many Americans would agree that such behavior is rude and boorish.)

Americans only speak English. Approximately 18% of the population over the age of 5 speaks another language at home. More than 28 million speak Spanish; 2 million speak Chinese languages; and French, Italian, German, Tagalog, Vietnamese, and Korean are each spoken in roughly a million households. Most of these people, however, are immigrants or the U.S.-born children of immigrants; most children born to American parents and raised in the United States are educated in English only. Most Americans study a second language (usually Spanish or French) for a year or two during their schooling, but relatively few Americans are fluent in two or more languages. Most Americans will expect you to speak at least basic English, and many will become impatient or frustrated if you don't. It is a strange American habit to speak loudly and slowly to a person who does not seem to understand English, as if an unfamiliar language is easier to understand when the person speaking it sounds annoyed. Fortunately, if you ever need help from a government agency or a hospital, the staff can provide an interpreter. And you'll generally find a much more diverse population—a more colorful tapestry of languages as well as ethnicities, religions, cuisines, and music—in big cities than in smaller towns and the countryside.

Of course, Americans make plenty of unfair generalizations too. You will probably encounter, from time to time, some stereotypes and misconceptions about recent immigrants in general or your home country in particular. Some people will welcome you with not only respect, but warmth and appreciation; others will be unfair and insensitive. There are almost 300 million different individuals here to deal with. We often speak in generalizations even though we *know* they're flawed, because it's so hard to make precise statements about such a big melting pot. We even persist in referring to our nation as "America" and its people as "Americans," to the known annoyance of the inhabitants of South America, Central America, Mexico, and Canada. So please pardon a few oversimplifications and lapses of precision; we don't mean to offend anyone.

O say, does that that star-spangled banner yet wave
o'er the land of the free and the home of the brave?

— From the U.S. national anthem

Perhaps the biggest and most important difference between the United States and most other countries is the explicit constitutional protection of individual freedom. It's all spelled out in our first ten laws, the **Bill of Rights** attached to the Constitution: You can practice any religion you want, or none at all, and no government agency or private employer is allowed to discriminate against you because of it. You can criticize the government all you want, in private and in public, verbally and in print, as long as you don't call for violent insurrection or threaten anyone with physical harm. If you think the president is a stupid liar and the mayor is a lazy crook, you're welcome to say so. In fact, though it's no way to make friends here, the Constitution even guarantees you the right to burn the flag that symbolizes that freedom.

You don't need permission to travel within the country, and you don't need to register with the police, unless you've been convicted of a serious crime. With just a few exceptions, you're free to buy and sell any property you wish, though you are responsible for paying applicable taxes on property or transactions. Your children are entitled to attend your local public school for free.

If you are questioned or detained by the police, you have certain rights—most notably, the government cannot force you to confess to any crime or to make any statements that might implicate you in a crime. Persons suspected of a crime are also entitled to legal counsel and usually entitled to a prompt, public trial with a jury of ordinary citizens.

Though we do complain about our government, it's always the government we chose. Every adult U.S. citizen (beginning at age 18) has the right to vote unless convicted of a serious crime, and all appointed government officials—including military commanders and police chiefs—answer to elected civilian authorities.

SINCE SEPTEMBER 11

The government has been keeping a closer eye on individuals since September 11, 2001, when the terrorist attacks at the World Trade

Center and the Pentagon permanently changed the nation's approach
to security. Even earlier, after the 1995 domestic terrorist bombing of
a federal office building in Oklahoma City, many public buildings installed metal detectors and security checkpoints. You and your bags
may be searched at the entrance to certain buildings as well as at airports and train or bus stations. And you may be questioned about
certain activities that are not illegal but "suspicious," such as taking
photos or writing notes near federal buildings that are not tourist landmarks. It is also harder to change your visa status once you're here.

Other recent changes in government policy remain controversial and may yet be ruled unconstitutional by the courts. For example,
some aliens have been detained without being charged with a crime,
and the government has classified them as "enemy combatants" on
the basis of alleged connections to groups that may have planned or
conducted terrorist acts against U.S. citizens. In June 2003, the *Washington Post* reported that minor technical violations of immigration
law, such as errors in visa paperwork, are more likely to draw close
scrutiny now—especially with regard to citizens of predominantly
Muslim countries. And since January 2004, most aliens who enter or
leave the United States by air or sea with a nonimmigrant visa must
be photographed and fingerprinted, and the Department of Homeland Security is authorized to collect other physical identifying information (such as eye scans, handwriting samples, and voice samples).
In a few cases, the government has even questioned some aliens on
the basis of national origin or ethnicity alone. But in general, compared to much of the world, the United States remains an extraordi-
narily open society.

You do need to carry an appropriate identity document—a **passport** or **Alien Registration Card** (green card)—and show it to any
law enforcement officer or immigration officer on request. Citizens,
too, are expected to carry a driver's license or other government-
issued identity card (commonly called **ID**—say "eye-dee"). Anyone
can be required to show ID when:

- entering guarded buildings, including some private office buildings;
- purchasing airline, rail, or intercity bus tickets;
- opening a bank account or withdrawing cash from a bank;
- obtaining prescription medicines;
- renting a car or moving van; or
- applying for a job.

You may also be asked to show ID when purchasing regulated goods such as alcoholic beverages or tobacco, or entering an establishment where alcoholic beverages are served. In this case, the merchant is not interested in your name, but in proof of age. (See Chapter 6.)

MILITARY SERVICE

The U.S. armed forces are currently an all-volunteer service; there has been no draft (conscription) since 1973. However, the President can order a draft should the need arise, and almost all male residents of the United States between ages 18 and 26 are required by law to *register* with the **Selective Service System**, the agency that would oversee conscription if so ordered. (Aliens with student or tourist visas are not required to register, nor are diplomatic or consular personnel or their families. But permanent residents, refugees, and persons receiving asylum must register.) The government *rarely* prosecutes individuals who fail to register, but it does deny their applications for government benefits (such as financial aid for college) or citizenship.

In the event of a draft, individuals who refuse on religious or moral grounds to bear arms or serve in the armed forces may ask to be certified as **conscientious objectors** and be assigned to alternative (civilian) service in the national interest. (This accommodation is available only to individuals categorically opposed to war—not to individuals with political objections to a particular war.) Even if drafted, some aliens are exempt from military service, depending on treaties and reciprocal policies in effect with their country of origin.

To register with Selective Service, ask for a registration form at your local post office. For more information, call 847-688-6888 or visit www.sss.gov.

HOW THE GOVERNMENT IS ORGANIZED

When we say "the government," we usually mean the federal **executive branch**, which is headed by the President and enforces the nation's laws; but the **legislative branch** and **judicial branch** are just as powerful. The legislature, or Congress, is divided into the Senate and the House of Representatives. Each state elects two Senators for a term of six years. The 435 seats in the House of Representatives (often just called "the House") are allotted to the states on the basis of state population, and members are elected to a term of two years. Each

Representative serves a particular district, while Senators are elected statewide—so every citizen is served in Congress by two Senators and one Representative. (Representatives are also known as *congressmen* and *congresswomen*.) The President is elected to a four-year term and cannot serve more than two terms.

The President commands the military and appoints judges, ambassadors, and secretaries (ministers), but cannot tell Congress what to do. Congress cannot negotiate with other nations, but must approve treaties and presidential appointments—and Congress controls the government's money. The courts cannot detain or punish anybody who has not been prosecuted by agents of the executive branch under laws made by the legislature. And, though it has never happened, Congress can remove a President who violates the law. The **separation of powers,** with each branch of the government having certain limited roles and responsibilities, results in a system of **checks and balances**—each branch of the government can prevent the other branches from overstepping their constitutional powers.

FEDERALISM

State governments each have a structure similar to the federal government, with three distinct branches—a state legislature, state courts, and an executive branch headed by a governor. Under the principle of *federalism,* the national government's power is limited to roles specifically listed in the Constitution, and any other government functions are left to the states to fulfill individually or to *delegate* to local governments of each city and county.

The federal government is responsible for foreign policy, currency, commerce, defense, and certain basic levels of consumer protection, environmental protection, health and welfare, highway construction, patents and trademarks, and other functions listed in the Constitution. State governments are responsible for laws concerning marriage, abortion rights, traffic, unemployment insurance, and education standards. Local governments are responsible for laws concerning housing, school enrollment, parking, and smoking. (And every level of government can collect taxes on the income you earn in the United States.) The Constitution requires states to extend *full faith and credit* to papers issued by the government of any other state; in other words, a driver's license, a marriage or divorce, or a high school diploma (finishing certificate) issued by one state is valid in every state.

THE CENSUS

The Constitution directs the government to count the population of the United States every 10 years in order to determine the number of seats each state will have in the House of Representatives. The national census is also used to estimate the need for a variety of government programs and services. Every house, every apartment, every remote shack, every inhabited cave in the mountains, every abandoned railway car with someone sleeping in it, every shelter for the homeless, every dwelling place of any kind is supposed to receive a census questionnaire either by mail or from a census agent. *Every person living in the United States at the time of the census* is to be counted—temporary residents on visas, newborn babies, even illegal aliens.

You are required by law to answer the Census Bureau's questions—truthfully, completely, and before the stated deadline. However, *your answers are strictly confidential and no other government agency can ever see the information you provide*—not the police, not the USCIS, nobody. The Census Bureau compiles individual and household information and provides Congress and the public with statistical reports about the U.S. population and the population of individual states, cities, and counties—it does not

All high government officials are either elected or appointed by an elected executive. Lower-ranking government workers are career civil servants who keep their jobs as governments come and go, so they're supposedly insulated from politics. **Warning:** *It is a serious crime to offer a bribe or gratuity to any government employee, or for a government employee to accept one.* (One lawyer who emigrated from Taiwan as an adult—and who now works for the U.S. government—says one of the hardest adjustments to make was to a new way of doing business in his profession: expecting the authorities to be honest. "It took a while to get used to the fact that you're *not* supposed to bribe people here. Other places I've been, it was expected.")

DEBATE & DISSENT

Americans value and exercise the right to criticize their own government. It is not considered disloyal—or even unpatriotic—to disagree with the nation's leaders and to march or rally in support of particular causes. Minority views are understood to be the "loyal opposition" and are a welcome and valued part of the democratic process. The U.S. Constitution establishes the most stable system of government in the modern world; no matter how bitterly an election is contested, everyone lives peacefully with the results.

POLITICAL PARTIES

THE CENSUS, CONT.

U.S. politics is dominated by the Democratic and Republican parties, though there are actually dozens of smaller parties that play a role in local politics in some parts of the country. The nation's founders did not anticipate the emergence of a two-party system, and indeed it arose only after the Civil War of 1861-1865. *In general,* the Democratic Party takes a liberal position in favor of government-funded social programs, a regulated market, and the taxes to pay for such policies, and the conservative Republican Party promotes low taxes, deregulation, and a minimal role for government.

reveal your personal information to anyone. (Not for 70 years, anyway. Eventually, historic census records are released to the public for the benefit of scholarly research.) Most of the statistical information in this book is derived from the 2000 Census.

A growing percentage of U.S. voters decline to join any political party, or join one of the minor parties. For example, there's the Green, Socialist Workers, and Labor parties to the left of center, and the Taxpayers and Constitution parties on the right. The Reform and Libertarian parties, among others, appeal to dissatisfied voters on the left and right alike, united by a belief that the people should rely less on the government and more on the private sector.

But political parties do not play the same role in U.S. government as they do in parliamentary systems. Voters vote for individual candidates, not for a party, and can vote for anyone they like—regardless of their own party affiliation or the candidate's. In 2002, there were two state governors and a U.S. senator who did not belong to any political party. It is not only possible, but fairly common, for the executive branch to be controlled by one party and the legislature to be controlled by another.

SOME CONTROVERSIES

So, what do Americans debate? Both major political parties and nearly all elected officials believe in capitalism; a generally free market with a few ground rules to protect public health and safety; civilian control of the military; and the right of corporations to be treated as persons under the law and to enjoy the same freedom as individuals. The fundamental system of government has not been altered since it was established in 1789—even the states that rebelled during the Civil War founded a structurally similar government for their confederacy. So what, in the United States, is the difference between liberals and conservatives?

Some of the persistent political controversies of the late 20th and early 21st centuries, briefly summarized, include:

Reproductive rights. A woman's right to abort a pregnancy is one of most emotionally charged debates in U.S. politics, and many voters choose candidates almost exclusively on the basis of this single issue. Under federal law, abortion is legal in the early stages of pregnancy and each state may set its own laws allowing, restricting, or banning abortion in advanced stages of pregnancy. Candidates for President are asked whether they would appoint federal judges who support existing law or judges who would seek to restrict states' freedom in this matter. Generally, most Democrats are *pro-choice* (they support abortion rights) and many Republicans oppose abortion rights; they call themselves *pro-life* and rivals call them *anti-choice*. There is little or no controversy, however, about the right to obtain and use contraceptives (birth control)—a right guaranteed to everyone in the United States since the 1970s.

Capital punishment. The United States is one of only a handful of countries that still impose the death penalty in some criminal cases. The federal government rarely executes anybody, but several states carry out dozens of executions every year; other states have banned capital punishment for crimes tried in state courts. This issue transcends party labels, though opponents of capital punishment are somewhat more likely to find allies among Democrats than among Republicans.

Gun control. The Constitution expressly protects the individual's right to own weapons. The nation's founders considered this an important means of limiting government power. (The American Revolution was fought largely by volunteers who used their own hunting muskets to repel the British army.) But today, 10,000 people are killed and half a million injured or threatened by criminals with guns in the United States every year. State laws generally require gun owners to get a license from the state and register with the police, and persons convicted of serious crimes may lose their right to own guns. Some states don't allow people to carry concealed weapons, and some states require a waiting period between the purchase and acquisition of a new gun (in order to prevent people from buying a gun when they're angry or upset). Generally, Democrats favor tough restrictions on gun sales and Republicans argue that such laws place an unfair burden on law-abiding people—while criminals will always find a way to obtain guns.

Privatization. Most Americans agree that the federal government is too big and too complex, with an inefficient and wasteful bureaucracy. But we don't agree on a solution. Republicans and conservative Democrats believe that the private sector operates more efficiently than the government, so they favor hiring private contractors with government money to administer various public programs. Contractors run some social service agencies, provide training for government workers, and even operate some federal prisons. City governments often hire private companies to clean and maintain the streets, provide emergency medical services, and enforce parking regulations. Liberals condemn this practice as an improper delegation of the government's duties, and argue that it makes it harder to hold the government accountable for the quality of services.

Environmental protection. Most Americans claim to be concerned about pollution, global warming, ozone depletion, habitat loss, and depletion of natural resources. However, few Americans are willing to make lifestyle changes to address these problems. And many Americans fear that increased environmental protection could cost businesses a lot of money and lead to the loss of jobs. Many Democrats and some Republicans favor expanded environmental protection laws; most Republicans and many Democrats say we have too much regulation already.

Globalization. Every President since 1980 has further deregulated international trade, to the delight of the business world and the concern of labor unions, consumers, and environmentalists. Modern trade agreements have undermined U.S. laws regarding various pesticides and chemicals, endangered species, and labor standards, and have made it easier for multinational corporations to abandon U.S. communities and move jobs away—often overseas—in search of cheap labor and permissive regulations. Not strictly a partisan issue, this trend toward deregulation pits labor unions and environmentalists on one hand against business-oriented Democrats and Republicans on the other. And it brings protesters out marching in the streets whenever the World Trade Organization or the International Monetary Fund has a meeting in the United States.

Campaign finance reform. Most politicians fund their campaigns with money donated by industry groups with an interest in particular legislation; ordinary citizens cannot hope to donate as much money to political campaigns as, for example, an association of real estate developers or pharmaceutical companies. Many Americans believe that campaign contributions buy a lawmaker's attention and interest—or, in effect, that most legislators' votes are basically for sale. Congress is perpetually considering new policies to limit the amount or source of campaign contributions. Critics point out, and the courts have agreed, that such laws unconstitutionally restrict the freedom of speech and expression—under the First Amendment, a donation of money is a form of expression. This debate does not reflect party labels, but rather a division between elite political insiders and working people.

Taxes. This is a simple and perpetual debate: most Democrats are willing to raise taxes to pay for social services and most Republicans want to reduce taxes and government spending. Everybody wants to simplify the tax code, but few leaders have offered fair and sensible plans to do so. And some Democrats want the tax code to be *progressive,* with the rich paying a greater percentage of their income than working people; Republicans tend to believe that tax cuts for the rich stimulate private spending and investments that *trickle down* through the economy and benefit everybody.

Notice that **foreign policy**, at least until recently, is *not* especially controversial. Americans do debate military and diplomatic policies, but in most elections, we tend to be preoccupied with domestic issues. Indeed, newcomers might be surprised by how much attention we pay to local controversies in our own neighborhoods—especially compared to how little attention we pay to international affairs most of the time.

Good morning, America, how are you?
Say, don't you know me? I'm your native son
I'm the train they call the City of New Orleans
I'll be gone five hundred miles when the day is done

— Steve Goodman

The United States is one of the few countries to use the English system of measurement instead of the metric system. Most Americans, with the notable exception of scientists, will look puzzled if you ask them how many kilometers it is to the next town, or announce that your newborn baby weighs three kilograms and is 50 centimeters long. Even temperatures and kitchen measurements are different—and, unlike the decimal basis of the metric system, the English units of measure are defined only by tradition.

LENGTH & HEIGHT

The standard units of linear measurement are the **inch** and the **foot**. An inch is 2.5 cm, and there are 12 inches (30 cm) in a foot. A single quotation mark (') after a numeral means feet, and a double quotation mark (") means inches—so 5'8" means five feet and eight inches. This is the usual format for noting a person's height or the dimensions of a room. Sometimes measurements are given only in inches (a 36" TV screen, referring to the diagonal length). A compact disc case is roughly 5" square, and a standard American magazine or business letter is 8½" inches wide and 11" long.

DISTANCE & SPEED

Short distances, such as the length of an athletic field, are noted in **yards**. One yard equals three feet (90 cm). Long distances are measured in **miles**. A mile is 1.6 km, or 5,280 feet, and any distance greater than a few hundred yards is usually noted in fractions of a mile. Highway distances are noted in miles and tenths, but locally, you're more likely to hear someone say the distance to the library or the post office is something like "three quarters of a mile" or "a mile and a quarter."

Speed is noted in **miles per hour** (mph). If a highway sign says "Speed Limit 65," that means 65 mph (104 kph).

A **nautical mile** is 1.15 miles, and nautical speed is measured in **knots**, nautical miles per hour. Some weather reports indicate wind speed in knots.

WEIGHT

The standard units of weight are the **pound**, 0.45 kg, and the **ounce**, 1/16 of a pound (or 28 g). By tradition, based on archaic forms of English, the abbreviation for pounds is *lbs.* and the abbreviation for ounces is *oz.* So an average adult might weigh 150 lbs., and a typical hamburger weighs 4 oz. Large objects, such as motor vehicles, are measured in **tons**. A ton is 2,000 lbs, or 0.9 metric tons.

• •

CONVERTING UNITS

There are many online unit calculators that convert metric units to English units. Some of the simplest are:
- www.digitaldutch.com/unitconverter
- www.sciencemadesimple.com/conversions.html
- www.convert-me.com

You can also find rulers, kitchen scales, thermometers, and other measuring instruments marked in both English and metric units. Still, it may be helpful to know some conversion formulas. These are approximate—not precise enough for scientific use, but suitable for everyday life and commerce, according to the National Institute of Standards and Technology:

mm x 0.04 = inches	inches x 25 = mm
m x 3.3 = feet	feet x 30 = cm
km x 0.6 = miles	miles x 1.6 = km
g x 0.035 = ounces	ounces x 28 = g
kg x 2.2 = pounds	pounds x 0.45 = kg
mL x 0.03 = fluid ounces	fluid ounces x 30 = mL
L x 0.26 = gallons	gallons x 3.8 = L
km^2 x 0.4 = square miles	square miles x 2.6 = km^2
hectares x 2.5 = acres	acres x 0.4 = hectares
m^2 x 11.1 = square feet*	square feet x 0.09 = m^2
(°C x 9/5) + 32 = °F	(°F - 32) x 5/9 = °C

* rough calculation not used by NIST

• •

LIQUID VOLUME & KITCHEN MEASUREMENTS

The standard units of liquid measurement are the **gallon**, 3.8 liters, and the **fluid ounce**, 1/128 of a gallon (or 30 mL). A typical bathtub holds about 40 gallons of water. Sodas are sold in liters (commonly 2-liter bottles), but other liquids are sold by the gallon or fraction of a gallon—milk, for instance, is available in gallons, half gallons, **quarts** (quarter gallons) and **pints** (1/8 gallon). A pint is 470 mL and is approximately the amount of water that weighs one pound. Cans or single-serving bottles of soda (soft drinks) or beer are usually 12 ounces (360 mL). Liquor and wine are sold in fifths, bottles measuring approximately 1/5 gallon and exactly 750 mL. Gasoline is sold in gallons and tenths.

If you use kitchen recipes published in the United States, you will not see ingredients listed by weight. For liquid and dry ingredients alike, the pint is further divided into the **cup** (½ pint) and quarters or thirds of a cup. Smaller quantities of liquid or dry ingredients are noted in **teaspoons** (tsp), equal to 5 mL, and **tablespoons** (tbsp), equal to 15 mL or 3 tsp. Measuring spoons and measuring cups in these standard volumes are available in any store that sells kitchen equipment, including most grocery stores and drugstores.

AREA

The geographic size of a city or state is noted in **square miles**, equal to 2.6 square km. The size of a parcel of land is noted in **acres**, equal to 0.4 hectares. The floor space of a room, home, or office is noted in **square feet**, equal to 0.09 square meters; one and a half pages of a standard American magazine would cover approximately one square foot.

CLOTHING SIZES

Some clothing—especially t-shirts and other casual apparel—is sold in just four standard sizes: small (S), medium (M), large (L) and extra large (XL). Most clothing, however, is cut in sizes that correspond to European standard sizes, but are numbered differently.

MEN'S CLOTHING

SHIRTS

USA	14½	15	15½	16	16½
EU	37	38	39	41	42

SUITS

USA	36	38	40	42	44
EU	46	48	50	52	54

SHOES

USA	6	6½	7½	8½	9
EU	39	40	41	42	43

WOMEN'S CLOTHING

SHIRTS, DRESSES

USA	8	10	12	14	16
EU	36	38	40	42	44

SHOES

USA	6	7	8	9	10
EU	37	38	39	40	41

For men and women, the size of pants (trousers, slacks) is measured in inches, and usually two sizes are indicated: the circumference of the waist and the length of the inseam. Sometimes only the waist size is given and the inseam is marked as *short, regular,* or *tall,* meaning the leg is left unfinished and is to be measured and hemmed after purchase. In more casual clothing, *short, regular,* and *tall* are often pre-set inseam lengths, such as 30", 32", and 34".

TEMPERATURE

Most weather reports, recipes, and other references to temperature in the United States use the Fahrenheit scale. Sometimes Celsius (standard international or centigrade) figures are also given, but unless otherwise noted, temperatures are shown in **degrees Fahrenheit**. On this scale, water freezes at 32°F and boils at 212°F; cooking temperatures range from 325°F to 450°F; human body temperature is 98.6°F; and most people are comfortable in a climate around 70°F.

To convert Fahrenheit to Celsius, subtract 32, divide the result by 9, and multiply that result by 5. To convert from Celsius to Fahrenheit, divide by 5, multiply the result by 9, and add 32.

TIME

Only in the military do Americans use the 24-hour clock. The rest of the country counts the hours from midnight to noon on a 12-hour clock and the hours from noon to midnight on a second 12-hour clock, distinguished by the abbreviations **a.m.** and **p.m.** Four o'clock in the morning (0400 in the European system) is 4:00 a.m., and 1600 in the European system is 4:00 p.m. or four o'clock in the afternoon. The colon separates hours and minutes, so the European hour of 1615 would be written as 4:15 p.m.—and a person might say "four-fifteen p.m." or "a quarter past four," meaning a quarter of an hour after 4 o'clock. The abbreviations stand for the Latin terms *ante meridiem* (meaning *before the Sun reaches the local meridian,* or *before noon*) and *post meridiem (after).*

When a British-educated English speaker would say it's "half three," meaning 3:30, an American would say it's *half past three* or it's *three-thirty.* Twenty minutes later, at 3:50, the American would say it's *ten 'til four* or, more casually, *ten of four*—or, simply, *three-fifty.*

The United States observes **daylight saving time** from April to October in order to conserve energy during the summer months. On the first weekend of April, clocks are set forward one hour; on the last weekend of October, clocks are set back to **standard time**—striking noon when the Sun is directly overhead. Newspapers, news broadcasts and some commercially printed calendars remind the public of the correct dates to make the adjustments. *The states of Arizona, Hawaii and Indiana do not observe daylight saving time,* though some parts of Indiana along the state's southern and northwestern borders do. (If you live in Indiana, have someone explain the state's special time zones; if you're just visiting, simply ask what time it is.) For a detailed explanation of the origins and purposes of daylight saving time, visit www.webexhibits.org/daylightsaving.

The so-called **continental** United States—all the states except Alaska and Hawaii, plus the District of Columbia—span four **time zones**; at noon in Los Angeles, it is 3 p.m. in New York. See Chapter 15 for details.

Other slang or jargon by which you might hear Americans refer to various times of day:

- **rush hour**—peak traffic times when most people are traveling to and from work; in most cities, morning rush is roughly 7-9 a.m. and evening rush is roughly 4:30-6:30 p.m.
- **happy hour**—a time for informal social gatherings after work and before dinner (supper), usually 5-7 p.m.
- **primetime**—8-11 p.m. (7-10 p.m. in the central time zone), the hours when TV networks broadcast their most popular programs
- **swing shift**—an evening shift (between the day and night shifts) in a 24-hour workplace
- **graveyard shift**—a shift working from midnight to dawn in a 24-hour workplace

DAYS & DATES

The days of the week are classified as **weekdays** (Monday through Friday) or **weekends** (Saturday and Sunday); the standard business week, except in the retail and hospitality industries, is Monday through Friday. The new calendar week begins on Sunday. Weeknights, however, are the evenings of Monday through Thursday; Friday evening is considered part of the weekend. A *school night* is any night before a day when school is in session.

Calendar dates are cited with the month (written out or abbreviated) and day followed by a comma, and then the year: July 4, 1776. Informally, dates may be written with numbers representing the month, day, and year in that order—7/4/1776.

CHAPTER FOUR

MONEY

You'll find out the banking system works completely different.

— *Monika Puglielli, German immigrant,*
writing advice to future immigrants

For many newcomers, the United States is almost synonymous with economic opportunity; many of the founders came here specifically so they could own land. Once you earn money here, what will you do with it? You'll need to get acquainted with the currency and coins; but once you've been here long enough to establish credit, you might find it easier to use a credit card for all but the smallest transactions. You should also take a close look at the variety of bank accounts and financial services available, and learn how and when to pay taxes.

CURRENCY

U.S. currency is all the same size and shape, and basically the same color: dark green bills measuring roughly 6" x 2½" (155 mm x 65 mm). Bills issued after 2003 have multicolored highlights, but are still basically green. Each denomination bears a different portrait, and each bill bears a unique serial number and the signatures of the Treasurer of the United States and the Secretary of the Treasury. The value is printed in numerals and in words, and each bill bears the words FEDERAL RESERVE NOTE, meaning the value is secured by the Federal Reserve banking system, and the words THIS NOTE IS LEGAL TENDER FOR ALL DEBTS, PUBLIC AND PRIVATE, meaning U.S. currency can be used in any transaction in the United States.

Bills of $1, $5, $10, $20 and $100 are in everyday use; the $50 bill is somewhat less common and the $2 bill, printed intermittently, is extremely rare. All denominations except the $1 bill were redesigned slightly in 1996 and again in 2003 to make them harder to counterfeit; the new bills are similar to the old ones (the portraits are larger and off-center, and a few other design features have a more modern look), but both old and new bills are circulated and accepted.

A common slang word for dollars is *bucks*. A $1 bill is sometimes called a *single,* and $100 bills are sometimes known as *C-notes* or *Benjamins* (referring to the portrait of Revolution leader Benjamin Franklin). A *grand* means a thousand, so you might hear it said that a $24,000 car costs "24 grand" or "24 G's." A salary or the price of a house might be cited using K, the metric symbol for a thousand, as in a $50K salary or a $140K house.

$1

Front: George Washington, first President of the United States, commanding general of the American Revolution

Back: the Great Seal of the United States, with Masonic symbols on one side (most of the nation's founders were Freemasons) and a bald eagle, a national symbol, on the other

$2

Front: Thomas Jefferson, 3rd President, drafted the Declaration of Independence

Back: signing the Declaration of Independence

$5

Front: Abraham Lincoln, 16th President, responsible for ending slavery

Back: the Lincoln Memorial in Washington, D.C.

$10

Front: Alexander Hamilton, first Secretary of the Treasury

Back: headquarters of the Department of the Treasury

$20

Front: Andrew Jackson, seventh President; on newer bills, the portrait has no frame

Back: the White House (shown from the north in bills printed in 1996 or later, and from the south on older bills)

$50

Front: Ulysses S. Grant, 18th President, commanding general during the American Civil War (1861-1865)
Back: the Capitol (headquarters of the U.S. Congress)

$100

Front: Benjamin Franklin, founding member of Congress and first U.S. ambassador
Back: Independence Hall in Philadelphia—first capital of the United States

COINS

The dollar is divided into 100 *cents*, written either as a decimal fraction of a dollar ($.30 means "30 cents") or as a numeral followed by a cents sign (¢, so 30¢ also means 30 cents). Coins in everyday use are the *penny* (1¢), the *nickel* (5¢), the *dime* (10¢), and the *quarter* (25¢).

Not all quarters look alike—in 1999, the U.S. Mint introduced a series of commemorative quarters honoring each of the 50 states, and each state's legislature was invited to submit a design to be struck on the back of the coin to celebrate that state's history, land, or culture. (The regular pre-1999 quarter has an eagle on the back, and quarters dated 1976 have a special design commemorating the nation's bicentennial.) For the purposes of exchange, it does not matter what state's image is displayed on the back; any quarter is worth 25¢ anywhere in the country.

The government has made several attempts to introduce a $1 coin, but it has never quite caught on. You might see the Sacagawea dollar coin or the silver Susan B. Anthony dollar coin dispensed as change in vending machines at post offices and in certain public transportation systems. Also occasionally seen in circulation are Eisenhower silver dollars and Kennedy 50¢ coins.

Though their value is not shown in numerals, coins of different value are different sizes and shapes (all shown actual size except as noted). All are made of silver-colored alloys except the copper penny and the gold alloy Sacagawea dollar.

1¢ (PENNY)

Front: Abraham Lincoln
Back: Lincoln Memorial

5¢ (NICKEL)

Front: Thomas Jefferson, third President, principal au-
thor of the Declaration of Independence
Back: Monticello (Jefferson's home), in Charlottesville,
Virginia*

10¢ (DIME)

Front: Franklin D. Roosevelt, 32nd President, only President ever elected to four terms
Back: torch and olive branch

25¢ (QUARTER)

Front: George Washington
Back: on quarters issued before 1999, bald eagle; on
quarters issued between 1999-2008, any of 50 designs
representing each of the states; on quarters issued in
1976, drummer boy from the colonial militia, commemorating the bicentennial of the American
Revolution

50¢ (HALF DOLLAR)

Front: John F. Kennedy, 35th President, assassinated in 1963
Back: Independence Hall

$1 (GOLDEN DOLLAR)

Front: Sacagawea, translator for early 19th-century U.S. surveyors
Meriwether Lewis and William Clark, depicted with her baby son,
Jean-Baptiste Charbonneau
Back: bald eagle

---

* This refers to nickels issued before 2004. Newer coins feature several different
  designs but are the same size and color.

$1 (SILVER DOLLAR)

Front: Susan B. Anthony, 19th-century advocate of voting rights for women
Back: emblem commemorating the Apollo XI mission to the Moon

$1 (SILVER DOLLAR)

Front: Dwight D. Eisenhower, 34th President, commanding general during World War II
Back: the Liberty Bell in Philadelphia (used in 1776 to signal the adoption of the Declaration of Independence) and the Moon

CURRENCY CALCULATORS ONLINE

Here are a few web sites that convert figures between U.S. dollars and foreign currency:
- www.x-rates.com
- www.xe.net
- www.exchangerate.com

BANKING & FINANCIAL SERVICES

Most Americans keep their money, except for small amounts of cash, in a bank—not only because it is automatically insured (up to $100,000) and protected against theft, but also because you earn **interest** as the bank makes investments using your money. But interest rates vary over time and from one type of bank account to another, and you need to shop around and compare specific accounts to make sure you will earn more in interest than you will pay the bank in service fees. This book provides only a brief introduction to banking in the United States; for a more detailed overview, visit *Money* magazine's "Banking 101" page at http://money.cnn.com.

CHECKING & DEBIT CARDS

The type of bank account most commonly used for everyday trans-actions is a **checking account**, which allows you to write checks (drafts) to pay obligations. This is an especially convenient way to pay bills by mail—for example, monthly phone services or the rent for a home. (It is not advisable to send cash through the mail.) The bank will provide you with personal checks preprinted with your name and address. When you write the name of a person or business on the check, in the space after the words PAY TO THE ORDER OF, you are instructing your bank to transfer the amount of money indicated to the account of that person or business. To protect against unauthorized alterations, it is customary to write the amount of money twice—

• • • • • • • • • • • • • • • • • •

OPENING A BANK ACCOUNT

When you open any type of bank account, you will be asked to:

- show two forms of ID (such as a passport, green card, driver's license, or birth certificate);
- show proof of address (such as a driver's license, current utility bill, or lease);
- provide the name and address of your employer; and
- make an opening deposit.

When you open a checking account, you will be given some *starter checks* (without a preprinted name and address) so you can pay immediate bills before your new checks arrive in the mail.

Under new laws intended to help the government detect terrorist activity, banks are required to report any deposits or withdrawals of more than $10,000 at a time. And deposits, withdrawals, or wire transfers of amounts close to $10,000 may be reported as "suspicious" activity. There's nothing illegal about it, but Treasury or USCIS officials might ask you to explain such transactions.

WITHOUT A BANK ACCOUNT

If you have just arrived in the United States (or you've just moved to a new city) and you don't yet have a local bank account, various financial services are available to you—for a fee:

- **Check cashing**. In most cities, especially in less affluent neighborhoods, there are businesses that specialize in cashing checks for people who do not have bank accounts. They usually require ID and proof of address, just like a bank, and they charge high fees—up to 10% of the value of the transaction.

once in numerals and once in words. If a check that is already *made out* (bearing your signature and the name of the recipient) gets lost or stolen and you notify your bank immediately, the bank can **stop payment** of the check. (There is usually a fee of $10 to $20 for this service.)

You must have enough money on deposit in your checking account to pay the amount indicated on the check, or you will be charged a penalty for a *bounced* or *returned* check, and you could face criminal charges of fraud if it is suspected that you wrote the check with deceptive intent. Most banks offer **overdraft protection** (insurance against bounced checks); if your checking account has this feature, your bank will go ahead and pay the check you have written and charge you interest until you pay the difference back into your checking account. If the amount of overdraft is small and you pay it back promptly, this is almost always cheaper than bounced check fees.

Most banks now offer **debit cards** to customers with checking accounts.

• • • • • • • • • • • • • • • • • •

These cards look and function like credit cards, but they deduct money directly from your checking account. They are accepted by most merchants who accept credit cards, they don't incur debt, and—unlike checks—they can be used for internet transactions. If you do not have a credit card, these cards can be especially helpful. However, if a debit card is stolen, a thief can empty your checking account in an instant; ATM cards and credit cards have more security features.

When you receive a check (for example, wages from an employer), write your signature in the space indicated on the back. If you want to **deposit** the money in your checking account, write your checking account number below your signature, fill out a deposit slip from your bank, and give both papers to the teller (or mail them to the bank). It can take several days for the value of a check to be credited to your checking account—to *clear*, as it is said. Your bank should provide a written statement of its **funds availability policy**, but in general, checks written by individu-

WITHOUT A BANK ACCOUNT, CONT.

These services are listed in the local Yellow Pages under CHECK CASHING SERVICE.

- **Money orders.** You can send money through the mail by purchasing a money order with cash—the value of the transaction plus a few dollars. All banks, post offices, and exchange bureaus sell money orders, but you can get them for lower fees from some convenience stores, photocopy shops, check cashing services, and liquor stores.

- **Traveler's Checks.** Banks and exchange bureaus sell these notes at face value (usually in denominations of $20 or $100) plus a small fee. They work like cash, but are not valid until you sign them and indicate a recipient. They are numbered, so if they get lost or stolen, you can notify the financial institution that sold them and get replacements.

- **Prepaid charge cards.** These are sometimes called "prepaid credit cards," but they actually don't involve credit. They are simply cards issued by a major credit card company, such as VISA or MasterCard, that record the amount of cash you have paid to the company; you then make purchases by allowing the merchant to deduct cash from the value encoded on the card. You can add value to the card by paying more cash to the issuing company. These cards are convenient because they're easy to get (you don't need a credit history) and they're accepted wherever credit cards are accepted. For a list of prepaid cards, visit **www.cardweb.com**.

als or bearing out-of-town addresses take longer to clear than checks from businesses or bearing local addresses. If you prefer, your bank will **cash** a check (give you the specified amount in cash) if you have at least that amount on deposit there.

Some checking accounts bear interest, some don't. Some checking accounts charge a monthly service fee, or limit the number of checks you may write each month, or charge a small fee for each check you write; most charge a fee for printing your blank checks. Generally, the more money you keep on deposit in a bank, the more services the bank will provide for free—but read the terms of a checking account before you actually set one up, and make sure you understand all the details.

SAVINGS

The simplest kind of bank account is a personal **savings account**. You deposit cash and it earns interest. You can withdraw cash whenever you want to. That's all. These accounts tend to pay interest at a higher rate than checking accounts, but lower than the more sophisticated kinds of savings accounts described below. As with checking accounts, they're usually free if you maintain a certain balance. These are sometimes called "passbook" accounts, recalling an earlier era when transactions were recorded in a little booklet similar to a passport.

AUTOMATED TELLER MACHINES (ATMS)

In the early 1990s, ATMs surpassed human tellers as the main point of service for everyday banking transactions. You'll find ATMs in banks, airports, train stations, shopping malls, supermarkets, restaurants, convenience stores, hotels, and college dormitories. And you might pay a lot of money for the convenience. There is usually no charge to use an ATM owned by your bank, but every time you use another bank's ATM, you can be charged $1 to $3 by that bank *and* another $1 to $3 by your own. If you use an ATM just once a week, that's several hundred dollars a year in fees. On the other hand, ATMs on an international network often give better currency exchange rates and lower international transaction fees than a bank or exchange bureau. And your own bank might charge a fee if you visit a human teller for a routine transaction that you could have made using an ATM!

Usually, an ATM card is included free with a bank account. For security, in case your card is lost or stolen, memorize your PIN (personal identification number, or ATM code) and never write it on your card or carry it in your wallet.

CERTIFICATES OF DEPOSIT (CDS)

Certificates of deposit offer higher interest rates than regular savings accounts, and they allow you to lock in a fixed interest rate for a predetermined period. You cannot routinely withdraw money from this type of account—CDs are intended for putting money away for months or years to earn interest. There are provisions for making withdrawals in an emergency, but you lose some or all of the interest accrued. Also, if interest rates go up, your money in a CD is stuck at the lower rate.

SAVINGS BONDS

Many Americans invest in the government by purchasing bonds from the U.S. Treasury. These are certificates that require, or *bond,* the Treasury to repay the face value of the note plus interest at the end of a fixed term, such as 10 years. Cities and counties also issue bonds to raise revenue for large projects and public expenditures not covered by taxes, but these are usually purchased by financial institutions and sold indirectly to customers through investment portfolios. Corporations also sell bonds as a way to borrow money from investors.

INVESTMENT FUNDS

These accounts invest your deposited money in a portfolio of corporate stock, government bonds, or currency. The portfolios are managed by investment professionals and often earn a higher interest rate than bank accounts, but there is usually a minimum balance of several thousand dollars and some restriction on withdrawals. A **money market account** might allow you to write checks drawn on the balance of your deposit, but only a few checks per year. Money market funds are generally considered more stable, but often yield less, than **mutual funds** (shared portfolios invested in the stock market). Employee retirement (pension) funds are often invested in money market funds or mutual funds.

INDIVIDUAL RETIREMENT ACCOUNTS (IRAS)

If you plan to retire in the United States, you'll need to consider long-term savings. Federal law allows you to place a certain amount of your own money every year in a designated savings account where it will be sheltered (exempt) from income tax; the account is invested by a financial institution to build an endowment bearing enough interest, after you retire, to provide you with monthly income. If you withdraw money from an IRA before you reach retirement age, you will lose the tax benefits and have to pay income tax on it. Some employers make annual contributions to an employee's IRA so the employee will not have to pay taxes on money that would be used for long-term savings anyway.

CASH MANAGEMENT ACCOUNTS

Brokerage firms can provide many of the same services as a bank—checking and debit cards, access to ATM networks, and accounts where you can deposit and withdraw cash as needed. These are *cash management accounts* invested in corporate stock or in mutual funds. Some banks, too, will invest your money in stock or mutual funds instead of bank loans. These accounts usually feature a high minimum balance and, accordingly, low fees.

• • • • • • • • • • • • • • •

LINKING BANK ACCOUNTS

Usually, all of your accounts at a particular bank—checking, savings, CDs, and investment funds—can be linked to allow you to transfer money instantly from one account to another. Also, the combined balance of your linked accounts will be used to determine whether you meet minimum balance requirements for various discounts, fee waivers, and special services. If your bank representative does not mention this option, ask about it.

• • • • • • • • • • • • • • •

OTHER ACCOUNT SERVICES

If you have an account of any kind at a bank, you can obtain **certified checks** from that bank for major purchases. These are checks on which the bank has stamped a guarantee that you have enough money on deposit to cover the transaction. You can also buy **cashier's checks**—checks drawn on the bank's own funds and in its own name—using money from your accounts or out of pocket. Cashier's checks work like money orders. Banks also sell traveler's checks and exchange currency, and if you have several thousand dollars on deposit, you might be offered these services for free.

LOANS

Banks lend money to individuals to pay for major purchases, such as a home or car; major expenses such as college tuition or *home improvement* (renovation or expansion of a house); or to start a small business. The terms of repayment are negotiable—if you agree to make large monthly payments, you can pay the debt quickly and minimize interest, or you can make smaller payments over a longer period and end up paying more interest. But in order to borrow money from a bank, you will need two things: an excellent **credit history** (see GETTING AND MAINTAINING GOOD CREDIT, below) and some **collateral**—some property of value equal to the amount of money you want to borrow. If you *default*, or fail to repay the loan as scheduled, the bank will be entitled to seize the collateral and sell it to recover its losses. (There is one exception: a **mortgage**, or loan to purchase a home. The home itself is collateral—so, in effect, the lender owns your house until you pay off the loan.)

ONLINE BANKING

Most banks allow you to make routine transactions using the internet—for example, you can direct your bank to pay a utility bill by debiting your account, so you don't need to mail a paper check. It's safe and convenient, and many banks offer online banking services at no charge other than the regular transaction fees. (Some banks charge a monthly fee for online services; others charge a few cents for each online transaction. Also, some banks let you make certain transactions by phone using touch-tone menus.) A few banks operate *only* on the internet, with no physical offices anywhere—and they tend to offer lower fees and higher interest rates than traditional banks:

- **American Bank**, www.pcbanker.com
- **Bank of Internet USA**, www.bankofinternet.com
- **Bank One**, www.bankone.com
- **E*Trade Bank**, www.etradebank.com
- **Everbank**, www.everbank.com
- **National InterBank**, www.nationalinterbank.com
- **NetBank**, www.netbank.com
- **Umbrellabank**, www.umbrellabank.com
- **VirtualBank**, www.virtualbank.com

Most banks' web sites feature tools that estimate the amount of money you might be qualified to borrow, based on your income, assets, and credit history. Online **loan calculators** let you experiment with different terms of payment at different interest rates—check out www.loanlizzard.com, www.411-loans.com, www.eloan.com, or www.financialpowertools.com, just for example.

CREDIT UNIONS

Credit unions are member-owned cooperatives that provide banking services to their members—and they usually offer lower fees than banks. Many large companies have employee credit unions, and so do some towns, communities, and universities. Other credit unions cater to members of a particular profession or trade. In most cases, if you belong to a group of people who are eligible to join a particular credit union, you and your family can become members for just a $5 fee and a $5 opening deposit. Like bank accounts, credit union deposits are insured up to $100,000. To find a credit union serving your community or industry, call the Credit Union National Association at 800-358-5710 or visit www.creditunion.coop.

CHOOSING A BANK AND ACCOUNTS

You can check the interest rates offered by banks throughout the country (both the interest paid on deposits and the interest charged on loans) at **www.bankrate.com,** and the financial section of your local newspaper will list interest rates at local banks and mortgage lenders at least once a week. For certain cities, you can download articles rating local banks from *Consumers' Checkbook* magazine, www.checkbook.org (see Chapter 7 for details).

Most banks' web sites include a **savings calculator** to determine how much interest your deposits will earn over various times at various interest rates. Many banks offer additional online tools for financial planning, and the *Money* magazine web site features dozens of financial calculators and tools to help you make sound decisions about exercising stock options, buying a home, refinancing a mortgage, planning a household budget, borrowing money for college, planning for retirement, and more. Visit http://cgi.money.cnn.com/tools.

The **National Institute for Consumer Education**, a program of Eastern Michigan University, offers some good educational materials at www.nice.emich.edu to help you choose a bank, apply for credit, and know your rights as a consumer of financial services.

THE FEDERAL RESERVE SYSTEM

The United States has a central bank, called the **Federal Reserve** (or simply *the Fed*), but the general public does not deposit money directly into it. The banks that serve individuals and businesses are corporations—they issue shares to be traded on the stock market. These banks are the Fed's customers. The Fed helps stabilize the U.S. economy by lending cash to commercial banks and by adjusting the interest rate it charges them. Among other services to commercial banks, the Fed processes checks and other transfers between bank accounts.

The Federal Reserve is a unique institution: it is chartered by Congress and run by a **Board of Governors** appointed by the President, but it is free to decide its own policies and does not need the government's approval to adjust interest rates. The Fed's lending policies essentially control the value of money in the United States, causing changes in inflation and unemployment domestically and ripples through financial markets around the world. The chairperson of the Federal Reserve Board is one of the most influential individuals in the world.

CREDIT CARDS

Cash and coin are endangered species in the United States. Most Americans use a credit card for all major purchases. Some fairly common transactions are impossible, or at least a huge hassle, without a credit card—renting a car, subscribing to an internet service, booking airline tickets, ordering theater or concert tickets by phone, or purchasing goods or services online. The concept is simple: a bank or other business issues you a *line of credit,* an amount of money the institution trusts you to repay; up to that amount, you may *charge* purchases to your credit card number and the lender will pay the merchant for you. You may pay the debt in full each month and avoid paying interest, or pay only a portion of the debt each month and pay interest on the remaining balance.

The problem, for international newcomers, is that the line of credit is based on your **credit history**—your record of borrowing money and repaying it on time. And a foreign credit history, even if it reflects the use of a credit card over many years, is not often accepted by

U.S. lenders. If you're going to be here for longer than a year or two, you should start to build a credit history in the United States as soon as possible.

GETTING AND MAINTAINING GOOD CREDIT

Several private companies called **credit bureaus** keep track of personal **credit ratings**—reports that indicate whether you always, sometimes, or rarely pay your debts on time. Credit bureaus cannot show anyone your credit rating without your consent, but you will have to give consent in order to be approved for a credit card or bank loan, or to lease (rent) a home. (If you are new to the country, just say so. Some lenders might be willing to consider other factors, such as an employment contract with an established U.S. company.) Credit ratings are based on a formula developed by a private company called Fair Isaac; for details about the factors that affect your credit rating, check out www.myfico.com.

If you have difficulty getting a regular credit card right away, you might be able to get a **secured** credit card—a card from a bank where you deposit money to serve as collateral for a line of credit. Secured credit will not enable you to make purchases that cost more than your immediate purchasing power (the money you deposit with the bank), but it will give you an opportunity to charge purchases, pay monthly bills, and establish a credit history. (You can also get **prepaid** credit cards, but they're just a surrogate for cash; they provide the convenience of a credit card, but do not affect your credit history.)

Relocation expert Deborah Stadtler, writing in *Mobility* magazine, recommends that you ask your employer to help you get credit: "Companies that transfer foreign nationals into the United States are implementing programs or processes that assist those expatriates in securing a personal credit card without a deposit." Some employers, Stadtler reports, will guarantee a new employee's credit card (take responsibility for the debt if the employee fails to pay it off). Other employers work with lenders to pay for interpretation of foreign credit records, or provide **letters of reference** to assure lenders that the applicant has a steady job and income. Also, many employers issue **company credit cards** to employees to pay for work-related expenses, such as restaurant meals that function as business meetings, or for relocation expenses. If you can get a company credit card issued in your name, you can build a credit history even though the debt is the employer's responsibility. According to Brenda Perrin, a relocation advisor quoted in Stadtler's article, it takes about three months to build enough credit to finance a car or major appliance.

The three major credit bureaus are:

- **Experian**, 888-397-3742 (formerly known as TRW)
- **TransUnion**, 800-916-8800
- **Equifax**, 800-685-1111

You're entitled to a free copy of your credit report from each bureau if you've been denied credit within the past 30 days; otherwise, you may be charged a small fee. You can challenge inaccurate information in your credit report—follow the credit bureau's instructions. (Avoid ordering reports more than once a year, though; frequent requests could have a negative effect on your credit rating.) For online access to all three credit bureaus, visit **www.icreditreport.com.**

CHOOSING A CREDIT CARD

Most banks issue credit cards, but so do airlines, telecommunications companies, car manufacturers, professional associations, magazine publishers, charities, and retailers. Credit cards from different lenders offer not only different fees and interest rates, but a variety of fringe benefits such as frequent-flier miles, discounts on phone service, donations to charity, and *automatic cash advances* (short-term, high-interest loans); so it pays to shop around, especially if you don't plan to pay off your balance every month. **CardWeb**, www.cardweb.com, is an excellent online directory of credit cards. You can search or browse the listings by interest rates, fees, special offers, or other features. Also look for ratings in *Consumers' Checkbook* (www.checkbook.org).

Most goods purchased with credit cards are automatically insured against loss or damage, at least for a few weeks. **VISA** cards, www.visa.com, and **MasterCard** cards, www.mastercard.com, are issued by thousands of different lenders and are accepted by almost all merchants. Other credit cards include:

- **American Express.** These prestigious cards have minimum income requirements (except for students) and annual fees. Until recently, American Express (or "Amex") only offered cards whose balance had to be paid off each month; now the company issues many different types of cards. Call 800-528-4800 or visit www.americanexpress.com.

SOCIAL SECURITY NUMBERS

All tax papers—and many other financial and legal documents—use your nine-digit Social Security number or Individual Taxpayer Identification Number (ITIN) for identification purposes. You must apply to the government to be issued one of these numbers if you are going to earn any money or transact any substantial business in the United States.

If your immigration status allows you to work in the United States and you are at least 18 years old, you can obtain a Social Security number from the Social Security Administration. You will have to apply in person at the nearest field office (there is at least one in every major city) and show your passport, birth certificate, and alien status papers. There is no fee. To find the local Social Security office, check the Blue Pages of the phone book or call 800-772-1213, or visit www.ssa.gov/immigration.

Sometimes a state or local government agency will ask for your Social Security number. If you are not eligible to work in the United States but you need a Social Security number, you can get one by completing the same application process and giving the field office an original letter (not a photocopy) on the letterhead of the state or local agency explaining why you need a number. You can also get a letter from the Social Security Administration stating that you are not eligible for a Social Security number, and that letter will satisfy many agencies that request your number—including schools, educational testing services, and agencies that manage subsidized housing.

Aliens not eligible for Social Security can get an ITIN from the IRS and use it in

• **Diner's Club.** These cards are accepted mainly by businesses in the travel and hospitality industries—hotels, restaurants, airlines, and travel agencies. Cardholders have access to special amenities at most major airports. Call 800-234-6377 or visit www.dinersclub.com.

• **Discover.** Discover and affiliated Novus/Private Issue cards give you an annual rebate based on the total value of purchases you charge each year. Some plans also let you earn discounts at certain hotels or stores. Call 800-347-2683 or visit www.discovercard.com.

Also, most **department stores** and other major retail chains issue charge cards, sometimes with lines of credit. Usually stores will issue these cards to anyone who already has a VISA or MasterCard account. Store charge accounts often have lower interest rates than bank-issued credit cards.

CREDIT SCAMS

Be suspicious of services that offer to "fix" or "repair" your credit history. Either your credit rating is accurate, in which case the only way to improve it is to establish good borrowing habits, or it is inaccurate and you can challenge it yourself and get errors corrected. (The National Institute for Consumer Education web site, mentioned above in the section on CHOOSING A BANK, explains how to challenge a

• • • • • • • • • • • • • • • •

SOCIAL SECURITY NUMBERS, CONT.

place of a Social Security number on tax forms or other financial papers. Get a copy of IRS Form W-7 from a public library or www.irs.gov and follow the instructions—and mail it at least six weeks before you need to file a tax return, to allow time for processing.

• • • • • • • • • • • • • • • •

credit report.) Credit "repair" services are almost always a scam or a ripoff. Also look closely at offers of "pre-approved" credit cards advertised by mail, especially those offering low interest or no fees. In most cases, the fine print will reveal that you are only pre-approved if you meet certain income requirements (so, in effect, you have to apply as you would for any other line of credit), and the low fees or interest rates are in effect only for several months and then increase substantially. If you have trouble paying your credit card bills, seek advice from a reputable nonprofit agency that helps consumers manage their debts; for a referral, contact the **National Foundation for Credit Counseling** at 800-388-2227 or www.debtadvice.org.

TAXES

The American Revolution was not fought for lofty principles of equal opportunity and religious freedom—the British colonies in North America were founded as havens for those principles, yes, but the Revolution itself was a fight against high taxes. Schoolchildren learn about the Boston Tea Party of 1773, a protest in which Sam Adams (brother of future President John Adams) and a handful of nationalists threw a shipment of British tea into the harbor to protest the excise tax on tea and other staple goods. Americans have been fighting—among themselves—about taxes ever since: we expect a lot of services from our government, but resent the taxes that pay for them.

INCOME TAX

The federal government and most state governments collect a tax on the income of every resident (permanent or not) earning a salary, wages, tips or money from self-employment. A portion of this tax is set aside for federal Social Security payments to retired or disabled citizens. Anyone working in the United States must obtain a Social Security number or taxpayer ID number and report U.S. income to the **Internal Revenue Service**. This income will be taxed at the same rate regardless of citizenship. Tax laws, including many opportunities to claim deductions or credits reducing one's tax liability, are complicated and may change every year. Newcomers are advised to consult an accountant or professional tax preparer, and may save more than enough money to pay for such services.

Most individuals have to file a disclosure of earnings, called a **tax return**, with the IRS every year between January 1 and April 15—and, since many people wait until the last minute, there are always long lines at the post office on April 15. (If April 15 is a Saturday or Sunday, the deadline is the next business day.) Some self-employed individuals have to file quarterly tax returns instead, on or before the 15th of April, July, October, and January. And persons who earn less than a certain amount aren't required to file a return or pay taxes; the amount depends on whether the person is married or single, is over or under age 65, and has dependents (children or elders living at home).

Every bookstore and public library has a variety of books to guide you through the process of preparing a tax return, and PROFESSIONAL TAX RETURN PREPARATION SERVICES are listed in the Yellow Pages. There is also a catalog of free pamphlets available from the IRS itself at 800-829-3676 or www.irs.gov. The most common tax forms, and **instruction booklets** that are updated every year, are available for free at libraries and post offices; for more specialized tax forms, you may need to make photocopies from a set of originals at the local library or print a copy from the IRS web site. Also, you can buy computer software that will prepare your tax return and file it online, or you can follow the IRS instructions to file an electronic tax return yourself (*e-file*).

Your employer is required to **withhold** a percentage of your pay (enough to cover your expected tax liability) and pass it along to the IRS. In January, your employer will mail you an IRS Form W-2, an official record of the total amount withheld in the previous year. Read the instruction booklet carefully to find out whether you are eligible for any tax **credits** or **deductions**—for example, your tax liability might be reduced to offset relocation expenses, medical bills, or college tuition payments. (These are policies that change every year as directed by Congress.) If your tax liability is less than the amount withheld, you will receive a **refund** from the government; if it is greater, you owe only the difference between the two figures.

State income tax laws vary and usually require separate paperwork. Check with the state government where you live or consult the appropriate **Newcomer's Handbook®** city guide. Generally, however, state income tax is based on a percentage of your federal income tax, and the state will ask for a copy of your federal tax return.

SALES TAXES

Most state governments collect a **sales tax** on consumer goods, and it is usually not reflected in the stated price of an item. Find out the sales tax where you live and expect to pay the marked price plus that percentage. (The state sales tax rate for most goods is listed below. The sales tax rate may be different for hotel and restaurant services than for consumer products, and usually groceries are not taxed. Also, some local jurisdictions levy their own sales tax in addition to the state tax.)

ALABAMA	4%	NEBRASKA	5.5%
ARIZONA	5.6%	NEVADA	6.5%
ARKANSAS	5.125%	NEW JERSEY	6%
CALIFORNIA	7.25%	NEW MEXICO	5%
COLORADO	2.9%	NEW YORK	4%
CONNECTICUT	6%	NORTH CAROLINA	4.5%
FLORIDA	6%	NORTH DAKOTA	5%
GEORGIA	4%	OHIO	5%
HAWAII	4%	OKLAHOMA	4.5%
IDAHO	5%	PENNSYLVANIA	6%
ILLINOIS	6.25%	RHODE ISLAND	7%
INDIANA	6%	SOUTH CAROLINA	5%
IOWA	5%	SOUTH DAKOTA	4%
KANSAS	5.3%	TENNESSEE	7%
KENTUCKY	6%	TEXAS	6.25%
LOUISIANA	4%	UTAH	4.75%
MAINE	5%	VERMONT	5%
MARYLAND	5%	VIRGINIA	4.5%
MASSACHUSETTS	5%	WASHINGTON	6.5%
MICHIGAN	6%	WEST VIRGINIA	6%
MINNESOTA	6.5%	WISCONSIN	5%
MISSISSIPPI	7%	WYOMING	4%
MISSOURI	4.225%	DISTRICT OF COLUMBIA	5.75%

Alaska, Delaware, Montana, New Hampshire, and Oregon do not have sales tax. **Note:** If you order goods by mail or internet from a merchant in another state, you may not have to pay sales tax.

OTHER TAXES

Homeowners—and, in some places, car owners—get an annual **property tax** bill in the mail. The *fair market value* of a home is appraised periodically by a local tax assessor, and this assessment is the basis for calculating the property tax. (The fairness of an assessment can usually be challenged though an appeals process.) Property taxes depend on the quality and condition of a building, and on its location and the reputation of the community. Public schools, police and fire departments, ambulance service, trash removal, recycling, roads, sewers, and other public works are funded largely by property taxes.

A **capital gains tax** is assessed on profits from the sale of real estate, stock, or other major assets, and an **estate tax** is assessed on money or property transferred by inheritance. These taxes primarily affect the rich and are a favorite target of conservative politicians. You will almost certainly need an accountant or tax lawyer to help you with these special situations.

No New Year's Day to celebrate, no chocolate-covered candy hearts to give away,
No first of Spring, no song to sing—in fact it's just another ordinary day...
I just called to say I love you; I just called to say how much I care.
I just called to say I love you and I mean it from the bottom of my heart.

— Stevie Wonder

Americans tend to spend a lot of time on the telephone, on the internet, or "hanging out" and visiting with friends. And with every advance in communications technology in the past 30 years—the answering machine, the pager, the fax machine, e-mail, the cellular and digital wireless phone, wireless internet, and whatever comes next—there's a new feeling of constant access and constant availability. As Stevie Wonder sang, it doesn't take a momentous event or a special occasion to draw people together—the infrastructure and the marketplace offer you lots of ways to keep in touch with the people you care about, wherever they are.

TELEPHONE

Most Americans have phone service in their homes; roughly half, based on industry statistics, also have wireless phones, but only a few use mobile or wireless phones at home instead of a wired phone line (landline). Telephones themselves are owned by the user, you, not by the phone company; you can buy telephones at department stores, home electronics stores, and some drugstores. All wireless phones, whether they use a cellular radio network or satellite technology, are commonly called *cell phones*. There are also **pay phones** (public telephones) in office buildings, supermarkets, shopping malls, and restaurants, and on street corners.

With just a few exceptions, phone numbers in the United States have 10 digits. The first three digits are the **area code** and, in many parts of the country, do not need to be dialed when placing a **local call** to a number with the same area code. (Originally, area codes were used only when placing **long distance calls**; in recent years, with the proliferation of phone lines, there are no longer enough unique phone numbers, and some densely populated regions have more than one area code.) In most of the country, when you are calling another area code, you have to dial **1** before it—and in some places, you have to dial the area code for all calls.

If you see a phone number that contains letters, such as 800-551-SEAT, dial the numbers associated with those letters on the telephone keypad (see p. 295). For example, 551-SEAT would be 551-7328.

Important: The area codes **800, 866, 877,** and **888** are used for **toll-free numbers**, phone numbers that can be called for free from any phone (including pay phones). These numbers are used by many businesses and government agencies to make it easier to call for service. The area codes **900, 915,** and **976** are used for phone lines that charge a **fee** by the minute. These numbers are used by fortune tellers, astrologers, and businesses that provide recorded advice by phone—or services that are politely called *adult entertainment,* such as sexually explicit dialogue. Also, there are several exceptions to the rule that phone numbers are 10 digits long: in most jurisdictions, **the phone number for emergency services (police, fire, and ambulance) is 911** and the number for **directory assistance** (to request the phone number of a specific person or business) is **411**. In some places, **311** is the number to call the police in a situation that is *not* an emergency.

When you pick up the phone, you should hear a **dial tone**, a steady, low-pitched hum that means the system is ready for you to dial a number. (Operator assistance is rarely used or needed.) After dialing, you will usually hear:

- a series of low-pitched tones, each roughly four seconds long, to indicate that the other person's phone is ringing;
- rapid, high-pitched tones less than one second long, to indicate that the other person's line is busy with another call; or
- a recorded voice explaining that the call cannot be completed—for example, if the number you dialed is no longer the correct number (in which case the recording will give you the new number) or if there is a technical problem with the phone lines.

PHONE ETIQUETTE

Americans usually answer the phone by saying **hello** or, at a place of business, by identifying the business and perhaps the person whose office you are calling. Most Americans, both at home and at work, have either an **answering machine** or **voicemail** (automated answering service provided by the phone company) to take calls in their absence. If a machine or voicemail answers the phone, you will hear a short recorded greeting from the person you called and then a high-pitched tone that signals you to start speaking. It's advisable to leave a message stating your name, the phone number where you can be reached, and the purpose of your call—but no more than that; keep it brief.

If the person who answers your call is not the person you want to talk with, you might be asked, "May I put you **on hold**?" This simply means you are advised to hold the phone and wait for the correct person to pick up the phone on the other end. As a matter of business phone etiquette, a person of very high rank in a company or government agency will usually have a secretary place calls and will pick up the phone only when the secretary reports that the other person has answered. (This is one of the few clear displays of social precedence in U.S. culture.)

A growing number of businesses and government agencies have **automated menus**, answering machines that greet you with a list of options; you select the appropriate option by pressing the corresponding number on the phone keypad. Some business phone numbers have an **extension**, a number that allows you to dial a specific person within the organization. For example, if you are calling someone at 555-1234 ext. 220, you would dial 555-1234 and wait for an answer. If your call is answered by a person, you would say "Extension 220, please"; if you reach an automated menu, you would dial 220 when invited to.

It is considered rude to have loud conversations on a wireless phone in a public place such as a restaurant or on a bus—yet many Americans do it. It is also considered rude to have a conversation on a wireless phone while you are in the company of other people socially or during a business meeting—yet many Americans do that too.

FINDING PHONE NUMBERS

You can look up residential and business phone numbers in the White Pages or by calling directory assistance (411 in most places, or 555-1212), and you can look up business toll-free numbers by calling 800-555-1212. Most phone companies charge a fee for each call to directory assistance. For a small fee, you can have your phone number listed under two or more different names—for example, if a relative with a different surname lives with you. And if you don't want people to be able to look up your number, you can request an *unlisted* (or *unpublished*) number. If you know what type of business you need (for example, a hotel, a taxi service, or a veterinarian) but not the name of a specific business you want to call, look in the Yellow Pages under the appropriate category; it will not do any good to call directory assistance and ask for the number of "a taxi service." And if there is a technical problem or you need help placing a call, you can always contact the **operator** of the local telephone company by simply dialing **0**—but ask about fees for operator-assisted phone calls.

SETTING UP PHONE SERVICE

The consumer information section of the local White Pages (available at the local public library if necessary) provides detailed instructions for setting up residential phone service. There are two basic types of service available: **unlimited** plans, in which there is a flat monthly fee for local service, and **economy** plans, in which a certain number of local calls are included with the monthly fee and additional local calls cost a few cents each. Most households find unlimited service more economical. In either case, there is no charge by the minute for local calls.

Until recently, every place in the United States was served by only one local phone company; the competitive market for local phone service is fairly new. The phone company that publishes your local Yellow Pages is probably the most established and widely used company in your area, but you can contact the state **public service commission** listed in the Blue Pages or on the state web site to get a list of all of the phone companies licensed to serve your location.

When you call a phone company to arrange for service, you will be offered a wide range of optional features that would increase your monthly phone bill. The consumer section of the White Pages describes all available services, and the phone company representative can answer any questions you have, but the most commonly used optional services are:

- **Voicemail**. This service works like an answering machine except that your recorded greeting and a caller's recorded message are stored on phone company equipment, not a machine in your home, and you dial a code number to retrieve your messages. Also, unlike an answering machine, voicemail can answer calls and record messages while you are talking to someone else on the phone.

- **Call waiting**. With this service, you can put one caller on hold while you answer a second incoming call on the same line and then switch back and forth between the two conversations as needed. Note, however, that this creates an etiquette problem: it is considered rude to make the first caller hold while you talk to the second caller, so the intended use of this feature is to arrange a time to call the second person back later. (If you must take the second person's call immediately, the polite protocol is to switch back to the first caller and quickly make plans to resume the conversation later.) Also, call waiting does not enable you to answer incoming calls while your phone line is in use for an internet connection; *internet call waiting* is a separate service available from your internet company.

- **Caller ID**. This service, along with a caller ID device connected to your phone, allows you to see who is calling you before you answer the phone. (You will see the caller's number and sometimes the caller's name—unless the caller has arranged to *suppress* caller ID, and there aren't many good reasons why an honest person or business would do that.)

- **Line service contract**. If there is a technical problem with the phone lines outside your home, the phone company is responsible for the cost of repairs; inside your home, you are responsible for the cost of repairs. For a small monthly fee, you can get insurance to cover wiring repairs in your home.

You may need to pay a **deposit** if you do not have credit history in the United States; the deposit is usually the equivalent of two months of basic phone service, and the amount will be refunded or credited to your account after you have paid your bills on time for a year. If you are satisfied with the way the phone jacks (connection sites) in your home are already arranged, the phone company can usually start your service without visiting your home; if you need jacks added or moved, you will need to make an appointment for the phone company to send someone to your home, and the cost of parts and labor will be added to your bill.

LONG DISTANCE CALLS

Long distance calls—to numbers outside your local service area—are billed by the minute. (Within a state, a number with the same area code as yours might be a long distance call from your location.) Some phone companies provide both local and long distance service, but more commonly, you sign up separately for local service and long distance. (You use the same phone line, but the long distance calls you make are billed at a different rate, and you might get a separate bill in the mail and pay a different company for them.)

The cost of long distance calls varies by time of day (cheaper in the evening), day of the week (cheaper on weekends), and on special deals offered by your service. Long distance companies compete fiercely with each other and are always introducing new features and discounts—for example, a reduced rate for calls to family members who have the same service. Look in the Yellow Pages under TELEPHONE - LONG DISTANCE or check out the **Telecommunications Research & Action Center**, an independent organization that provides information about long distance services. Call 202-263-2950 or visit http://trac.org.

Prepaid calling cards enable you to make long distance calls, including international calls, without a long distance service—especially convenient if you haven't opened a bank account or if you're traveling. These cards are available at convenience stores and many other locations and may be the cheapest way to make long distance calls, but it costs extra to use them at payphones. The rates per minute are very low, but there may be hidden charges such as a connection fee or an activation fee. Each time you place a call with the card, a computer voice will tell you how much encoded money value remains on the card and how long you will be able to talk.

If you need to make a long distance call without a prepaid card or long distance service, you can always place a **collect call**. The person who receives the call will be billed for it—at a much higher rate than ordinary long distance calls. (An operator or computer voice will ask the person's permission before putting you on the line.) As a matter of etiquette, collect calls should be used for emergencies or quick messages only. Collect calling service is available nationwide by calling 800-COLLECT (800-265-5328) or 800-CALL ATT (800-225-5288), or by dialing the local operator, **0**.

TELEPHONE FRAUD & ABUSE

Occasionally, you might discover that your long distance service has been changed without your permission—an illegal practice known as **slamming**. Or you might notice that your monthly bill includes charges for special features you did not order or calls you did not make; that's called **cramming**. You cannot be forced to pay these charges, but you need to report the problem to your *local* phone company in order to clear it up. You can also file formal complaints with the **Federal Communications Commission** at 888-225-5322, www.fcc.gov, or **the Federal Trade Commission** at 202-382-4357, www.ftc.gov. Both agencies can impose fines against companies that engage in fraudulent or dishonest practices in interstate commerce. Meanwhile, you can protect against slamming by asking your local phone company to *freeze* your chosen long distance service so it cannot be changed without your authorization.

The Federal Trade Commission can also help if you have been the victim of scams or deceptive solicitations by phone. Many businesses—some reputable, some not—call people at home to peddle goods and services. (Some charities call to solicit donations.) This is called **telemarketing** and almost everybody claims to hate it, but businesses would not keep doing it if it didn't make a profit. Telemarketers often call at dinnertime, because they expect to find most people home at that time; it is perfectly acceptable to tell a caller that you do not accept phone calls during dinner, and you are never obligated (or even expected) to return a telemarketer's call. The people who work for telemarketing firms are just doing their jobs and should not be treated rudely, but etiquette does not require you to allow anyone to bring advertising into your home without your consent—and you should never feel obligated to answer any questions on the phone with a stranger. Many companies will take your number off their telemarketing lists if you ask them to—simply say "Please put me on your *do not call* list."

You can also place your phone number on the Federal Trade Commission's **National Do Not Call Registry**. Telemarketers who call numbers on this list can be fined by the government or sued by individuals. To register, for free, call 800-382-1222 or visit www.donotcall.gov. (Note that charitable or political solicitors are exempt—only commercial sales calls are forbidden.)

If you receive any phone call from an unidentified person who makes obscene or threatening remarks, or if you are being harassed over the phone by someone you know, report the incident to your local phone company. The company may be able to trace the source of the calls and refer the matter to a law enforcement agency. You can also determine the phone number where a call originated if you dial *69 right after you hang up—but it will only work if the call originated locally, and you will be charged a fee for this service. **Note**: *No legitimate business or agency will ever call you and ask for your credit card number or any other financial information.* Nor will any phone company or government agency ever place a collect call to you. (If you call a merchant to place an order, you will of course be asked for a credit card or debit card number—but the merchant did not call you.) Anyone who calls you to obtain financial information, or anyone posing as a government agent and asking you to accept the charges for a collect call, is attempting to rob you of money or valuable information; don't give it to them. Hang up the phone.

WIRELESS PHONE SERVICE AND PAGERS

Some Americans seem to be growing a phone out their ear. You'll see people who are constantly on the phone—walking down the street, sitting in a restaurant, and even while driving.* As with long distance service, competition is fierce and promotional deals vary every week. Check advertisements in the local newspaper or listings in the Yellow Pages under CELLULAR—or visit www.getconnected.com or www.point.com, online vendors of wireless phone service. Most plans include a certain amount of airtime each month and charge by the minute if you exceed that time; some offer free long distance or free airtime at night and on weekends. Watch out for **roaming** charges— higher rates that add up quickly if you use your phone outside a designated home calling area. Long-term contracts often offer the best rates, but have cancellation fees if you change services before your contract expires. If you want to avoid long contracts, deposits, and credit checks, you can get **prepaid wireless service** from one of the

---

*   Illegal in some places. Also, if you are talking on a wireless phone while driving and you're involved in a collision, the courts and the insurance companies can take that into consideration as they decide who is at fault and responsible for the cost of damages.

regular wireless companies or by buying prepaid cellular calling cards, available at many convenience stores and drugstores.

Some people still carry **pagers** (beepers), though they're not as widely used as they were before the emergence of the cell phone. A pager alerts you when someone is trying to reach you; the caller can transmit a phone number he or she wants you to call. Many pagers also allow the caller to leave a voice message or transmit a brief text message. Look in the Yellow Pages under PAGING.

MAIL

Americans like to complain about it, but the U.S. Postal Service is remarkably reliable and fast, considering the volume of mail it handles. It's also fairly inexpensive. Although the price of postage has tripled in the past 25 years, you can still send a letter anywhere in the country for about the same price as the cost of a local call from a pay phone, and it will reach almost any U.S. address within two or three days. In fact, it's *because* the mail is so reliable and affordable that Americans tend to get annoyed when a piece of mail does get lost or delayed.

"When we first got here, we thought the mailboxes were trash bins. I put my banana peels in them." — Victoria Kao, who immigrated from Taiwan at age 8

Mail is also convenient. You do not have to go to the post office to send first class letters under 16 ounces. You can drop them in any of the blue metal **mailboxes** you see on streetcorners or outside public buildings. If mail is delivered to your home in a letterbox at the curb or the front door, you can also leave outbound mail there to be picked up. (Some homes don't have a letterbox, but instead, a slot in the front door.)

Every community in the United States has a **post office** where you can mail packages, buy postage stamps, and arrange for special services such as proof of delivery. Mailing services include:

- **First class mail** for letters and packages. This is regular mail, whether domestic or international.

- **Certified mail** for important documents. For a small fee, the postal service will keep track of the letter and have the addressee sign a receipt to confirm that it was delivered.
- **Registered mail** for valuables, such as jewelry or stock certificates. For a fee, the post office will take special security measures during delivery.
- **Priority mail** for packages that must be delivered in three days or less. You will be charged a certain minimum fee no matter how little the package weighs.
- **Express mail** for letters and packages that must be delivered the next day. Expensive, but cheaper than private overnight delivery services.

The post office can also sell **insurance** to pay for loss of goods sent through the mail; **money orders** (see Chapter 4); and mailing supplies such as boxes, padded envelopes, and cardboard mailing tubes for posters or large documents.

Post offices in cities tend to have long lines around noon, when people take a lunch break from work; post offices also get crowded just before April 15 (the deadline for paying income taxes) and during the winter holiday season. If you have a credit card or debit card, you can order postage stamps delivered to your home—call 800-275-8777 or visit www.usps.com. That's also the phone number and web site to use if you need to look up the zip code for a particular address, calculate the postage for a parcel of a certain weight, find the nearest post office, or notify the postal service when you move. If you have a complaint, you can contact this number or web site to get the number of the postal service's regional **customer service** office.

POST OFFICE BOXES

Sometimes a person or business arranges to receive mail at a **post office box**—a locked bin at the local post office that is rented by the month or the year. For people who move around a lot, this can be more convenient than changing a mailing address every few years. (You can arrange for mail to be *forwarded* to you from any address.) If there are no boxes currently available at a convenient post office, you can also find private mailboxes at **The UPS Store/Mail Boxes Etc.**, a nationwide chain of mailing supply stores: call 800-789-4623 or visit www.mbe.com.

JUNK MAIL

Just as telemarketers use the phone lines to bring advertising into your home, junk mail (the industry prefers the term **direct mail marketing**) is the practice of sending advertisements, product catalogs, and sometimes official-looking letters or phony checks through the mail to promote products or services. And, as with telemarketing, the business advertised might be legitimate or it might not. The difference is that telemarketers waste your time, while junk mailers waste your planet's natural resources.

In most communities, the paper can be recycled. But you can try to reduce the volume of junk mail in the first place by registering your address with the **Mail Preference Service**:

> MAIL PREFERENCE SERVICE
> DIRECT MARKETING ASSOCIATION
> PO BOX 1559
> CARMEL NY 10512

This will deter most direct mail companies, but only those that subscribe to the service and keep their lists up to date. You can register online at www.dmaconsumers.org, and your request will be processed faster, but you will be charged a $5 fee. Also, the major **credit bureaus** share a phone number you can call to ask that your address be removed from any lists they sell to direct mail companies: 888-567-8688.

PRIVATE DELIVERY SERVICES

There are businesses that compete with the postal service for fast shipping of parcels. Some guarantee overnight delivery for a certain price; others handle bulky items at a lower price than the postal service. In many cities, businesses pay courier services to deliver papers or small parcels immediately by bicycle. For overnight delivery, the major nationwide companies are **DHL Worldwide Express**, 800-225-5345 or www.dhl-usa.com, and **FedEx**, 800-238-5355 or www.fedex.com/us. For bulk domestic shipping by air or land, the leading nationwide company is **UPS** (United Parcel Service), 800-742-5877 or www.ups.com. Smaller shipping companies are listed in the Yellow Pages under DELIVERY. And local couriers are listed in the Yellow Pages under COURIER SERVICES and MESSENGERS.

ADDRESSES

Every home, place of business, and public building in the United States has a street address identifying its location by street number; city; state or territory; and **zip code** (postal code). Every state and territory has a two-letter **postal abbreviation**, written in capital letters with no periods, and certain abbreviations are commonly used to identify streets, roads, avenues, boulevards, and other types of thoroughfares. The zip code is nine digits, but only the first five (which represent a geographic area) are required; the use of the four-digit suffix is optional and less common, but it will help ensure fast delivery.

In written English, the city and the state abbreviation are separated by a comma (Baltimore, MD); however, the postal service recommends that an address be printed on a piece of mail in ALL CAPITAL LETTERS WITH NO PUNCTUATION MARKS AT ALL.* As in most countries, the address is printed in the center of the envelope or parcel, and the sender's address is printed in the upper left corner (or on the flap of the envelope) in case the piece cannot be delivered or the addressee had moved. So, for example, a letter might be addressed like this:

JANE DOE
PRESIDENT
APPLE COLLEGE
2280 APPLEVIEW DR
APPLETON OR 97223

STATES & TERRITORIES

For most states and territories, there are two recognized abbreviations: a two-letter postal abbreviation, always in capital letters with no period, and an abbreviation that starts with a capital letter and is followed by a period. The postal abbreviation is always used on mail or in a written address, and it may also be used in general writing. The second abbreviation shown here, if any, is the older style of abbreviation still used in formal writing and in newspapers. (Some states' names are not abbreviated in formal writing—states whose names are not more than six letters long.)

---

* One exception is the symbol ℅, meaning *in care of.* You could write to the author of this book in care of the publisher—MIKE LIVINGSTON ℅ FIRST BOOKS, 6750 SW FRANKLIN ST, PORTLAND OR 97223.

	POSTAL	FORMAL
ALABAMA	AL	Ala.
ALASKA	AK	—
ARIZONA	AZ	Ariz.
ARKANSAS	AR	Ark.
CALIFORNIA	CA	Calif.
COLORADO	CO	Colo.
CONNECTICUT	CT	Conn.
DELAWARE	DE	Del.
FLORIDA	FL	Fla.
GEORGIA	GA	Ga.
HAWAII	HI	—
IDAHO	ID	—
ILLINOIS	IL	Ill.
INDIANA	IN	Ind.
IOWA	IA	—
KANSAS	KS	Kan.
KENTUCKY	KY	Ky.
LOUISIANA	LA	La.
MAINE	ME	—
MARYLAND	MD	Md.
MASSACHUSETTS	MA	Mass.
MICHIGAN	MI	Mich.
MINNESOTA	MN	Minn.
MISSISSIPPI	MS	Miss.
MISSOURI	MO	Mo.
MONTANA	MT	Mont.
NEBRASKA	NE	Neb.
NEVADA	NV	Nev.
NEW JERSEY	NJ	N.J.
NEW HAMPSHIRE	NH	N.H.
NEW MEXICO	NM	N.M.
NEW YORK	NY	N.Y.
NORTH CAROLINA	NC	N.C.
NORTH DAKOTA	ND	N.D.
OHIO	OH	—
OKLAHOMA	OK	Okla.
OREGON	OR	Ore.
PENNSYLVANIA	PA	Pa.
RHODE ISLAND	RI	R.I.
SOUTH CAROLINA	SC	S.C.

	POSTAL	FORMAL
SOUTH DAKOTA	SD	S.D.
TENNESSEE	TN	Tenn.
TEXAS	TX	—
UTAH	UT	—
VERMONT	VT	Vt.
VIRGINIA	VA	Va.
WASHINGTON	WA	Wash.
WEST VIRGINIA	WV	W.Va.
WISCONSIN	WI	Wis.
WYOMING	WY	Wyo.
AMERICAN SAMOA	AS	A.S.
DISTRICT OF COLUMBIA	DC	D.C.
GUAM	GU	—
PUERTO RICO	PR	P.R.
NORTHERN MARIANAS	—	—
U.S. VIRGIN ISLANDS	USVI	USVI

OTHER POSTAL ABBREVIATIONS

These are the abbreviations preferred by the postal service for the most common types of streets, roads, and thoroughfares in U.S. addresses, and for other words often found in addresses:

APARTMENT	APT
AVENUE	AVE
BOULEVARD	BLVD
CIRCLE	CIR
COURT	CT
DEPARTMENT	DEPT
DIVISION	DIV
DRIVE	DR
EXPRESSWAY	EXPY
FLOOR	FL
FORT	FT
FREEWAY	FWY
HEIGHTS	HTS
HIGHWAY	HWY
LANE	LN
MOUNT	MT
MOUNTAIN	MTN

PARKWAY	PKWY
PLACE	PL
ROAD	RD
ROUTE	RTE
RURAL ROUTE	RR
STREET	ST
SQUARE	SQ
STATION	STA
SUITE	STE
TERRACE	TER
TOWNSHIP	TWP
TURNPIKE	TPK

INTERNET

A growing majority of the U.S. population has access to the internet at home, at work, or both. In addition to dial-up service through a phone line, high-speed internet connections such as DSL lines are available in most urban areas. You can also connect to the internet through a cable TV provider's lines and, in some places, by wireless modem (*wi-fi*). Most **internet service providers (ISPs)** charge a flat monthly rate, not a rate based on minutes or hours.

The biggest complaints of U.S. internet users are the high rates of **spam**, or unwanted commercial e-mail messages (often advertising pornography, scams, or both) and the prospect of young children finding and viewing inappropriate images on the web. Most of the nation's 7,000 ISPs, and all of the major nationwide ones, offer software to help block spam and to let parents set some restrictions on their children's unsupervised internet use. Almost all ISPs require you to use a credit card or debit card to set up an account and pay the monthly bill. Some ISPs offer a few weeks of free service on a trial basis—and if you don't cancel the trial subscription before the trial period ends, you automatically become a paying subscriber and your credit card or bank account will be charged at the beginning of each month.

ISPs are listed in the Yellow Pages under INTERNET and prominently advertised in many magazines and newspapers. The biggest nationwide services are:

- **America Online (AOL)**, 800-827-6364, www.aol.com
- **Earthlink**, 800-395-8425, www.earthlink.net
- **Microsoft Network (MSN)**, 800-426-9400, www.msn.com

In some communities, you can find **internet cafés** (cybercafés)—casual restaurants or coffee bars that have internet terminals you can rent by the hour. Look for one at www.cybercafes.com. **FedEx Kinko's**, 800-254-6567 or www.fedexkinkos.com, is a nationwide chain of photocopy shops where you can rent computers by the hour for internet purposes or other uses; you can find local businesses that provide similar services in the Yellow Pages under COPY. (And remember, you can connect to the internet for free at any public library.)

• • • • • • • • • • • • • • •

INTEGRATED TELECOM SERVICES

Some telecommunications companies offer local phone service, long distance phone service, cable TV, and internet service all on one account with one monthly bill. Each of the services is cheaper if you buy several services from the same provider—for instance, the cheapest way to get a high-speed DSL connection to the internet is to subscribe to DSL service provided by your phone company.

• • • • • • • • • • • • • • •

TELEVISION & RADIO

Throughout the United States, traditional **broadcast TV** stations carry both national network programming and local programming—typically just a dozen or so stations in each city or viewing area. These broadcasts are free; all you need is a TV set with an antenna. Depending on your location, reception might be clear or fuzzy. Most U.S. households subscribe to either **cable TV** or **satellite TV** service, which provides hundreds of channels and perfectly clear images, for a monthly fee. **Basic cable** service typically includes 60 to 80 channels of entertainment, educational programming, news, weather, sports, music, and old movies; **premium cable** service includes additional channels you select, such as movie channels that show recent films. Some premium channels show movies and sporting events on a **pay-per-view** basis instead of charging a flat monthly fee.

Cable TV is a locally regulated industry. Look in the Yellow Pages under TELEVISION - CABLE to find the companies authorized to provide service in your city or county and check the Blue Pages for the local government's office of cable communications, the agency to call if you have any complaints about service. If your home is already equipped for cable TV, the company will simply supply you with a control box to hook up to your TV set; if you want to rearrange or add cable outlets (sockets), the company will send technicians in and bill you for parts and labor. Only the oldest TV sets you might find in a resale store (see Chapter 7) need special adapters to accommodate a cable.

Satellite TV is similar to cable, but is beamed to your home through a satellite dish antenna. The leading nationwide providers of satellite TV service are **DirecTV**, 800-494-4388 or www.directv.com, and **DISH Network**, 800-333-3474 or www.dishnetwork.com. These services feature more channels than most cable systems.

Local newspapers carry daily and weekly schedules of TV programs on broadcast and cable channels available in the area, and regional editions of *TV Guide* magazine (with weekly program listings) are available at newsstands, drugstores, and supermarkets. You can also look up the TV listings for your zip code at www.tvguide.com.

Most areas have a variety of **radio stations**— some devoted to popular or current music; some to classical, jazz, rap, country-western, gospel, *oldies* (music from the 1950s and '60s), or *golden oldies* (music from the 1940s and

PUBLIC RADIO & TELEVISION

There is no government radio station broadcasting within the United States; radio stations are dependent on advertising fees paid by sponsors. There are, however, two *public radio networks*—independent nonprofit corporations that are funded by charitable donations and government subsidies—that carry public affairs programming, fine arts, special-interest talk shows, and other material that might not be able to compete in a media market that revolves around the needs of corporate sponsors. Most large cities have at least one station that carries programming from either **National Public Radio (NPR)**, www.npr.gov, or **Pacifica Radio**, www.pacifica.org.

There is no national government TV station either (except the NASA channel, which shows live video from the International Space Station and the Space Shuttle). The **Public Broadcasting Service (PBS)** is a TV network whose affiliated local stations, like their public radio counterparts, carry public affairs, educational, and cultural programming. PBS stations receive charitable donations and some government aid. For information, visit www.pbs.org. Most local governments have cable TV stations that carry local public affairs programs. Also, by federal law, every cable system must provide a public access channel for programs produced by members of the community. (So you can start your own cable TV show in your jurisdiction by simply signing up for a time slot and taking some required orientation classes.)

Finally, on cable TV and broadcast radio, you can watch or hear **C-SPAN** (Cable-Satellite Public Affairs Network) provide unedited coverage of the day's proceedings in Congress or federal agencies. The network's web site, www.cspan.org, offers lots of background information about the U.S. government.

earlier); and some to news, sports, or discussion of current events. In general, music stations are found on the FM band (88 MHz to 108 MHz) and *talk radio* (news, sports, and discussion) stations are found on the AM band (530 KHz to 1700 KHz). The arts section of your local newspaper might feature a list of local radio stations, their frequencies, and their formats or type of programming; if not, just explore the dial.

In 2002, a *satellite radio* network started offering a menu of several dozen nationwide radio stations transmitted by digital signals (with CD sound quality) to special radio receivers. Like satellite TV, this is a service that requires a monthly subscription—but the variety of programming available is much more diverse than broadcast radio. For information, contact **XM Satellite Radio** at 800-852-9696 or www.xmradio.com.

LANGUAGE

American English, like the rest of American culture, is a "melting pot" of diverse influences—it's constantly evolving. There's regional variation in dialect and pronunciation, and various ethnic groups in the United States have distinctive speech patterns. There is no single authority (like the French Academy) to rule on questions of proper English. Still, American English is a far more universal language than, for example, the regional languages spoken within China or many African nations.

Americans use many **idioms** or **figures of speech** that are not to be taken literally. New slang words or idiomatic phrases are always appearing and others disappearing from common use. Advertising copy and commercial products or companies are especially stylized in their spelling and usage. If you haven't been exposed to a lot of U.S. culture through film and TV, you might find it helpful—even if you're fluent in English—to check out a phrasebook of American figures of speech. *What Are Those Crazy Americans Saying?* by Jarold Kieffer (Kieffer Publications) is an excellent one.

NOT THE QUEEN'S ENGLISH

Newcomers who learned English in a British school or from a British teacher will find many little differences between American and British expressions and forms. A Yankee and a Brit can understand each other without difficulty, but there are lots of words and phrases—especially colloquialisms—that need to be translated. In England, *knocked up* means *awakened with a knock on the door*; in the United States, it's a rude synonym for *pregnant*. In England, the front lid of a car is the *bonnet* and the rear storage compartment is the *boot*; here, the front is the *hood* and the rear is the *trunk*, and if you try to *hire* a *lorry*, the American clerk might not know you want to *rent* a *truck*. And these are just a few examples. If you speak in a British manner, don't be surprised if some Americans seem puzzled occasionally. Spelling, too, is sometimes different—but you've probably noticed that already.

> BRIT: Do you have a favourite programme on the tele?
>
> YANK: No, I have a favorite program on TV.

Also, certain conventions of style in writing and typesetting are different from European styles, as you may have noticed throughout this book. For instance, in Europe, a decimal fraction is separated from a whole number by a comma; in the United States, a decimal fraction is separated by a point (dot), and a comma is used to separate each multiple of a thousand. So the number twenty-one thousand two and a half, written **21 002,50** in Europe, is written **21,002.50** here. European quotation marks look like «this» whereas American quotation marks look like "this." And the numerals **1** and **7** also look slightly different here than in Europe.

LANGUAGE AND THE LAW

The United States does not have an official language. Some government agencies are required by law to accommodate the language needs of any resident in need of service. Some conservative political leaders propose to make English the official language, which would mean the government is not required to interact with anybody in other languages. There are areas in many cities where another language is prevalent—usually Spanish, Korean, or a Chinese dialect. Every child in public school studies English; many study a second language, at least at a basic level. All public schools must provide **English as a Second Language (ESL)** classes to any student who needs them, as determined by a test of reading and writing skills. (See Chapter 11.)

If you ever have to deal with the police, the courts, the USCIS, Homeland Security, or other law enforcement officials—or a hospital, or a public school that your child attends—you can always ask for an interpreter. Never try to guess at the meaning of contracts or other legal documents if the legal jargon is beyond your comfort level with written English—have a trusted person explain it to you.

BODY LANGUAGE

Body language—hand gestures, eye contact, posture, and other non-verbal clues to a person's mood and meaning—is an important part of communication, and newcomers should learn the meaning of certain gestures. Some "hands-on" gestures, such as a handshake or a hug, are discussed in Chapter 13, but here are some additional points of body language:

- Americans normally make **eye contact** when speaking to each other; if you come from a culture in which it is respectful to look down when facing a superior, such as a boss or schoolteacher, you will probably hear such people say "Look at me when I'm talking to you!" Eye contact is considered a sign of attention, interest, and honesty.

- If you shake or **nod** your head up and down, it means *yes*; if you twist your head from side to side, it means *no*. Americans also make certain tonal humming or guttural sounds that mean *yes* or *no*. These sounds are best expressed in print as "uh-huh" or "mm-hmm," a pair of vague murmurs that derive their meaning from pitch: a low tone followed by a higher one means yes and a high tone followed by a lower one means no. (Ask an American friend to demonstrate "uh-huh" and "mm-hmm" for you.)

- Two **hand gestures** that indicate approval or readiness are similar to gestures that have rude or obscene meanings in some cultures. It's important to know that, in the United States, it's a positive statement when you point your thumb straight up while curling your other fingers tight like a fist, or when you make a circle with your thumb and forefinger and extend your other three fingers upward. Oh, and sticking your middle finger straight up is considered vulgar and rude.

  When Americans count with their fingers, they usually start with the forefinger and count the thumb last, in contrast to the European habit. The first and second fingers held up like a **V** can therefore mean two, but it is also a gesture that can mean, curiously, either peace or victory.

"OK" gesture - everything is all right.

- In a classroom or a large meeting, you can indicate that you wish to speak by **raising your hand** above your head.
- One hand held up at shoulder or eye level, palm forward, can mean *stop* if it's held still and *hello* or *goodbye* if it is waved from side to side.
- Holding both hands high above your head is the gesture of **surrender** to the police or to an armed criminal.

Another important aspect of body language is **social distance**—how close to another person you normally stand during a conversation. This is not something people often think about, much less talk about, but on a subconscious or instinctive level, your American acquaintances will habitually step away from you if you are standing too close or step toward you if you are standing too far away. After this happens a few times, you'll develop a feel for the proper distance—but typically, two people who are not intimate partners will stand or sit about an arm's length apart, a distance at which you could just place your hand on top of the other person's shoulder.

And one final consideration is **hygiene**. Lorin Kleinman, an Anglo-American etiquette columnist who grew up in Germany, observes that Americans tend to be more concerned about hygiene than most people. It may seem extravagant, but most Americans shower or bathe every day. We also, men and women alike, use a variety of scented toiletries (colognes and perfumes, deodorants, antiperspirants, aftershave lotions, soaps, oils, and powders) to hide our natural human odors—and we brush our teeth two or three times a day and chew minty lozenges to conceal breath odors. (Curiously, however, many Americans are lazy about washing their hands after going to the bathroom. In restaurants, you will see signs reminding customers and employees to wash their hands.) If your culture does not equate floral or spicy scents with cleanliness and health, then some Americans—however friendly they may be—will probably think you "smell funny." And nobody wants to be so rude as to say so. You will make friends who will accept and appreciate you as you are, but in a workplace or among new acquaintances, try to smell like soap.

CHAPTER SIX

STREET SMARTS

> If you feel your dream holiday to the U.S. or Canada could turn
> into a nightmare of medical bills and muggings...
>
> — *Advertisement in London for travel
> insurance*

A n American from New York was talking with an Israeli soldier
in Gaza. The soldier, wearing bandoliers of live ammunition
and holding a machine gun, seemed almost oblivious to the
sound of rocket fire and distant gunshots as he asked the American:
"New York? Isn't it dangerous there?"

Actually, your chance of being robbed, kidnapped, or assaulted
in the United States is pretty low, but there are things you can do to
minimize that risk—and things that could attract the wrong kind of
attention and make you seem like an easy target for crime or fraud.
And even nonviolent crime, such as dishonest business or *con games*
(taking advantage of a person's confidence), can cost you a lot of
money and inconvenience if you're not alert.

It's also important to know some basic laws and expectations.
Activities that might be perfectly acceptable in your native country
might be illegal here, and we might routinely engage in behavior that
would be illegal back home. You'll need to become familiar with social norms and be able to recognize appropriate and inappropriate
behavior; or, as Americans say, you'll need to develop some *street smarts*.

PUBLIC RESTROOMS

You will not, in most U.S. cities, find free-standing restrooms or "water closets" except in parks. Public restrooms—also called *bathrooms,
lavatories,* or *the men's room* and *the women's* or *ladies' room*—are found in
almost all public buildings, restaurants, indoor shopping malls, and
gas (petrol) stations; all airports, train stations, and bus stations; and
some department stores, supermarkets, parks, tourist landmarks, and
subway (metro) stations. Only in the fanciest hotels or restaurants is
the restroom staffed by an attendant, and in most places, you do not
have to pay to use the facilities. In some fast-food restaurants and gas
stations, the restroom is locked and you have to ask the cashier (clerk)
for the key.

Men's and women's restrooms are usually separate and marked by internationally recognizable icons
or by the words *men* or *gentlemen* and *women* or *ladies*.
In some smaller establishments, such as cafés or
bookstores, you might see a door with both men's
and women's icons on it; that means it's a small
restroom, like the one in a private home, available
to only one person at a time. The door will be locked
if anyone is inside.

Symbols designat-
ing women's and
men's restrooms.

At an outdoor festival or concert, or in a park,
you may see *portable toilets*—plastic booths that contain a single com-
mode and urinal. These, like small restrooms, can be locked from the
inside when in use.

American men's rooms include toilets in separate stalls, individual
urinals, lavatories (sinks), and sometimes a table or shelf for changing a baby's diaper. Women's rooms include toilets in stalls, lavatories, a shelf for changing diapers, and receptacles for used sanitary
items. Standard plumbing fixtures in the United States will become
clogged if you flush anything other than human waste and toilet paper (bathroom tissue). Bidets are very rare here.

It is generally acceptable for young children (up to 6 years old)
to accompany a parent into a public restroom regardless of gender.

CONTROLLED SUBSTANCES

Alcohol, tobacco, narcotics, and various mood-altering drugs and
medications are regulated by federal and state laws. Some are sold
only under certain circumstances and only to adults; some are available only with a doctor's prescription; and some are prohibited. Penalties for drug violations can be very severe.

ALCOHOLIC BEVERAGES

Alcoholic beverages are regulated by state governments, and in most
states, you must be at least 21 years old to buy or consume alcohol.
These laws do not apply to religious rituals and are generally not
enforced with regard to family meals in private homes. You may be
asked to show ID (a passport or driver's license) when you purchase
alcohol to prove your age. At many bars and nightclubs, it is the
owner's policy to "card" everyone (check ID) at the door and not
allow anyone under 21 to come in.

Alcoholic beverages are taxed by the state and federal governments and command much higher prices in restaurants than at retail stores. (Restaurants rely on the sale of alcoholic drinks to make a large portion of their profit; you might pay $4 for a bottle of beer in a restaurant and then see the same beer in a store for $1.) In some states, retail sale of hard liquor is limited to state-run stores, and in some states, only specially licensed stores may sell beer and wine.

The standard serving of beer in the United States is 12 ounces (about 375 mL) and some bars and restaurants serve a pint (470 mL). A glass of wine is 4 ounces, and a shot of liquor or a mixed drink usually contains 1 ounce of liquor. These standard servings each contain roughly the same amount of alcohol—half an ounce (15 mL). *Know your capacity.* Even if you don't do anything that actually hurts anybody, public drunkenness itself is a petty crime in most jurisdictions—you could be ordered to pay a fine or spend a night in jail for *disorderly conduct.*

Driving while intoxicated (DWI) is a serious crime that can result in jail time or in loss of your driver's license. In addition to criminal penalties, a drunk driver will be held responsible for property damage and medical bills. Every state sets a level of *blood alcohol content* that automatically constitutes the crime of DWI. If the police suspect you are under the influence of alcohol, they will stop you and administer a series of tests. If you appear to have difficulty speaking, walking, or following directions, they will analyze a sample of your breath. In most states, if your blood alcohol level is higher than 0.08%, you will automatically be charged with DWI. If it's lower, but it appears that alcohol was a factor in reckless driving, you may be charged with **driving under the influence** (DUI), a crime with somewhat less severe penalties.

For these reasons, and for safety, any group of people going to a bar or party where alcohol is served should have a **designated driver**—one person who agrees to stay sober and give everyone else a ride home. (Better yet, take public transportation.) A bartender or the host of a party cannot allow you to drive away in an impaired condition; he or she could face legal sanctions. If you've been drinking, a friend or co-worker—or the bartender—may take away your car keys. They're not stealing; they're looking after your safety and may well save your life and others.

If you find yourself drinking too much alcohol—for example, if your drinking habits start to affect your work or your family life—

you can get free help in every city from the local chapter of Alcoholics Anonymous, a network of people who work together to help each other quit drinking alcohol.

TOBACCO

Tobacco has been a leading export from North America since the first European colonists learned about the plant from the indigenous people. Tobacco is still a $45 billion industry; in 2001, U.S. companies produced more than half a trillion cigarettes.

Yet Americans' attitudes toward tobacco are changing. A series of lawsuits in the 1990s exposed the fact that cigarette manufacturers had been concealing information about the health effects of smoking, and as part of the legal settlement, tobacco companies paid millions of dollars into state funds to produce educational materials and advertisements urging young people not to smoke. Since 1970, the number of smokers in the United States has declined by 32%, to roughly ¼ of the adult population, according to World Health Organization figures.

Some cities and counties prohibit smoking in public buildings and commercial establishments, and many private workplaces restrict or prohibit smoking. It is illegal everywhere to smoke in confined spaces such as buses, subways, and elevators. Most restaurants have a nonsmoking section; some allow smoking only at the bar. Cigar and pipe smoking is not welcome in many indoor places, but some bars and restaurants specifically offer a cigar lounge. Chewing tobacco, likewise, is considered an outdoor activity.

You must be at least 18 years old in order to buy tobacco products.

ILLEGAL DRUGS

Alcohol, tobacco, and federally approved medications are the only legal drugs in the United States. In many places, there is underground trade in marijuana, cocaine/crack, heroin, LSD ("acid"), methamphetamines (notably "ecstasy"), and other controlled (restricted) substances. Aliens convicted of selling or possessing illegal drugs are likely to be deported, and citizens face long prison sentences and large fines. Possession of more than a tiny quantity of illegal drugs may be treated by the courts as evidence of *intent to distribute,* so a drug user may be tried and sentenced as a dealer, subject to much tougher penalties. And it's illegal to buy, sell, or possess prescription medications without a doctor's orders.

RESTRICTED ACTIVITIES

These activities are limited by law to certain circumstances:

- **Gambling.** It is illegal to place bets (wagers) on games of chance or sporting events except at licensed casinos and horse racetracks; in state lotteries; or in certain regulated situations where games of chance raise money for a recognized charity. These laws are usually not enforced with regard to low-stakes "friendly" wagers, such as workplace bets on sporting events. Many businesses—especially radio stations—sponsor *contests* or *sweepstakes* in which participants are selected at random to win prizes; however, by law, the business cannot require you to make a purchase in order to participate.

- **Prostitution.** It is illegal in every state except Nevada to accept *or offer* money in exchange for sexual favors. In most cities, prostitution is closely related to trade in illegal drugs.

- **Pornography.** You must be 18 years old (in some states, 21) to buy or rent sexually explicit publications or films. The courts have recognized that it is hard to say exactly what constitutes pornography—for example, Michelangelo's *David* could be classified as obscene if some state laws were applied too literally—but any sexually graphic material that the *local community* considers obscene may be restricted.

- **Movies.** In 1968, the film industry feared that the government would ban movies that depicted too much sex, violence, or offensive language. To avoid government interference, the Motion Picture Association of America began to label movies with ratings to warn parents if a film might be unsuitable for children. The ratings in use today are:

G	general audiences—all ages admitted
PG	parental guidance suggested—some material may not be suitable for children
PG-13	parents strongly cautioned—some material may be inappropriate for children under 13

R   restricted—under 17 requires accompanying parent or adult guardian

NC-17 no one 17 and under admitted

X   sexually explicit

NR   not rated (documentaries and films not widely distributed)

• •

PARENTAL ADVISORIES

TV programs, like movies, carry ratings to warn parents of sexual or violent themes. These ratings are just informational—unlike movie ratings, they don't prevent children from viewing the material.

TVY   program suitable for young children

TVY7   program suitable for children ages 7 and above

TVY7-FV   program suitable for children ages 7 and above, but depicts fantasy violence

TVG   program suitable for general audience (all ages)

TVPG   parental guidance suggested for young viewers; program depicts moderate levels of violence (V), sexual situations (S), or adult language (L) or dialogue (D)

TV14   parents strongly cautioned; program depicts intense violence (V), sexual situations (S), or adult language (L) or dialogue (D)

TVMA   mature audience only; program depicts graphic violence (V), sex (S) or crude language (L)

Recorded music with graphic sexual or violent lyrics usually has a parental advisory label on the package, but it is up to the individual merchant to decide whether to sell the recording to children. And computer games carry these advisory ratings:

Ao   suitable for adults only

E   suitable for everyone

eC   suitable for early childhood

M   suitable for mature users

T   suitable for teens

• •

- **Hunting & fishing.** Game animals may be hunted only during certain designated seasons and in limited numbers, and you must purchase a state hunting or fishing permit. (Under federal law, ecologically threatened or endangered species may not be hunted at all.) In most states, a *fish & game service* or a *natural resources* agency is responsible for these permits and regulations.
- **Marriage.** In order to get married in a manner recognized by civil authorities, you must get a marriage license from the state, regardless of arrangements with a religious institution. The appropriate agency is usually listed in the Blue Pages under MARRIAGE LICENSES. Civil marriages (secular wedding ceremonies) are performed by a local court official called a *justice of the peace*. A few states recognize civil union or marriage of same-sex couples; for information about same-sex partnership rights in your state, contact the Lambda Legal Defense & Education Fund at 212-809-8585 or www.lambdalegal.org.
- **Licensed professions.** There are dozens of professions and trades that may not be practiced without a license. The list varies from one state to another; most states have an *occupational licensing bureau* to administer exams and collect license fees.

DRIVING

Driver's licenses are issued by state governments. In most states, drivers must be at least 16 years old and pass a vision test and a written test on traffic law as well as a test of actual driving skills. You pay a fee when your license is issued and to renew it every few years. If you do not already have a driver's license from a country whose licenses are recognized by your new home state, you will have to apply first for a **learner's permit**, which allows you to drive under the supervision of a licensed driver while you practice for the driving test.

The agency that issues driver's licenses—known in most states as the *Department of Motor Vehicles* or the *Motor Vehicle Administration*—also issues **registration** papers and **license plates** (tags) to vehicle owners. All vehicles on public roads must display a government-issued license plate with a current registration sticker showing that registration fees for the current year have been paid. To register a vehicle, you will have to show proof of ownership (such as a bill of sale) and pay a state tax, usually a percentage of the sale price; many states also require that a vehicle be tested for safety and clean emissions. You will also need to show proof of **insurance**.

Because driver's licenses, vehicle registrations, and license plates are issued by the state, you must get new ones if you move from one state to another—usually within 30 or 60 days after you move. **Motorcycles** must be registered and licensed just like cars, and operators must have a motorcycle driver's license.

Check the state web site or the Blue Pages of the phone book to find the nearest office of your state's motor vehicle agency.

AUTO INSURANCE

It is illegal to drive without **liability insurance** to cover, in the event of an accident, the cost of medical care for anyone you might injure and the cost of any property you might damage. The amount of coverage required by law varies from one state to another—but you only need to meet the requirements of the state where your vehicle is registered, not every state you might visit. The basic principles of insurance are presented in more detail in Chapter 10; essentially, in return for a monthly contribution or *premium,* an insurance fund will compensate anyone injured or deprived of property in a collision that is found to be your fault. (Liability insurance is not the same as **collision insurance**, which pays for damage to *your* vehicle after a collision that is your fault. Collision insurance is not required by law, but is advisable if you would have difficulty paying for unexpected car repairs.)

The price you will be charged for liability insurance is based on your **driving record**—the number of times you have been found to violate traffic laws or cause an accident. The state keeps track of this information, and insurance companies will ask for it. (So will employers if you apply for a job that involves driving.) Insurance companies also consider your age, gender, marital status, and where you learned to drive. Before you buy an insurance policy, get several quotes from different companies listed in the Yellow Pages under INSURANCE. For more information about insurance companies, visit www.checkbook.org and www.consumerreports.org.

Sometimes newcomers have difficulty getting auto insurance because they do not have an official driving record. Ask an insurance agent about state insurance funds for persons who are considered "high risk" drivers and cannot get private insurance policies. It's an expensive alternative, but after a year of safe driving, you should have a record that enables you to get cheaper insurance.

TRAFFIC LAWS & CUSTOMS

Someone who learned to drive in Paris might think U.S. drivers are remarkably disciplined. Someone who learned to drive in Singapore might think U.S. drivers are a bunch of anarchists. They would both have a point. Every state has many detailed traffic rules, signs, and signals that must be obeyed, both for legal reasons and for safety; but many American drivers operate just barely within the law, or just outside it—especially with regard to the posted speed limit. The result is a fairly predictable standard of behavior on the road most of the time—it's not a chaotic free-for-all, but there are dangerous surprises.

Unless a serious crime is involved, such as DWI or resisting arrest (fleeing from the police), most traffic violations do not require you to appear in court and will not appear on criminal background checks. **Moving violations** (violations of traffic laws) and **parking violations** (parking in a restricted space) are enforced with written citations, or **tickets**, stating that a law enforcement officer witnessed the violation and that you must pay a fine. If you get a ticket, you must either pay the fine within a certain period (usually 30 or 45 days) or *appeal* (challenge) the citation. You can pay the fine by mail or at an address shown on the ticket, and in some jurisdictions, you can file an appeal by mail; in others, if you want to challenge the ticket and try to avoid the fine, you have to go to traffic court and plead your case to a judge. Local governments rely on the fact that the appeals process is usually so long and tedious that most people find it easier to just pay the fine whether they think it is fair or not.

Traffic laws vary from one state to another, but the most basic law is that local traffic signs and signals must be obeyed—or, if there is a police officer or other public safety official directing traffic, he or she overrules any signs or signals and must be obeyed. Still, you should know these general rules and customs observed throughout most of the country:

- Traffic moves on the **right side** of the road, and on multi-lane highways, slower traffic is supposed to keep to the right and faster traffic moves to the left for passing. Passing on the right is discouraged and, in some places, illegal.

Drivers are advised to follow the vehicle ahead of theirs at a distance no less than twice the length of their own vehicle; following a vehicle too closely is called *tailgating* and is both dangerous and rude.

- **Red lights** always mean *stop* and **green lights** always mean *go*. **Yellow lights** usually mean *proceed with caution,* but in some cities, it is illegal to enter an intersection when the light is yellow. In most places, the signal lights at intersections are stacked vertically with red on top, yellow in the middle, and green on the bottom. A colored arrow governs traffic that is turning in the direction indicated.

- The **speed limit** on most interstate highways outside of urban areas is 65 or 70 miles per hour, but the local speed limit is always indicated by signs and may be enforced by hidden radar or, in a few cities, by hidden cameras. (Your speed can be determined by the distance travelled between two photos, and your legal address can be determined from your license plate number. So you might get a speeding ticket in the mail.)

- In most states, it is mandatory for everyone in a moving car to wear a **seatbelt** at all times. In some states, you can be stopped by the police and fined for not wearing a seatbelt. *Children must ride in a federally approved* **child safety seat** *up to a certain age and weight specified by state law,* usually six years and 40 pounds; the nonprofit National Safe Kids Campaign recommends using child safety seats up to eight years and 65 pounds. (Contact Safe Kids at 202-662-0600, www.safekids.org, or the National Highway Traffic Safety Administration at www.nhtsa.dot.gov for details about the proper use of passenger restraints.) Many foreign-made child safety seats are not legal for use in the United States—if you bring one with you, get it inspected by a local Child Passenger Safety Technician listed on the Safe Kids web site. (This is a free service.)

- Unless otherwise posted, in most areas it is permissible to **turn right at a red light** after first coming to a complete stop. A red octagonal STOP sign, used at intersections not busy enough to warrant traffic lights, requires you to come to a complete stop and then proceed; if more than one vehicle reaches an intersection at once, and each vehicle is subject to a STOP sign, the vehicle on the right (counterclockwise) has the right of way. And a *flashing* red light means the same thing as a STOP sign.

• Other distinctive **traffic signs** used throughout much of the country include:

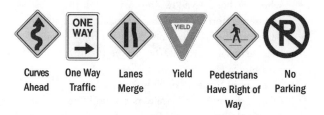

| Curves Ahead | One Way Traffic | Lanes Merge | Yield | Pedestrians Have Right of Way | No Parking |

• It is customary and, in many states, mandatory to use electronic **turn signals** when preparing to turn or to change lanes. The horn is intended as a warning device for emergencies or hazardous situations, and may provoke hostile reactions if used in congested traffic.

• Many major bridges and tunnels, and some highways, are subject to **tolls**. In some cases you pay a fixed toll to enter; on some highways, instead, you receive a ticket upon entry and present it to the gatekeeper on exit, and pay a toll based on the distance traveled. If you are a frequent user of a toll road, you can arrange to make a monthly payment and get a sticker or placard indicating payment, or get an electronic pass that lets you go through the tollgate and receive a bill in the mail for your tolls each month.

• If you hear **sirens** or see **flashing lights**, move to the right and allow the emergency vehicle to pass. If you see flashing red lights on a stopped **schoolbus**, do not pass; not even emergency vehicles are allowed to pass a schoolbus that is loading or discharging passengers. (Most schoolbuses are painted a distinctive yellowish-orange.) Public safety vehicles have red and blue warning lights; construction, utility, and sanitation vehicles that may disrupt traffic have amber-colored warning lights.

• If you are involved in a **collision**, *you must stop and wait for the police.* If you can help any injured people at the scene, you must do so—for example, if you have a wireless phone, you have a legal duty to call for an ambulance. You should not make any statements about the incident or discuss who was at fault; if you even say "I'm sorry" to a person whose vehicle collided with yours, a lawyer can argue in court that you admitted some measure of responsibility. The only information you should (and must) exchange with other drivers involved is your name and the name and policy number of your auto insurance plan. Beyond that, just wait for the police and answer their questions, and don't hesitate to request an interpreter. Leaving the scene of a collision in which you are involved is a crime known as *hit-and-run driving*.

- If you are stopped by the **police**, pull to the shoulder (side) of the road in a well-lit area and remain seated in your car. Keep your hands where the police officer can see them—either on the steering wheel or above your head—until the officer asks for your papers. (You will be required to show your driver's license and the vehicle registration papers, which must be kept in the vehicle at all times.) Do not make any sudden moves or reach for anything out of sight—if the police think you are reaching for a weapon, they could panic and shoot you. Most traffic stops go smoothly and result in a ticket

RECOGNIZING THE POLICE

If you think you're talking to a police officer, make sure he or she is the real thing. Sometimes thieves pose as police officers in order to get inside people's homes or to make drivers stop on a remote stretch of highway. (This is rare, but newcomers may be especially vulnerable to such tricks.) A law enforcement officer will always wear a numbered metal badge when in uniform, and the uniform should display the officer's name on an engraved bar or embroidered patch. An *undercover* officer (dressed in plain clothes) will show you a badge and a police department ID in a wallet or case. Police cars might not bear distinctive markings, but they are always equipped with red and blue warning lights (perhaps concealed when not in use); a loudspeaker or bullhorn; a bright searchlight; and two-way radio equipment. Impersonating a police officer is a serious crime.

or a written warning, but misunderstandings can be very dangerous.

PEDESTRIAN SAFETY & LAWS

Pedestrians are required to cross the street at a corner; *jaywalking,* or crossing the street in the middle of a block, leads to thousands of deaths and injuries every year and in most places it's illegal. On large or busy streets, look for a **crosswalk**—a set of lines painted across the road to mark the area where pedestrians should cross. Drivers must yield to pedestrians crossing in the crosswalk. At intersections with traffic lights, cross only when the light *facing you* is *green*—and even then, always look both ways and don't assume all drivers will obey the traffic signals.

At the largest or busiest intersections, there may be special traffic lights for pedestrians. Older **walk signals** flash the word WALK in white when it's safe to cross and the words DON'T WALK in red when it's not safe; newer walk signals flash the "walking person" icon in white and the "hand" icon, palm forward, in red. In some places, you must press a button on the pole holding the walk signal in order to activate the signals.

Some residential streets have no sidewalks. If you must walk in the street, always walk on the left side (where you'll be facing oncoming traffic)—and be aware that American drivers tend to pay little attention to pedestrians and cyclists. At night, it's a good idea to avoid wearing dark clothing while walking, and even to put some reflective tape (available at bicycle shops) on your outerwear.

CRIME & SAFETY

Violent crime is nowhere near as common in daily life as it is on TV, but it is more common than in many other prosperous countries. Every city has its "good" and "bad" neighborhoods; the street gangs and turf wars that accompany the drug trade tend to be fairly localized. The most effective way to avoid violent crime is to learn which neighborhoods are hospitable to strangers and which are best avoided until you know the city well; even then, it is seldom advisable to walk city streets alone late at night. U.S. cities tend to be fairly safe places if you are alert and attentive to your surroundings—and *most* violent crime does not take place between strangers.

In 2000, there were an estimated 6.3 million violent crimes committed in the United States—homicide, rape/sexual assault, robbery, and aggravated assault. Approximately 533,000 of these crimes (8%) involved guns—but guns were used in 66% of the 15,000 murders that year. Those are frightening numbers, but remember, the population of the United States is roughly 300 million; and, according to the British Home Office, the crime rate declined more in the United States in the 1990s than in the United Kingdom, Japan, or any European Union country.

Of course, as in any country, violent crime is not the only security concern here. More than a million cars are stolen in the United States each year, and property is stolen from parked cars—often through a smashed window. Homes can be burglarized. And unsuspecting people, especially the elderly or poorly educated, can be robbed of money through deceitful schemes.

WHEN A CRIME HAS BEEN COMMITTED

In most parts of the country, **911** is the emergency phone number for the local police, fire department, and ambulance service.* A central operator will answer this number and ask whether you need police, fire, or medical assistance, and will connect you to an appropriate dispatcher. Interpreters are available. (But find out, as soon as you arrive in a new city, whether 911 is the general emergency number. In some small towns, the police department and the fire/rescue service have their own separate emergency numbers.)

If you are the **victim** of a crime, get to a safe place and call the police. Avoid touching or moving anything that might be useful to the police as evidence. Be prepared to give the police as much detailed information as you can remember, and promptly write down your own recollection of events to help you remember details later in court. If you are robbed, *immediately* report any credit cards, ATM cards, passport or other ID stolen. This will not only help the authorities find the thieves, but also relieve you of *liability* (legal responsibility) for charges or cash withdrawals made after you report

---

* This is why many taxicabs are equipped with illuminated signs that say CALL 911. These signs do *not* mean that 911 is the number to call to request a taxi! When a taxi's CALL 911 sign is lit, it means the driver is being threatened and is asking bystanders to call the police.

SEXUAL ASSAULT

In some countries, a woman who accuses a man of rape or sexual assault cannot expect to be taken seriously by the authorities, especially if the man is her husband or a relative. In the United States, the saying taught to college students is: *if she says 'no,' it's rape.* It does not matter if the victim is the perpetrator's wife, or they're on a date, or the victim was wearing revealing clothing, or the victim accepted a gift or a drink. Forcing or coercing *any* person to perform *any* sexual act is a serious crime in every state and on federal territory, under *any* circumstances. And American juries, courts, and even prison inmates tend to reserve their deepest animosity for those who take sexual advantage of children.

Still, according to most organizations that advocate for the rights of crime victims, the majority of sexual assaults go unreported—many victims do not wish to discuss the incident with strangers in court, or they do not expect a jury to believe them, and they're afraid the accused will seek revenge. As a result, many rapists go free and continue to prey upon vulnerable women and children (and, less commonly, men).

In order to bring a sexual assailant to justice, experts advise, it is important to call the police immediately after getting to the theft. If you are not a permanent resident, notify your country's embassy or consulate that your passport has been stolen.

If you **witness** a crime, get to a safe place and call the police. The police will ask you to report what you saw in as much detail as possible, and you may be asked later to testify in court or in a pretrial proceeding. In the U.S. legal system, a person on trial for a crime has a right to confront and question accusing witnesses in court; many people are therefore reluctant to testify in cases of violent crime, but reliable witness testimony is considered an important part of a fair trial. If either the government or the defense in a criminal trial thinks your testimony may shed light on the facts of the case, you may be ordered by a judge to give testimony and face criminal penalties if you refuse or give false testimony.

ROBBERY

As in most cities around the world, crowded places in the United States—train stations, shopping malls, and buses and subways—attract pickpockets and purse-snatchers. So do maps, large rolls of cash, conspicuous jewelry, and other signs that you have money or you're new in town. Be alert. A stranger who asks you what time it is, or asks for a cigarette, or "accidentally" bumps into you, might be trying to get you to stop walking for a moment so a partner can grab your wallet or purse. (Of course, not always. You should not go around assuming everyone you meet is trying to take advantage of you—but you should be conscious of situations where you might be vulnerable.)

Armed robbery is most likely to occur at night and in relatively deserted areas; if you stick to crowded, well-lit streets, you dramatically reduce your chances of being *mugged* or *held up*—forced by a threat of violence to hand over your money or valuables. Just as you may have seen in movies or on TV, a robber might say "stick 'em up" (meaning *put your hands up above your head*) or "freeze" (meaning *don't move,* act as if frozen) and then demand your wallet. A thief might also claim to have a "nine," a "22," or a "45" concealed in a pocket; those are types of handguns. Threats should be taken seriously, and it is unlikely that the contents of your wallet are worth getting shot or stabbed to protect.

• • • • • • • • • • • • • •

SEXUAL ASSAULT, CONT.

a place of safety and to go with them to a hospital or health clinic for an immediate medical exam. If this is done *before* the victim changes clothes, or takes a shower or bath, or has anything to eat or drink, there is a good chance that a specially trained medical team can collect enough samples of skin and hair to isolate the assailant's DNA—and establish identity and win a conviction in court. It is difficult, in such an emotionally stressful situation, to resist the temptation to wash up and put on clean clothes; but if evidence is washed away, lost, or damaged, it might be much harder to stop the rapist from striking again.

It is also illegal to ask or induce anyone under a certain age to engage in sexual acts; the minimum *age of consent* varies from one state to another and it may depend on the difference in age between the persons involved.

• • • • • • • • • • • • • •

In addition to forcible theft of money or valuables, you can be robbed of your identity. The simplest and most common form of **identity theft** is the unauthorized use of a telephone code. If you use a calling card to place long-distance calls from a public phone, make sure no one can see you dial—a skilled thief can figure out your dialing code from the way your arms or hands move when you dial. In more elaborate identity theft schemes, a thief might search your household trash (rubbish) or recycling bins to find bank statements, credit card bills, or other financial papers, and start using your account numbers for various transactions. Just as if your credit card or ATM card had been stolen, report any such theft immediately—not only to set the authorities on the trail of the thief but also to protect yourself from financial responsibility for further losses. Also, never give your Social Security number to a stranger, and remember, wireless phone conversations can be intercepted.

PROPERTY CRIMES

The easiest way to deter burglars is not to try to make your house burglar-proof, but to make it a bit less vulnerable than the next house. A dedicated thief can foil almost any security system—but few will bother if an easier target is available. The first and most basic deterrent is to *keep your doors locked*, whether you're home or not. (Always lock the doors of your car, too.) If a stranger knocks on your door, trust your instincts; especially in cities, it is not considered rude to ask unexpected visitors to state their business before you open your door. If someone claims to be a law enforcement officer, building inspector, or other public official, ask to see official ID before you let the person enter. And if someone approaches you while you're driving (for instance, offering to clean your windshield while you wait at a red light), it could be an attempt to rob you and you should not open your window or door.

If you ride a bicycle, keep it locked when not in use. Have a bicycle salesperson show you the proper way to use U-locks and cable (chain) locks, and always lock your bike to a bike rack or fence—not a signpost that could be lifted straight up through the lock. Many urban cyclists carry their bicycle seat with them when they leave their bike locked in a public space—even if a thief can break a lock, a bike without a seat is not likely to be taken.

Some people rent (hire) a **safe deposit box** at a local bank to store their valuable papers and jewelry. For a monthly or yearly fee, the bank gives you exclusive access to a locked drawer in its fortified vault. Many police departments will engrave your name on valuable items if you ask them to, and department stores, gift shops, and jewelry stores will do so for a small fee. It's also a good idea to make a list of all of your valuables and keep one copy in a safe place and another copy on file with your insurance company. (This is a useful precaution not only against theft, but also damage caused by fire or natural disaster.)

For added security at home, consider an **alarm system**. Look in the Yellow Pages under BURGLAR ALARM SYSTEMS for companies that install and operate a variety of home security features—motion detectors, motion-sensitive lighting, door and window alarms, surveillance cameras, and devices that automatically call the police if any of these systems are triggered when you're not home. You could also buy or adopt a trained **watchdog** (see PETS in Chapter 8) or, indeed, any loud canine. Even **signs** that warn of an alarm system or vicious dog will help deter burglars. To help prevent car theft, consider buying a security clamp that locks onto the steering wheel and prevents it from being turned.

Many communities organize **citizen watch groups** that patrol the neighborhood and call the police if they see any suspicious activity. And **civic associations** meet regularly with the police to discuss ways to improve neighborhood security.

FRAUD & SCAMS

A man walks along the sidewalk near a major tourist attraction, calling out: "Oakleys, Oakley sunglasses!" Maybe they're genuine designer shades and maybe they're cheap imitations; maybe they're honest merchandise and maybe they've been stolen. It doesn't matter. As soon as you take your wallet out of your pocket or purse, the vendor will grab it and run away.

You park your car on a city street. A stranger greets you and offers to "watch your car" for $5 to make sure it doesn't get stolen or damaged. If you choose not to pay for his services, guess what? He will make sure your car *does* get damaged—he'll see to it personally. You'd be wiser to park somewhere else.

An ad in the back of a magazine promises you thousands of dollars a week, in cash, working at home, with no immigration papers required. You send in $100 for a "starter kit" to set up your own business. The kit, when it finally comes in the mail, is just a bunch of order forms for merchandise you assemble and send back to the wholesaler. You do some calculations and find that you *could* earn thousands of dollars a week—*if* you, your spouse, and your children work 20 hours a day every day. And the company will probably find minor faults with the items you do assemble and buy them at a much lower price than it quoted.

If a deal seems "too good to be true," it probably is. Americans and visitors, old and young, with or without a lot of education, are targeted every day by unscrupulous dealers and deceptive advertisements. Sometimes the deals are illegal—for example, luring customers by advertising a low-priced product that is not actually available and then offering a higher-priced product instead—and sometimes the deals are so carefully crafted that they just barely satisfy the law but are still dishonest. So you should always—but *especially* when you are new to the country and a particular city—check the reputation of a business before making a major purchase or signing any sales contracts or papers.

To avoid fraud, scams, and ripoffs:

- Read—and make sure you understand—all the details and legalistic *fine print* of a sales contract before you sign it.
- Make sure you're dealing with a legitimate business. Many professionals, including most tradespeople who make repairs in customers' homes, must be **licensed** by the state, and you can ask to see their license and check with the licensing agency to make sure it is authentic. Tradespeople should also be **bonded**, meaning an insurance company has agreed to take financial responsibility if the individual steals or damages your property. Many (but by no means all) small businesses belong to the local **chamber of commerce** or merchants' association; a business that *does* is probably reputable.
- Contact the regional **Better Business Bureau** (listed at www.bbb.org or in the business section of the local White Pages) to find out whether there are any unresolved customer complaints about the business. The BBB is an association of businesses that promote good customer service and accountability.
- Ask for references from satisfied customers—or, better yet, ask a friend or coworker to recommend an appropriate company for your needs.

If you take all these precautions and still get conned or cheated, you have several levels of recourse available:

- Either in person or by phone, ask to speak with the supervisor of the person with whom you have a dispute. Often the manager or owner of a small business will be eager to resolve a legitimate complaint before you talk to all your friends and damage the company's reputation. If the business is a **chain**—a regional or national company with many locations—you might want to write to a regional manager or vice president. Always state specifically what **remedy** you are seeking—do you want a refund of the money you paid? Do you want to exchange defective goods for new ones? Do you want free repairs? If your request is reasonable and would fix the problem without humiliating the company, it is likely to be granted; if you insist that an employee who offended you be fired or punished, you probably won't get results, as the manager will not want to be seen letting a customer dictate company policy in a matter of discipline.

- If you have already tried to negotiate directly with the offending business, you can ask the Better Business Bureau to step in and help resolve the dispute. If the company is not a member of the BBB, you can file a complaint with the **Federal Trade Commission** at 202-382-4357 or www.ftc.gov—but this process will be slow and involve lots of paperwork.

- Shoddy or defective products that could be dangerous—for example, an appliance that catches on fire or a toy that has loose parts that a small child might choke on—should be reported to the **Consumer Product Safety Commission** at 800-638-2772 or www.cpsc.gov. This federal agency also keeps a list of product **recalls**—voluntary or court-ordered notices from the manufacturer inviting customers to exchange faulty products for improved ones or for a refund.

- If a business has done something fraudulent or deceptive, you can file a complaint with the state agency responsible for **consumer protection**—usually an *office of consumer affairs* or a consumer protection division of the *state attorney general's office*. Check the state government web site or the Blue Pages.*

---

* If a business has defrauded the public (for example, by inflating prices or exaggerating costs in a contract with the government) and you report it to the authorities, you may be awarded a percentage of the taxpayer money you help recover. Individuals who report their own employers for fraud are called **whistleblowers** and are legally protected from retaliation. If you discover your employer or another firm dealing dishonestly with the government, get advice from a lawyer specializing in whistleblower protection or from the Government Accountability Project, 202-408-0034 or www.whistleblower.org.

- Finally, if all else fails, you can sue someone in civil court.

COURTS AND THE LEGAL SYSTEM

For any offense committed against another person or another's property, a person may face two separate legal proceedings: a criminal case argued by the government and a civil suit argued by the injured party. A criminal conviction can result in fines, incarceration, mandatory community service, or deportation; a civil judgment can result in court-ordered payments to the injured party, and if necessary, seizure of property to pay for damages.

POLICE

In 1966, the Supreme Court reviewed the case of *Miranda v. Arizona*, in which a suspect in police custody was coerced into making a confession that he later said was false—he had confessed because he was afraid of the police. The Supreme Court ruled that a confession coerced by the police could not be considered valid. Today, as you may have seen in movies or on TV, the police must advise you of certain rights before they ask you any questions. The police must tell you, in a language you understand, that you have the right to remain silent; you have the right to consult with an attorney; if you cannot afford an attorney, the court will provide one for you at no cost; and any statement you make after receiving these warnings can be used against you in court. In other words, *in the United States, you never have to talk to a law enforcement officer without a lawyer present to advise you.* If you start answering questions and decide later that you want a lawyer present, you can always stop answering questions and demand one. (But if you exercise your right to a free lawyer provided by the court—a *public defender*—you will eventually have to prove that you can't afford to pay legal fees.)

Does that mean the police never mistreat or deceive suspects? No. But the legal system does recognize that a confession made after harsh treatment should be taken less seriously than a confession made after decent treatment—and if the police go too far, the government will not be able to win a conviction in court. The cornerstone of the U.S. legal system is the belief that it is better to let some criminals go free than to let even one innocent person be wrongly punished. It's not a perfect system—there are certainly innocent people in U.S. prisons—but it's an ideal to which we aspire.

CRIMINAL COURT

Since a crime is considered an offense against the general public, crime victims do not decide whether a crime suspect will be prosecuted or what charges he or she will face. Those decisions are usually made by the *prosecutor*, the government's lawyer in criminal matters. In federal cases, the prosecutor is an agent of the Attorney General, the presidential appointee who heads the Justice Department. State crimes are prosecuted by agents of an elected *state attorney general* or *state's attorney*. At the federal level and in some states, the prosecutor must present evidence to a **grand jury**—a panel of randomly selected citizens meeting behind closed doors—and convince the jurors that the government has enough evidence to justify bringing the accused person to trial. This is intended to prevent the government from prosecuting its critics just to harass or intimidate them.

Detention of the accused is one of the areas of law that has begun to change since September 11, 2001. Hundreds of people, mostly aliens, have been detained without specific criminal charges—the government simply claims that they're tied to a terrorist organization and labels them "enemy combatants." There may or may not be a solid basis for that claim, but the government does not have to prove it in open court. In the vast majority of criminal cases, however, the nation's well-established safeguards for the rights of the accused still apply.

Generally, you cannot be held in custody for more than 48 hours (until the next business day) without being **arraigned**—brought before a judge or magistrate to be told of the charges against you. At an arraignment hearing, you will be asked to *enter a plea*—to say whether you *plead guilty* and confess to the charges or *plead not guilty* and choose to go to trial. The judge will set a trial date and decide whether you must stay in custody until then. Unless accused of a very serious crime, a person with a job and family in the community is often allowed to go home until the trial; a person who does not have ties to the community is thought to be more likely to flee and not return for trial, and may be released only on **bail**. The accused pays the specified amount of money (bail) to the court as a guarantee, or *bond,* that he or she will show up for trial; the money is returned if the accused is acquitted. Persons accused of a violent crime, or who have been convicted of other crimes in the past, are usually not released before trial.

Defendants who plead guilty do not face trial, but proceed directly to a sentencing hearing. Those who plead not guilty face trial before a jury of ordinary citizens. The jury decides the facts of the case—who seems to be telling the truth, who doesn't, and ultimately, whether the defendant is guilty or innocent. The judge ensures that the evidence presented is legitimate and that the contending lawyers' arguments are fair. The prosecution and the defense each get a chance to question the other side's witnesses, and the defendant cannot be forced to testify; the Fifth Amendment to the Constitution guarantees freedom from self-incrimination. (It is said that someone "takes the Fifth" when he or she declines to answer questions.)

Most states require the jury's decision, or *verdict,* in a criminal case to be unanimous. In criminal cases, in order to declare the defendant guilty, the jury must be convinced of the defendant's guilt **beyond a reasonable doubt**. This is the legal **burden of proof** in a criminal trial: the government must prove its accusations beyond a reasonable doubt, or the defendant is innocent.

If convicted (found guilty), the defendant can **appeal**, or ask a higher court to review the legal integrity of the trial and perhaps overturn the conviction. If the defendant is acquitted (found not guilty), the government *cannot* appeal and you can never face criminal charges again for the same act.

Persons convicted of a serious crime or **felony** may be sentenced to a year or more in prison and a fine of more than $1,000. Persons convicted of a less serious crime or **misdemeanor** may be incarcerated for up to a year, fined up to $1,000, or ordered to perform a certain amount of community service—picking up trash along a highway, for example. Sometimes a person who is convicted of a nonviolent crime and has never been in trouble with the authorities before will be sentenced to **probation**, a period during which the person is free to live and work normally but must report every week to a court officer and may not travel without permission. If the person completes the probation without breaking any more laws or violating any court orders, the conviction may be erased from the person's court records. But these are penalties usually imposed against citizens; aliens convicted of a serious crime are usually deported.

The defense and the prosecution often have one thing in common: the desire to avoid the expense and stress of a trial. To encourage the defendant to plead guilty, the prosecutor might be willing to substitute less serious charges or recommend a mild sentence. This is called **plea bargaining**; most judges support it and go along with prosecutors' recommendations.

CIVIL COURT

Americans, more than most people, are quick to turn to the courts to settle personal or business disputes. We are *not* as violent a society as some people think, and most Americans do not try to resolve disputes by fighting. We're more likely to sue somebody. It is also, in part, a result of the American desire and pressure to get rich: some people file lawsuits just to try to collect money from people or companies that might pay a settlement in order to avoid the hassle of a trial.

Conservative politicians call for new laws to limit the amount of money a court can award to an injured or inconvenienced person, to protect businesses from unjustified lawsuits; liberal politicians argue that the ability to win court-ordered payment for damages is the only protection ordinary people have against the dangerous effects of shoddy goods and services. So this may be the only country where—to take an extreme example—a customer could successfully sue a restaurant because her coffee was too hot and she spilled it and burned herself. And this is why you see ridiculous warning labels on so many American products—not because the manufacturer really believes we're all such idiots that we need to be warned that a cup of coffee might be hot, but to provide some legal protection: the manufacturers can always say they warned you.

A civil lawsuit is concerned with *liability* or legal responsibility, not with criminal behavior, and can only result in orders to pay money to an injured person or to refrain from certain activity; it cannot result in anyone going to jail or paying a fine to the government. The proceedings are therefore slightly more relaxed than in a criminal case. A jury in a civil trial might be smaller than the standard 12-person jury and may not have to reach a unanimous decision. Also, the burden of proof is lighter: either side must prove its case only by a **preponderance of evidence**, not "beyond a reasonable doubt." In other words, the *plaintiff* (complaining party) or the defendant only needs to convince the jury that its own argument is more likely true than the other side's.

Petty disputes—in most states, matters involving less than $1,000—may be settled in **small claims court**, where the two parties argue their cases to a judge themselves, without lawyers or jury. And Americans are beginning to embrace various kinds of **alternative dispute resolution** (ADR), such as *mediation,* where a neutral third party helps the contending parties reach an agreement, or *arbitration,* where a neutral

• • • • • • • • • • • • • •

CLASS ACTION SUITS

You will occasionally see news reports about *class action suits*, and you may even be involved in one and not know it. These are cases where a few people make a legal claim on behalf of a larger group of people who have suffered similar damages—for example, everyone who bought a particular brand of soap that has been shown to injure the skin, or every shareholder of a company whose stock has declined in value due to misconduct by its top executives. If a payment is ordered, the plaintiffs and "all others similarly situated" are entitled to a share.

• • • • • • • • • • • • • • •

third party makes a ruling. Agreements reached through ADR can be enforced in court. Your local courts are listed in the Blue Pages, and the civil division can refer you to ADR services.

LAWYERS AND LEGAL AID

If you are accused of a crime, you need a lawyer. If you are sued, you need a lawyer. If you want to sue somebody, you need a lawyer. And there are many other times when you should consult with a lawyer—for instance, when you buy a home, start a business, or write a **will** (a binding legal statement indicating who will inherit your property when you die). There are plenty of lawyers at your service: by some estimates, 3 million—more than 1% of the U.S. population.

How do you choose one? Most lawyers specialize in a certain area of law, so it probably won't help to just pick a random lawyer listed in the Yellow Pages.

If you've entered the United States to become a permanent resident or a citizen, you've probably worked with an immigration lawyer. He or she can probably refer you to a trusted colleague in another field if you need help with a specific legal issue. Unions and professional associations often have lawyers available to answer questions or provide referrals, and in many communities, there are local immigrant support groups that can help—ask the local USCIS office or your country's consulate for a list. If you work for a large company, there may be an employee assistance program that can offer legal advice.

State **bar associations** (lawyers' professional organizations) have referral services to connect you with appropriate lawyers in your community. You can find your state bar association at **www.findlaw.com** or in the business section of the White Pages. Most cities and counties also have a **legal aid bureau**—a network of lawyers who donate a certain percentage of their time to provide *pro bono* (free) legal counsel to low-income clients.

AGE OF MAJORITY

Any person in the United States is legally considered an adult upon reaching his or her 18th birthday. A person younger than 18 is called a **minor** in matters of law, but is an **emancipated minor** with the same rights as an adult if pregnant, legally married, or declared emancipated by a court order. Minors generally cannot enter into legally binding contracts. State laws determine the age at which a person may obtain a driver's license; purchase or consume alcohol; get married without parental consent; *drop out* of school (stop attending school without earning a diploma); and work for wages. A minor accused of a crime may be tried as a *juvenile* (child), in which case any resulting criminal record will be sealed or *expunged* (erased) when the person turns 18; or, at the discretion of the court, a minor may be treated as an adult and face adult penalties if the alleged crime is very serious and the authorities believe that the accused was fully aware of the nature of the alleged act.

NOTARY SERVICES AND YOUR SIGNATURE

You may occasionally need the services of a **notary public,** a certified witness who attests to the valid signature of important documents. If a bank, insurance company, school, or other institution asks you to get a document *notarized,* it means you should not sign it until you are in the presence of a notary public. (Banks, courthouses, real estate agencies, and car dealerships often have a notary on staff— just walk in and ask.) The notary will ask you for ID, watch you sign the papers, and stamp the papers with a **notary seal** and sign them. The notary may charge a few dollars for this service.

Whether a document is notarized or not, in the United States, an adult's **signature** implies that the signer has read and understood the document, agrees to its terms, and has not made any false statements in it. If you are found to have signed a document that contains statements that you knew to be false, you could face criminal charges of fraud or perjury. And **forgery,** the act of signing another person's name on a document, is illegal.

What are you going to miss most when you leave?

"Half-and-half. In Germany, there's no half-and-half—you either have milk or you have cream. And I'll miss being able to buy groceries on Sunday."

— Nika Greger, a German citizen returning to Berlin after two years in Washington, D.C.

A mericans may seem to spend money liberally, and we're certainly wasteful in some ways—for example, we tend to replace broken household items instead of repairing them, and we consume more energy and water per capita than anyone else in the world. But we're also quite thrifty in some ways. As a Chinese poet, Yang Lian, recalls in *Granta* magazine (Spring 2002): she took an American friend to a restaurant in Beijing and was surprised when her guest asked if they could take their unfinished meal home with them. In the United States, it's a perfectly accepted practice; a waiter in a restaurant might even ask you if you want a *doggie bag,* because the custom originated when people would take table scraps home to the family dog. Nobody wants to waste food. Clever American shoppers visit several different stores—or call them on the phone—to compare prices before making a purchase. It might surprise you to see someone who earns $75,000 a year worrying about ways to save $1 or $2 on groceries, but the American view was best expressed by Ben Franklin: "A penny saved is a penny earned."

WHERE AMERICANS SHOP

If you're moving from a place where you buy bread from the baker, meat from the butcher, and vegetables from the greengrocer, you may find it hard to keep those habits in most U.S. communities. By the late 20th century, the average American relied largely on two stores: the supermarket, for every kind of food, and the department store or discount store, for almost everything else. There are still plenty of specialized stores around, but—even though Americans claim to value variety and diversity—if you visit a dozen shopping malls in a dozen cities, you won't notice much difference.

- **Supermarkets.** These large grocery stores usually include a butcher, a deli, a bakery, a seafood counter, and sometimes a pharmacy in addition to a dozen or more aisles of packaged goods and refrigerated aisles of dairy products and frozen foods. Some are open 24 hours.
- **Department stores.** These huge stores—often several stories tall—are divided into departments that sell clothing, furniture, linens, jewelry, cosmetics, shoes, electronics, appliances, kitchenware, tools, and almost anything else you can think of.
- **Drugstores.** Also called *pharmacies* (in Europe, *chemists* or *apothecaries*), drugstores mainly sell medications and related health and hygiene supplies, but most also sell tobacco products, shaving and beauty supplies, batteries, greeting cards, candy and snack foods, magazines, and a few small appliances such as clocks and hair dryers.
- **Discount stores.** These are department stores or drugstores that emphasize low prices on everyday clothing and practical items for the home. Wal-Mart, Target and Kmart are examples.
- **Warehouse stores.** These are combined supermarkets and department stores that emphasize large quantities at low prices. Some charge an annual membership fee. These stores offer good deals if you have a large household or you run a small business. Costco and Sam's Club are examples.
- **Convenience stores.** These are small stores that sell a basic selection of snack foods, beverages, motor oil, medications, tobacco products, newspapers, and milk. Many are open 24 hours a day and are combined with a gas (petrol) station; they're intended to give drivers and commuters a place to stop for a quick snack and any items needed right away.
- **Hardware stores.** Called *DIY stores* in the United Kingdom, these stores sell tools, lumber, and other supplies for home repair and home improvement.
- **Specialty stores.** If a department store or discount store does not have the specific item you want, there are dedicated jewelry stores, furniture stores, bookstores, music stores, computer stores, toy stores, shoe stores, sporting

goods stores, and ethnic grocery stores. And there are clothing stores that focus on a certain style or age group, or that just sell shoes, or formal wear, or athletic wear, or clothing by a certain designer. Look around, explore—you can probably find anything you want and all sorts of things you hadn't even imagined.

- **Outlet stores.** Outlets sell *factory seconds*—goods that do not meet the manufacturer's specifications but that are still in decent condition. For example, if a clothing designer orders the mill to produce 2,000 shirts and they're not exactly the color the designer wanted, they will probably not be sold in regular clothing stores; instead, they'll be sent to an outlet store and sold at a lower price.

- **Resale stores.** Several types of stores sell used goods no longer wanted by the original purchaser. Though the selection of merchandise is unpredictable, these stores can be a very inexpensive source of furniture, clothing, kitchen equipment and dishes, books, and even small appliances. A **thrift store** sells donated goods, often to raise money for a charitable purpose; a **consignment store** sells goods on behalf of people who own them and entrust them to the store to sell; and a **pawn shop** (pawnbroker) sells valuable items seized as collateral to pay overdue loans.

- **Specialty food markets.** Some grocery stores specialize in **health food**—items with fewer artificial ingredients and less sugar and fat than most processed foods—or in **organic food**. There are also stores that emphasize **gourmet** foods—rare ingredients, special imports, and foods of premium quality. A **deli** (from the German word *delicatessen*) is a sandwich shop or café that also sells sliced meats and cheeses in bulk (not prepackaged). A **food co-op** is a member-owned or worker-owned nonprofit grocery store—usually, but not necessarily, specializing in health food. A **farmers' market** is an event where local farmers gather sell fresh produce. And there *are* bakeries, butcher shops, and greengrocers—just not as many as you might expect.

- **Shopping malls.** In many suburban areas, dozens of specialty stores and two or three department stores are grouped together under one roof. These are **shopping**

malls—convenient places to hunt for the best prices and selection from several different retailers. Some malls are considered *upscale,* with a lot of shops that cater to fashionable and expensive tastes, while other malls feature more practical and economical shops. There are also smaller clusters of stores known as **strip malls** or **shopping centers**. These do not have a common indoor promenade as malls do; they just share a common parking lot and perhaps a covered walkway in front of the shops.

- **Internet.** Some of the nation's biggest retailers are online companies. Originally a bookseller, Amazon.com has evolved into an online department store that sells just about everything. Most retail **chains** (companies with many stores) have web sites that allow you to order merchandise with a credit card or debit card—or through an internet payment agency such as **PayPal**, www.paypal.com. And online **auction houses** such as eBay, www.ebay.com, allow individuals and businesses to sell items to the highest bidder.

- **Classified ads.** If you're looking for cheap secondhand (used) furniture, computers, stereos, musical instruments, cameras, or other household goods—even cars—start by looking in the *classified advertising* section of your local newspaper. These ads list thousands of items for sale by individuals who no longer want them (for example, people who are moving away and don't want to take all of their furniture to their new home, or who have bought a new computer and no longer need the old one). You contact the seller directly and make arrangements to see the goods and negotiate a price.

RETAIL BUSINESS HOURS

Most retail stores open every morning between 8 and 10 a.m. (perhaps as late as noon on weekends) and stay open until 7 to 10 p.m. Some close earlier on Sundays. Some grocery stores, drugstores, and convenience stores are open 24 hours every day, or close only on major holidays. **Restaurant** hours depend on the character of the neighborhood—for example, a restaurant in a downtown office district might be open only at lunchtime and for early dinners or *happy hour,* usually from 5 to 7 p.m., when reduced-price beer or cocktails attract an after-work crowd. Some bars and restaurants in areas known for nightlife don't even open until evening. Some restaurants close in the afternoon, opening only for a few hours at lunchtime and again in the evening.

Of course, **online shopping** can be done at any hour that suits you, and most **mail-order** retailers have 24-hour phone numbers to take your orders.

TIPPING

Originally, a tip or gratuity was considered a gift in recognition of exceptional service. Now, it is an expected part of certain transactions, and withholding a tip is considered a rebuke. But tipping is not as complicated as many visitors fear.

Tipping is expected in all restaurants with table service (not in fast-food restaurants or self-service buffets). Waiters and waitresses are paid lower wages than service workers in other industries, because it is expected that they will receive a certain percentage of their income in the form of tips. The general rule is that a tip is 15% of the amount of the bill. It is polite but not compulsory to round the tip up to the nearest dollar. In major cities, where the cost of living is high, 15% to 20% is customary. The tip may be left on the table in cash or, if you're paying by credit card, simply written on the credit slip when you sign for the transaction. Sometimes, for a large party, a service charge of 15% or 18% will be added to the bill, in which case you are not expected to leave an additional tip.

Other service workers who expect to be tipped are taxi drivers, bartenders, newspaper delivery workers (add a tip to the monthly bill), barbers and hairdressers, and delivery workers for pizza parlors and other restaurants that deliver hot food to your door. Again, tip 15% or at least $1. It is also customary to give hotel porters $1 per bag; to leave a tip for the housekeeping staff at the end of a hotel stay; and to give $1 or more to musicians in bars or restaurants that do not collect a *cover charge* (an amount added to the bill, or collected at the door, to pay for entertainment). One is generally not expected to tip bus drivers, train conductors, or flight attendants.

Never tip any government official, especially one involved with law enforcement, security, or any kind of licensing, permits, or immigration. It would be considered a bribe and a serious crime.

PRICES

In most cases, merchants in the United States mark their wares with a price tag and there is no haggling—the price marked is the price you pay, along with any sales tax charged by the state. There are two exceptions:

- For major purchases such as a house, car, boat, or maybe a computer, it is entirely proper and routine to negotiate about price, payment arrangements, and optional features to be included. Often, a major purchase will be made with a combination of a **down payment** (paid immediately) and **installment payments** (paid each month until the full price has been paid). You pay the merchant a **finance charge** (interest) in exchange for the privilege of taking possession of the goods.

- If the seller is not a professional merchant—for example, if you're buying used furniture through the classified ads, or if somebody is selling old trinkets at a flea market or yard sale—the stated price is understood to be a starting point for negotiations. (A **flea market** is a gathering of people selling used goods from their own homes. At a **yard sale,** also known as *garage sale, rummage sale* or *tag sale,* a single household is selling used goods on its own front lawn.)

Most retailers occasionally reduce the price of some or all of their goods during an advertised

• • • • • • • • • • • • • •

PRICES: A MATTER OF EQUALITY

The concept of fixed, predetermined prices was introduced by the Quakers, a religious sect that believes in treating everyone equally. Thomas D. Horne, a master electrician and a Quaker, has had some misunderstandings with customers from cultures where haggling is expected—customers who "seem to take a refusal to bargain as an insult to them personally, as if you are saying they are not worth the time." But, he explains, "If I charge two or more different prices for the same work... then one of those customers has been cheated. If the lower price is fair for one customer it is fair for all." Some merchants do offer a **discount** (reduced price) for certain categories of people, such as students, the elderly, or military veterans—but the discount is a fixed percentage of the price of the goods, and the customer either qualifies for the discount or does not. (Note: For the purposes of discounts and other privileges, the elderly are often called **senior citizens.** That's just a polite term—anyone over the age of 65, whether a U.S. citizen or not, is a "senior citizen.")

• • • • • • • • • • • • • •

sale or **special,** often on holiday weekends or at the turn of seasons. If an item advertised at a discount is *sold out* (no longer available) while the reduced price is still in effect, you can sometimes get a **raincheck,** a voucher that will let you buy the same item later at the reduced price.

Many stores or manufacturers—especially grocery stores and manufacturers of food products—print **coupons** in the local newspaper that can be cut out and redeemed at the store for reduced prices on specified items. Some grocery stores issue **discount cards** to customers who register their name and address with the store. The cardholder is offered a reduced price on many items, and the store makes money by selling lists of customers' addresses to companies that advertise products by mail.

The price of household goods, clothing, food, and other items— even houses—can vary significantly from one part of the country to another. The average cost of essential goods and services, combined with average housing costs and taxes, is called the **cost of living** and can be used to compare one city or region to another. To determine how your cost of living would change if you moved to another city, check out the online **salary calculators** at www.homefair.com or http://cgi.money.cnn.com/tools. These tools show that, for example, if you earn $50,000 a year in Washington, D.C., you would need to earn $84,000 in New York City to maintain the same standard of living there—but that you could live just as comfortably on $38,000 in Atlanta. A similar tool on the Coldwell Banker real estate web site, www.coldwellbanker.com, compares the cost of similar homes in different cities.

Other factors that can affect the price of goods include:

- **Brand name.** Sometimes the only differences between two pairs of blue jeans are the designer's label and the price. For some kinds of products—such as tools, appliances, outerwear, or health foods—a respected brand name may indeed signify a well-made and reliable product compared to similar goods made by an obscure manufacturer. But often, especially for clothing, expensive brands are prized for a trendy image and not necessarily for quality.
- **Merchant's reputation.** Some retailers have earned an excellent reputation for service and integrity; others are just considered fashionable. If customer service is not an issue—if you know what you want and how to find

and select it—then the store with the lowest price is just as good as the store with the best reputation.

- **Time of year.** The best time to buy Christmas decorations is early January, and the best time to buy shorts and sandals is at the end of the summer. The demand for the product has just peaked for the year and merchants are eager to get rid of leftover stock in a *clearance sale*.

- **New technology.** Between 1985 and 1995, the price of VCRs dropped gradually from $300 to $60. Computers that sold for $2,000 five years ago are now sold for $100 in classified ads. Wait six months and the price will come down; wait a year and the price will come down a lot.

- **Condition.** You can sometimes find slightly damaged goods that are still perfectly functional. For example, most supermarkets have a rack or bin of items whose packaging has been dented; the food inside is not affected, but the store wants its shelves to be neat and attractive, so the items are marked *reduced for quick sale*. Day-old bread and other baked goods are sometimes available at half the price of fresh goods. And if a store has an item on display that is not in stock, you can offer to buy the display model at a reduced price—but you'll get the item "as is," with no packaging or instructions or guarantees of its good condition.

To get a good idea of the average price of various goods in your region, and of the ranges of goods offered by area stores, check out the **advertising supplement** to the Sunday edition of the local newspaper. Bundled inside the Sunday paper is a stack of glossy advertising pages that show items currently *on sale* (at a reduced price) at major local stores. Grocery stores' advertising supplements might be included on another day of the week.

Finally, do some math. Look at the weight of packaged goods, not just the size of the container. You'll notice that one 16-ounce container costs less than two eight-ounce containers of the same product. Sometimes fruit, baked goods, and other items have quantity discounts—you'll see prices like *50¢ each or $5/dozen*. (Dozen means 12.) The **unit price**, ounce for ounce, is usually highest for the smallest quantities. You may be new to the country, but you *are allowed* to bring your common sense with you.

CONSUMER PROTECTION

If you have a dispute with a merchant or contractor, see the section on FRAUD & SCAMS in Chapter 6. But there are lots of steps you can take to avoid disputes in the first place and to make sure you're dealing with a reputable business that sells reliable products and services. In addition to the **Better Business Bureau** and the **Consumer Product Safety Commission** mentioned in Chapter 6, check out these helpful resources:

- **Federal Consumer Information Center.** This federal agency provides free background information about various industries to help consumers choose specific vendors and products—and avoid common mistakes and ripoffs. For free catalog of publications, call 800-688-9889 or visit www.pueblo.gsa.gov.
- *Consumers' Checkbook.* This magazine, published by the nonprofit Center for the Study of Services, rates thousands of products and services—not only household goods, but also financial institutions, insurance companies, doctors, telephone companies, and more. The magazine does not carry advertising, so it has no financial incentive to favor any business. Local editions of the magazine are published for seven metropolitan areas: **Boston, Chicago, Philadelphia, San Francisco, Seattle,** the **Twin Cities** (Minneapolis and St. Paul), and **Washington, D.C.** The organization also provides special services and resources for people who are buying a car (see below) and national directories of the top-rated health care providers (see Chapter 10). Call 800-213-7283 or visit www.checkbook.org.
- *Consumer Reports.* This magazine is published by Consumers Union, a nonprofit organization that tests thousands of products to find out whether they fulfill the manufacturer's advertised claims. Like *Consumers' Checkbook,* the magazine does not sell advertising. Some articles offering general advice about choosing reliable goods are available for free on the organization's web site, but you have to pay to get the detailed reports. Call 800-208-9696 or visit www.consumerreports.org.
- **Good Housekeeping Institute.** This private lab tests a variety of home electronics, lawn and garden tools, small

appliances, baby products, fitness (exercise) equipment, power tools, and other products and provides reviews on the "Savvy Consumer" page at http:// magazines.ivillage.com/goodhousekeeping. (Note, however, that the institute publishes *Good Housekeeping* magazine, which does accept paid advertisements.)

- **Magazine articles.** At any newsstand or bookstore, you can find monthly magazines devoted to cars, computers, cooking, bicycling, musical instruments, photography, home improvement, investment and finance, travel services, and every sport and recreational activity imaginable. Most topical magazines feature product reviews and ratings in their subject area.

- **Internet ScamBusters.** This online magazine exposes the latest scams, frauds, and dirty tricks in use on the internet (circulating by e-mail) and by credit card companies. The site also provides information about counterfeit goods and *urban legends* (sensational and frightening stories that tend to be widely retold but that are not true—ask any American college student for examples). Visit www.scambusters.org.

- **Referrals.** Ultimately, there's no substitute for a first-hand account of personal experience, positive or negative, with a specific local business. Ask a friend or co-worker to recommend a good auto mechanic, a good dentist, or a good place to buy fresh bread. Not only will you learn which local businesses are most likely to give you a fair deal and courteous service, but it's also a good way to learn what's available in your neighborhood— and to start a conversation. (Americans tend to be opinionated in general, and to have especially strong opinions about their favorite local businesses—and any business that has treated them dishonestly or discourteously in the past.)

WARRANTIES

Most household goods are sold with a **warranty**, a written policy stating that the manufacturer will repair or replace a defective product within the first few months after it is sold. Most states also have implied warranty laws that require manufacturers to replace defective goods even if there is no written warranty. Many department stores offer service contracts on the appliances, electronics, and other major items they sell; for a fee, you get an extended term of warranty protection or free repairs. (Do some math and decide carefully whether a service contract is worth the price.) Also, note: usually a warranty or service contract is *void* (canceled automatically) if you try to repair the item yourself or if it was damaged by misuse. And most goods purchased with a credit card are automatically insured for several weeks or months.

Many household items, especially small appliances and electronics, come with a product registration card inside the packaging. This is a short questionnaire printed on a prepaid postcard, and the manufacturer wants you to fill it out and mail it. You are *not* required to do this. It will help the manufacturer with business-related research, but it will also cause you to receive junk mail (see Chapter 5). Sometimes you are offered extra warranty protection if you register your purchase—and if the model is *recalled* for safety reasons, the manufacturer will be able to notify you.

STORE SECURITY

Do not be alarmed if a uniformed guard or other store employee approaches you as you enter and ask you for your bags. Shoplifting, theft of merchandise from stores, is a widespread crime that causes merchants to raise prices; to help prevent shoplifting, some stores require you to *check* your bags while you shop (leave them with a clerk, just as you might check your coat at a theater or fancy restaurant). Shopping malls and large stores often have their own private security forces that resemble small police departments—complete with guards who carry guns and patrol the parking lot in marked cars. And some merchandise is marked with an electronic anti-theft tag that must be removed by the cashier; if you've paid for an item and an alarm sounds when you walk out the door, it means the tag was not removed. Wait for a security guard and show your receipt (proof of payment).

FOOD LABELING

Federal law requires that processed foods be labeled with a list of ingredients in order of proportion, along with information about the levels of certain beneficial and harmful **nutrients**—vitamins, sugars, carbohydrates, and fats. Where food labels in some countries report *energy,* U.S. food labels say **calories**, and they actually mean kilocalories. Labels must disclose the use of preservatives, artificial flavors and colors, and certain other additives. However, food manufacturers are *not* required to disclose the use of pesticides, fungicides, genetically modified organisms (GMOs), natural or recombinant (genetically modified) growth hormones, or irradiation. The Agricultural Marketing Service, an agency of the **U.S. Department of Agriculture**, decides which pesticides, feed, and other agricultural ingredients may be considered organic; products made with at least 95% organic ingredients may be labeled ORGANIC and may bear the **USDA Organic** symbol. Products may bear the label MADE WITH ORGANIC INGREDIENTS if they contain at least 70% organic ingredients. For details, visit www.ams.usda.gov.

USDA Organic Symbol

Labeling and **food safety**—the handling and processing of food products and the use of ingredients that pose a risk to human health—are regulated by the federal **Food & Drug Administration**. If you have questions about nutrition labels or the safety standards that food products must meet, call the FDA Consumer Hotline at 888-463-6332 or visit www.foodsafety.gov. (If your question is about meat or poultry, contact the USDA instead, at 800-535-4555; for questions about seafood, call the FDA Seafood Hotline at 800-332-4010.)

Certain agricultural products are inspected and graded by the USDA according to quality:

- **Meat.** On the basis of fat marbling, age, and tissue health, the USDA awards one of eight grades to inspected beef. The top grades are *prime, choice, select,* and *standard,* and those are the grades you will see in grocery stores; lower grades are sold to commercial producers of processed food products. Other types of meat are graded *prime, choice, good* or *standard,* and *cull.*
- **Milk.** Almost all milk sold directly to consumers in the United States is Grade A, the highest quality. Cow's milk is also classified by fat content: *whole* (3%-4% fat by volume), *lowfat* (1%-2%), or *skim* (fat-free). Other classifications of dairy liquid include **acidophilus milk**, a type

of cultured milk with beneficial bacteria; **buttermilk**, the liquid left over after butter has been churned from cream; **heavy cream** (also known as whipping cream), at least 36% fat by volume; **table cream**, less than 36% fat, used mainly as a condiment in coffee or tea; and **half-and-half**, a blend of milk and cream, also used mainly with coffee and tea. (If you order *cream* in a restaurant, you will usually be served half-and-half.) All milk sold in retail stores is *pasteurized* (heated to kill harmful bacteria) and *homogenized* (blended to dissolve lumps of fat). Goat's and sheep's milk can be purchased from dairy farm co-ops and health food stores. **Milk substitutes** made from soy, rice, or almonds are available in unflavored and flavored varieties for people who follow a **vegan** diet (with no animal products) or who cannot digest lactose (the sugar that occurs naturally in milk). So are a variety of **nondairy creamers**—powdered or liquid cream substitutes used in coffee or tea.

- **Butter.** Based on flavor, texture, and color, butter is graded AA (best), A (good), or B (standard). A variety of butter substitutes (**margarine** and other condiments made from solidified vegetable oils) are available for people who follow a vegan diet or wish to avoid saturated fats, though some nutrition experts caution that the hydrogenated oils in margarine may be just as unhealthy as the animal fats in butter.

- **Eggs.** Eggs are labeled with a quality grade like those assigned to butter (AA, A, or B) and with a weight classification (*Jumbo, Extra Large, Large, Medium, Small,* and *Peewee*). Most eggs sold in grocery stores are Extra Large or Large, and recipes assume those sizes are used in cooking. If the eggs come from free-range chickens (not kept in cages) or from chickens raised on an organic diet, the manufacturer will indicate that on the package.

In addition to USDA inspection grades, some dairy products bear the **Real Seal**, an industry association mark that indicates that the item does not contain any synthetic ingredients, vegetable oils, imported dairy ingredients, or other substitutes for domestic dairy products. And most processed foods

Real Seal

are made and packaged in kitchens certified **kosher** by a rabbi; consumers who follow Old Testament dietary laws can look for a small **κ** on the packaging (or a **u** for the Union of Orthodox Rabbis of North America), along with the word *pareve* if the product contains neither meat nor dairy ingredients.

The FDA also regulates **dietary supplements**—pills, capsules, extracts, and other products that provide extra vitamins, minerals, amino acids, or other nutrients. These preparations do not need to be approved by the FDA, but the agency can ban supplements that are found to be unsafe. For more information, contact the Center for Food Safety and Applied Nutrition at 888-723-3366 or www.cfsan.fda.gov.

WATER

Practically every home in the United States has hot and cold running water. In most areas, water is provided by a **public utility**— a company that is granted a legal monopoly in return for government regulation of its prices. Federal law sets the standards for the purity of drinking water. Under the **Safe Drinking Water Act**, *tap water* (water piped into homes by a utility) must be monitored for certain contaminants, including **arsenic**; harmful microbes such as **cryptosporidium**; **MTBE**

VEGETARIAN AND VEGAN LIVING

The vegetarian lifestyle is increasingly popular in the United States, especially among college students and young adults. According to the nonprofit Vegetarian Resource Group's analysis of commercial polls and industry statistics, about 5% of adult U.S. residents say they never eat red meat; 3% never eat meat, poultry, or fish (6% of young adults); and 20% to 30% of U.S. adults who are not strict vegetarians do avoid red meat or actively seek meatless options on restaurant menus. Commercial meat substitutes made from soy, vegetable protein, or wheat gluten—practically nonexistent 20 years ago—are now available in most supermarkets. Strictly vegetarian restaurants and grocery stores are uncommon, but most restaurants offer some satisfying vegetarian meals. About 1% of the adults in the United States (2% of the adults in major U.S. cities) are **vegan** and do not eat any animal products, including eggs or dairy ingredients in processed foods; some vegans also avoid wearing leather shoes and clothing. A vegan diet can present some difficulties in the United States—not only socially, but in terms of finding a satisfying and varied diet that meets nutritional needs. Contact the **Vegetarian Resource Group** at 410-366-8343 or www.vrs.org for more information.

(methyl-t-butyl ether, an additive in motor vehicle fuel); **nitrates**, which can be dangerous to young children and which cannot be removed by boiling; and **radon** and other radioactive contaminants. Utilities must have their water supplies tested regularly by government-certified labs to ensure compliance with these limits, and the U.S. **Environmental Protection Agency** (EPA) can order utilities to advise their customers to boil their tap water or use bottled water if violations are found. State environmental agencies are required to monitor the levels of dozens of other contaminants that are not regulated but which *may* be regulated someday, depending on the outcome of further scientific research. And water utilities or the state government must make water quality test results available to the public. (Check the Blue Pages or your state government web site to find the state environmental agency.)

The EPA publishes a free booklet, *Water On Tap: What You Need To Know,* that explains where drinking water comes from, how to find out whether it's safe, what to do if it isn't, and how you can help keep water sources clean. The text (and lots of related information, some of it technical and scientific) is available online at www.epa.gov/ safewater, or you can order printed information from the **Safe Drinking Water Hotline** at 800-426-4791.

Many rural homes get their tap water from a **well** connected to the plumbing system, and the EPA does not oversee testing of water from private wells. However, the Safe Drinking Water Hotline and web site offer advice about private lab testing of wells. (Labs are listed in the Yellow Pages under LABORATORIES-TESTING.) Nitrates and certain bacteria can be detected in inexpensive tests that should be performed every year; other contaminants, such as pesticides, may require special tests that will be more expensive. You can do some testing yourself with kits available from hardware stores or from the nonprofit Water Quality Association, 800-749-0234 or www.wqa.org.

Most municipal tap water is treated with **chlorine** to kill harmful bacteria and **fluoride** to help young children grow healthy teeth. Some people consider these additives a form of contamination, and some people believe the federal standards for drinking water do not sufficiently protect public health. As a result, household **water filters** are increasingly popular. Inexpensive filters such as the Brita system are available at drugstores and supermarkets. They remove the taste and odor of chlorine, but they don't eliminate most pollutants. Heavy-duty water filters that remove almost all microbes, lead, chlorine, and other toxic trace elements from tap water are available by mail from Gaiam, 800-869-3446 or www.gaiam.com; Real Goods, 800-762-7325 or www.realgoods.com; and some department stores. Some filters hook up to your sink to filter water as you draw it from the tap, while others attach to free-standing jugs or coolers.

If you prefer **bottled water,** you can arrange to have it delivered to your home on a weekly or monthly basis by dealers listed in the Yellow Pages under WATER COMPANIES. Bottled water is also available at any grocery store or drugstore; many supermarkets have dispensers to refill your own jugs with filtered water. Bottled water is considered a food product and is regulated by the FDA Center for Food Safety and Applied Nutrition, not the EPA, but the purity standards are the same. For details, call 888-723-3366 or www.cfsan.fda.gov.

APPLIANCES

When you purchase a household appliance in the United States, you own it—it is not recovered by the manufacturer for recycling. If the model is found to be defective or unsafe due to a design flaw, the Consumer Product Safety Commission can order the manufacturer to issue a recall notice inviting users to return the item and get their money back or get a replacement model. The EPA and the U.S. Department of Energy jointly award the **Energy Star** seal to appliances that meet certain energy efficiency guidelines; compared to products that do not meet Energy Star guidelines, these goods saved U.S. residents an estimated $6 billion in 2002 alone.

Energy Star Seal

Household electrical current in the United States is 60 Hz. Practically all U.S. appliances run on 110V—the only common exception is laundry dryers, which run on 220V. If you want to use appliances not designed for U.S. use, you will need a **transformer**. To use imported appliances designed for 110V, you will need an **adapter** if the plug does not fit one of the outlets illustrated below. These devices are available at hardware stores. Transformers, depending on the wattage rating, can be expensive; adapters are not. (You might need an adapter with certain appliances you buy in the United States—some older homes only have nonpolarized two-prong outlets, and many devices have three-prong plugs or polarized two-prong plugs.) Computers and other sensitive electronic equipment can be damaged by minor variations in the electrical current, so they should always be plugged into a **surge protector.** These devices are available both for individual appliances and as a feature on a *power strip*, an accessory that allows you to plug several appliances into one wall outlet safely. Follow the manufacturer's instructions carefully—incorrect use of transformers, adapters, or power strips can be dangerous. When you buy appliances or electrical accessories in the United States, look for a mark that says **UL Listed**—the seal of approval from **Underwriters Laboratories**, a respected safety testing agency founded by the insurance industry to help prevent electrical fires.

NONPOLARIZED   most common in older homes

POLARIZED   for plugs on which one prong is wider than the other

GROUNDED   for three-prong plugs

GFCI   (ground fault circuit interrupter) with built-in circuit breaker for safety

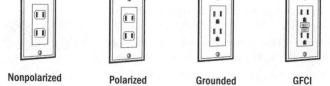

Nonpolarized   Polarized   Grounded   GFCI

Almost all U.S. households have a refrigerator, a gas or electric oven, a gas or electric stove, a vacuum cleaner, and a TV set and some kind of stereo equipment. Almost all houses, and all apartment buildings, have a furnace or boiler to heat the air and a water heater to heat the tap water. About 78% of households have a laundry washer and dryer; 53% have an electric dishwasher; 86% have a microwave oven; 89% have a VCR or DVD player; and 78% have air conditioning units—either central ones that serve the whole house or window units that serve a single room. Some kitchen sinks are equipped with an electric garbage disposal, a device that shreds food residue after it is rinsed down the drain. The most common **small appliances** are toasters, kitchen blenders or mixers, electric coffeemakers, steam irons to press clothing, sewing machines, vacuum cleaners, electric fans, hairdryers, and answering machines for the phone.

Major appliances—refrigerators, ovens, dishwashers, laundry machines, furnaces, and water heaters—are usually sold or leased (rented) along with the home. You will not need to buy major appliances unless one breaks down or you wish to replace an existing model with a more efficient one.

If you overload an electrical circuit in your home by running too many appliances at once, one of two safety devices will be activated: in an older home, a **fuse** will break, interrupting the circuit and cutting off power; in a modern home, a **circuit breaker** switch will automatically turn off. If your home is equipped with circuit breakers, you can reconnect the circuit by simply throwing the switch; a broken fuse, however, must be replaced. (Fuses are available at hardware stores.) As soon as you move into a new home, make sure you know where the fuse box or the circuit breaker cabinet is mounted—usually in a basement or utility closet.

If you have to dispose of an old appliance, contact your city or county solid waste agency (see the section on UTILITIES in Chapter 9) to find out whether it can be recycled or how you can arrange for it to be picked up.

AUTOMOBILES

If you're going to be in the United States for a long time and you think you want to buy a car, plan to spend some time shopping around for the best deal. Buying a new car is a complicated transaction, and it often involves borrowing money. (Many auto *dealerships,* or retailers, offer their own financing programs, but a loan from a financial institution will usually have more favorable terms.) The annual car buyer's edition of *Consumer Reports* magazine is a good place to start (see CONSUMER PROTECTION above).

A car is one of the few purchases in the United States that you *are* expected to haggle over—nobody pays the sticker price for a car. Negotiable points include optional features (usually just called **options**) and terms of financing (down payment, monthly payments, and interest). Rarely is a customer more experienced in bargaining than a professional salesperson—so watch out for sales tricks such as unexplained fees or unreasonable attempts to rush you into a decision. Two suggestions: avoid any car dealer who will not let you take a vehicle on a short **test drive**, and never sign a sales contract on the same day it's negotiated; go think it over and come back the next day. (The American expression is "sleep on it.")

If you have mechanical problems with a new car, you may be entitled to return it for a refund—state laws that protect car buyers are called **lemon laws** (*lemon* is slang for a mechanically faulty car). For details, visit www.carlemon.com.

If you're looking for a **used car**, you can call or visit used car dealerships; shop around online through www.carmax.com or www.carsdirect.com; or look in the classified ads in the newspaper. The **Kelley Blue Book** is the standard reference for the value of used cars based on *make* (manufacturer), model, year, and mileage. It's available in libraries and bookstores or at www.kbb.com. **Edmunds** also rates used cars at www.edmunds.com. Also, check with the **National Highway Traffic Safety Administration** to find out if a model has ever been recalled from the market for safety reasons—call 800-424-9393 or visit www.nhtsa.dot.gov—and visit **www.carfax.com** to find out whether a specific vehicle has ever been in a collision. Finally, have the car **inspected** by a mechanic before you finalize the deal; look in the Yellow Pages under AUTOMOBILE REPAIRS AND SERVICE. Note: Auto shops that display the **ASE** seal have met voluntary high standards set by the National Institute for Automotive Service Excellence.

ASE seal

For general advice about buying a car and specific information about cars and financing, check out **www.cars.com** or **Autosite**, www.autosite.com, as well as the resources listed under CONSUMER PROTECTION above. Local dealerships are listed in the Yellow Pages under AUTOMOBILE DEALERS, NEW and USED; most dealers, however, sell at least a few used cars that they have accepted for their *trade-in* value toward the purchase of a new car.

LEASING & SHARING

You don't have to buy a car. If you plan to be in the country for just a year or two, it might make sense to **lease** a car instead. The monthly payments can be almost as expensive as the installment payments on a new car you would buy, but there's no expensive down payment and you can often lease a better car than you could buy for the same monthly payment. You can also exchange cars easily under a leasing arrangement, so it's like getting a new car every year. Look in the Yellow Pages under AUTOMOBILE LEASING and visit **www.leaseguide.com** for general advice. Read the fine print, however, before you sign a lease agreement. Some automobile leases can end up *costing more* than the price of a new car.

A relatively new option in some major cities is **car-sharing** networks. If you need a car occasionally, but not often enough to own one, you can join one of these programs. Members share a fleet of cars kept at central locations such as public transportation stations; whenever you need a car, you make reservations by phone and you'll be billed for the time and mileage. The fees cover gas, insurance, and the cost of maintenance. If you're planning a weekend road trip, car-sharing fees would be much higher than ordinary car rentals where you pay a flat fee per day; however, for local errands such as grocery shopping, this can be an economical alternative to car ownership. Contact **Flexcar**, 206-332-0330 or www.flexcar.com, or **Zipcar**, 866-494-7227 or www.zipcar.com. The list of cities with car-sharing services is still small, but growing.

Inch by inch, row by row, gonna make this garden grow —
All I need is a rake and a hoe and a piece of fertile ground.
Inch by inch, row by row, please bless these seeds I sow
And warm them from below 'til the rains come tumbling down

— Dave Mallett

O nce you've found a new home and moved into it, you'll want to start living in your new community. You'll want to explore your new surroundings, find fun things to do and interesting places to go, discover the local restaurants and music and arts and sports and countless other institutions that make a community something more than just a place on a map. You'll want to go out and play. In short, you probably didn't come here just to live; you probably came here, like most Americans' ancestors, to improve your *quality of life*—or, like most travelers, to experience things you wouldn't experience at home.

Most of the information in this book is general background material. It's no substitute for the information you can gather from local sources. As noted throughout this book, you can gather a lot of information from your local **telephone directories**, your local **public library** and your **state government web site**. Along with these essential resources, your most valuable sources of information about your new city or county are local **newspapers** and their web sites; local government web sites listed at **www.citysearch.com** or **www.officialcitysites.org**; and the local **Newcomer's Handbook®** or other resources available from First Books.

NEWCOMER'S HANDBOOKS®

Newcomer's Handbook® city guides are excellent resources for relocating or getting to know your city better. Published by **First Books,** they are written by local authors, frequently updated and full of useful information. Newcomer's Handbooks® are unbiased and do not contain advertising. Available for **Atlanta, Boston, Chicago, Los Angeles, Minneapolis/St. Paul, New York City, San Francisco, Seattle,** and **Washington, D.C.** First Books also sells other guidebooks and Welcome Packages for dozens of cities. Order by phone at 503-968-6777 or visit www.firstbooks.com.

NEWSPAPERS

Daily newspapers offer a wealth of information about a community in addition to the current news. Most major newspapers include special sections about business and finance, the arts and entertainment, the weather, sports, real estate, health care, restaurants, home improvement, and recreation. Most papers also have a *classified advertising* section where readers offer to buy or sell all kinds of property—from household goods to cars, homes, and land.

Most newspapers also devote two or three pages to essays of opinion and commentary. These include *editorials* written by the newspaper staff and representing the political voice of the newspaper; *op-ed* columns written by guest writers with expertise in a certain field and appearing opposite the editorial page; and *letters to the editor* submitted by ordinary readers with comments about recent news stories. If you read the opinion pages every day, you will quickly get a sense of the range of political opinions reflected in your community and its elected government. Good newspapers try hard to keep opinions and factual reporting strictly separate. The American approach to journalism calls for unbiased reporting of the facts, and readers expect that; opinion columns are offered in a separate section to help readers consider different perspectives.

PERSONAL ADS

Americans buy and sell just about everything through the classified ads in the newspaper—old furniture, concert tickets, pet lizards, boats, accordions, and services such as massage or babysitting. But some Americans also use the classified ads to meet people and find romance. Some people are comfortable flirting with strangers at a bar or a social gathering, but others prefer to know a few personal details about a stranger before going out on a date. Personal ads give people an opportunity to mention a few of their interests and the basic attributes (such as age, race, and gender) of the kind of person they would like to date; people who fit the description can respond by phone or e-mail. Even if you're not looking for someone to date, reading the personal ads can be a fascinating way to learn about the culture of your new community. **Remember:** In the United States, it is perfectly acceptable for men and women to socialize with each other—whether married or not—and an American woman is not necessarily indicating an interest in having sex just by spending time socially with a man. (See the section on SEXUAL ASSAULT in Chapter 6.)

Newspapers in the United States are private businesses, independent of the state, and the government cannot interfere with the publisher's or editor's decisions about content. So the press is an important institution that helps Americans hold our leaders accountable for their actions—but it's also an in-depth guide to the community, updated every day.

Most cities have just one major daily newspaper. Many also have one or more **alternative** newspapers—weekly papers that usually cater to young adults. These are often free (paid for by advertisements) and provide relatively little news, but very extensive listings of cultural events and lots of classified ads. You might also find some weekly or monthly **neighborhood** newspapers that cover a very small area in great detail, reporting stories that would not interest anyone who does not live or work in the neighborhood but might be very important to those who do. These are almost always free and are sometimes delivered to every home in the neighborhood. And many cities are served by **special-interest** papers catering to the local African-American community, Latino community, Jewish community, other ethnic groups, or the local gay and lesbian community or local business owners.

MAKING NEW FRIENDS

If you don't already know someone in town who can show you around a bit and start introducing you to people, you might want to join a few clubs or attend some community events where you're likely to meet people who share some of your interests. For example, if you play a sport or pursue a hobby, you can probably find other enthusiasts through the local **recreation department** (known in some places as the *parks and rec department*). These are city or county agencies that offer classes in a wide range of recreational activities—for all ages and skill levels. Many also operate public gymnasiums, swimming pools, tennis courts, and other athletic facilities. You might also meet people through a local chapter of a **professional association** or an **ethnic heritage society**. (Ask your native country's embassy or consulate to refer you to an expatriates' group in your new city.) Some communities even have **newcomers' clubs** or "Welcome Wagon" programs to help new residents get settled and connect with their neighbors. A real estate agent or local government office should be able to tell you about these services. **Places of worship** can provide an instant sense of community. And a great way to meet kind, caring people and learn a lot about your community at the same time is to volunteer with a local charity or civic group (see Chapter 16). Finally, the **National Council for International Visitors** matches foreign newcomers with American counterparts in the same profession—for details, call 202-842-1414 or visit www.nciv.org.

CULTURAL AND SPORTING EVENTS

The cheapest, but seldom the most convenient, way to get tickets to a concert, play, ballgame, or other live event is to go in advance to the venue and buy tickets at the box office—after you call to make sure it's open for business. Most people find it easier to order tickets through a **ticket agency** either by phone or online; the agent usually adds $2 or $3 to the price of each ticket as a service charge, but it may be worth it for the convenience. It's easiest if you have a credit card or debit card, but some venues let you reserve tickets by phone and pay cash when you pick them up at the **will call** window. When you go to the event, be sure to take your ID *and the card you used to pay for the tickets*—you'll need to show both.

Three major nationwide ticket agencies handle practically all live cultural and sporting events—as well as many museum exhibits and attractions:

- **Ticketmaster**, 800-551-SEAT, www.ticketmaster.com
- **All Sports & Concerts**, 800-786-8425, www.ascticket.com
- **Encore Tickets**, 800-296-3626, www.encoretix.com

Performing arts events are listed in the local newspaper, but you can also get advance notice of future performances by contacting theaters directly. Many of the nation's performing arts venues are listed on the web at www.culturefinder.com. Most theater companies, orchestras, operas, and dance companies are funded by a combination of ticket sales, grants from private donors, grants from government agencies (to a much smaller extent than in many countries), and **membership** dues; you do not have to be a member of a theater or arts organization in order to attend performances, but members get discount tickets and preferred seating.

SETTING UP YOUR HOME

As soon as you move into a new home—probably the very same day—you'll want to find the nearest **hardware store**. (The British term is *ironmonger's* or *DIY store*.) In addition to the tools and supplies you need for maintenance and small repairs around the house, hardware stores can provide free advice about home improvement. Your neighborhood hardware store can help you conserve energy, plant a garden, build a set of bookshelves, or choose the right kind of paint.

If you need to furnish a home right away and you don't have time to shop around, you can usually rent anything you need—look in the Yellow Pages under RENTAL. Be careful, though: if you rent household items for more than a month or two, you will almost always end up paying more than if you had bought new furniture— even credit purchases are usually cheaper in the long run than "rent-to-own" plans. Use these services sparingly.

TRANSPORTATION

If your city has a subway or local railway, stop by a station and get a map—and spend some time studying it, especially lines that serve your neighborhood or your workplace. Same with buses. If you take a few hours to familiarize yourself with local **public transportation** options (routes, fares, and schedules), you could save yourself hundreds of hours a year by finding the most convenient way to get around. Many Americans simply assume that driving is the fastest and easiest way to navigate a city, and they're often mistaken; they pay for it in wasted time, avoidable stress, and the costs of gas and parking. (Yes, gasoline is much cheaper here than in most countries— or at least it seems like it, because we pay part of the cost through taxes and pay a subsidized price at the pump—but in many circumstances, public transportation is actually cheaper.) If your city has a **commuter information bureau**, stop by and ask for advice about your commute; such services are free, and the agency might even have a newcomer's guide to the local transit systems. In most communities, the consumer information section of the Yellow Pages is the best place to start looking for transit information.

If you plan to get around town by **bicycle**, know the local laws. In some cities, a bicycle is considered a vehicle and is supposed to obey the same signs and traffic patterns as cars; in other places, it's OK to ride a bike on the sidewalk. In some states, cyclists under age 16 are required by law to wear a federally approved safety helmet. (Expert cyclists recommend that *everyone* wear a helmet at all times when riding a bike.)

CHILD CARE

In approximately 60% of the households in the United States, two adults work for pay. It is no longer assumed that a mother stays at home to raise children while a father works to support the family. (Aside from more modern notions of gender equality, it's not easy in many cities for one parent to earn enough money to support a family of three or more.) As a result, many children spend part of the day with a childcare professional, either at a **day care center** with other children or in the child's home.

Some parents of young children arrange to work at home, or work a reduced schedule, in order to spend time with the kids. If that option isn't available to you, and you don't have relatives in the area who can help with child care, you'll want to choose childcare services *very carefully*. The vast majority of day care providers are reliable, loving people who chose the profession because of a sincere desire to nurture kids; a few, however, are unscrupulous, and with your children, there's no room for error. (And integrity isn't the only issue. Check out the provider's child-rearing philosophy, including any religious or academic aspects, in detail. It's perfectly appropriate to ask a lot of questions—in fact, avoid any childcare agency that does not welcome and encourage your questions.)

Start by looking up the state laws and regulations that govern childcare facilities. The **National Resource Center for Health & Safety in Child Care** keeps track of that information—call 800-598-KIDS or visit http://nrc.uchsc.edu. For advice about choosing a provider, licensing requirements, health and safety tips, and links to related services and agencies, check out the **National Child Care Information Center**, www.nccic.org.

Hiring a **nanny** is generally the most expensive childcare option, but it can be a very rewarding arrangement for everyone involved. The tax implications and employment laws involved can be complicated, so unless you become an expert in U.S. employment law very quickly, it might be best to go through a nanny agency that handles all the paperwork for you—including the criminal background checks and reference screening that you would want to do before placing your children in the care of a stranger. Look in the Yellow Pages under NANNY SERVICE or search online at www.nannynetwork.com.

For **babysitting** (an occasional evening of child care), you can probably find a reliable teenager or college student whose parents are your friends, neighbors, or co-workers. Ask other parents in the neighborhood how much they usually pay a babysitter, and make sure the babysitter is aware of any food allergies or special needs your child has—and what to do in an emergency. If you don't know any suitable young people (or if the ones you know are in great demand), try asking for referrals at a local **place of worship**—most will be happy to help regardless of your religious affiliation—or contact the student employment office at a nearby **college or university**.

PETS

The population of the United States includes 73 million domesticated cats and 68 million domesticated dogs, according to research conducted by a pet food industry group; roughly 40% of U.S. households include at least one dog and 36% include at least one cat. People also keep pet fish, birds, small mammals (typically hamsters, gerbils, or rabbits), and small reptiles. In rural areas, pet horses and goats are a possibility.

It's not easy to bring a pet into the United States. Contact the **Bureau of Customs & Border Protection** at 202-354-1000 or www.cbp.gov *several months in advance* to check the latest policies, because some animals may need to be quarantined before entry. Then you'll need to look up the local laws in your city or county. If you're renting a home, ask about pet policies when negotiating the terms of a lease. And you'll need to find a local veterinarian, pet supply store, and reputable pet sitter or kennel to look after your companion animal when you travel—look in the Yellow Pages under PET. If you want to adopt or buy a new pet once you're here, look for animals raised in humane conditions and avoid doing business with factory-style "puppy mills"—and then, at the appropriate time, have your pet spayed or neutered to prevent further overpopulation of homeless domestic animals. For general information about pet care and domestic animal issues in the United States, contact the **Humane Society of the United States** at www.hsus.org or the **American Society for Prevention of Cruelty to Animals**, 212-876-7700 or www.aspca.org.

LICENSING & REGULATION

In most cities and counties, dogs must be licensed by the local government to show proof of vaccination against rabies. The dog should wear the license tag on a collar. There is usually a fee for the license (typically $10 to $20). Look in the Blue Pages or on the local government web site for ANIMAL CONTROL or PET LICENSING. In most jurisdictions, you can get a license by mail. Generally, other pets do not have to be licensed, but most jurisdictions do not allow residents to keep **exotic or vicious animals** as pets—for example, in some places it is illegal to keep a half-breed wolf dog or a pit bull terrier. Many places have *leash laws*—outside the fenced yard of your home, your dog must be kept on a leash at all times—and animals are generally not allowed on public transportation vehicles or in stores, restaurants, or offices. (**Service animals**, such as guide dogs for the blind, are allowed everywhere.) And any animal who bites or seriously injures a human can be seized by the local **animal control** agency and be killed. It is also illegal to keep animals listed by the U.S. Fish & Wildlife Service as **endangered or threatened** due to ecological conditions; the Endangered Species List is available at http:// endangered.fws.gov.

ADOPTING A PET

Local **animal shelters** always have cats and dogs in need of loving homes. Shelter staff will interview everyone in your household and perhaps visit your home to make sure your family is prepared to take proper care of a companion animal. For information about your community's animal shelter, look up HUMANE SOCIETY in the business White Pages or ANIMAL CONTROL in the Blue Pages, or ask a local veterinarian. Also, in the classified ads in a local newspaper, you can find pet owners who are moving out of town and seeking good homes for animals who cannot go along.

SERVICES FOR PEOPLE WITH DISABILITIES

Federal law requires all public buildings to be accessible to people in wheelchairs and to make certain provisions for the blind and deaf. It also protects people from unreasonable job discrimination based on such conditions and requires employers to make *reasonable accommodations* for qualified people with disabilities. (See EMPLOYMENT LAW in Chapter 12.) The controlling law is called the **Americans with Disabilities Act (ADA)**, but it protects everyone in the United States, not just Americans. Almost all large office buildings, shopping malls, hotels, and other major private properties are fully accessible.

Individual stores and restaurants, however, are not covered by the ADA. Your local government's **tourism agency** or **visitor's**

bureau (listed in the Blue Pages) should have a list of accessible, ADA-compliant stores and restaurants; also, on the Internet at **www.wiredonwheels.org**, restaurants nationwide are given ratings for wheelchair access.

State and local governments have agencies to help people who have disabilities. The government can help you find any special equipment or services you need, as well as any charitable programs that offer free resources. Unfortunately, there is no standard name for state or local government agencies for the disabled, so you will have to look carefully through the Blue Pages or search a government web site. Federal programs and services for people with special needs are listed at **www.disability.gov**, and general information is available also from the **International Center for Disability Resources on the Internet**, www.icdri.org.

TELEPHONE

Local phone companies provide **telecommunications relay service,** often just called *relay,* that allows deaf and hearing persons to communicate with each other by phone through a trained operator using text telephones. The relay operator translates both parties' words verbatim and is required by law to keep all conversations strictly confidential. The service is free. Hearing-impaired phone customers can also get **text telephones** to communicate with businesses and agencies that publish a **TDD** or **TTY** number.* Check the consumer information section of the local White Pages for details about these services. A directory of federal agencies' TDD numbers is available from the Federal Consumer information Center, www.pueblo.gsa.gov, and the federal government offers its own free relay service for deaf persons contacting government agencies: 800-877-8339.

TRANSPORTATION & TRAVEL

Most airlines, railways, bus companies, and other passenger carriers make any needed accommodations for passengers with special needs with at least 24 hours' notice. In most cities, there is a public van service to drive disabled residents and their companions to the

---

*   These devices are known mainly by their initials, but the letters stand for **Telecommunications Device for the Deaf** and **Text Teletype**—two names for the same technology.

nearest public transportation station, or on other errands, by appointment. For general information about travel services for people with special needs, check out:

- **Travelocity.com** online
- **Mobility International USA**, 541-343-1284 (voice and TDD) or www.miusa.org
- **Society for the Advancement of Travel for the Handicapped**, 212-447-7284 or www.sath.org

Here are some sources of detailed information about specific arrangements offered by nationwide passenger carriers:

- **Airlines**: *Air Transportation of Handicapped Persons* is a free pamphlet available from the U.S. Department of Transportation. Write to:

  FREE ADVISORY CIRCULAR NO AC12032
  DISTRIBUTION UNIT
  USDOT PUBLICATIONS DIVISION M-4332
  WASHINGTON DC 20590

- **Amtrak** (railway): 800-USA-RAIL or TDD 800-523-6590
- **Greyhound** (intercity bus company): 800-752-4841 or TDD 800-345-3109 to arrange for special accommodations; 800-231-2222 to arrange for free travel for companions attending passengers with special needs
- **Rental cars**: The car rental companies listed in Chapter 15 can accommodate special needs with 48 to 72 hours' notice. **Wheelchair Getaways**, 800-873-4973, www.blvd.com/wg, specializes in renting lift-equipped vehicles.

All public buildings and most private ones have parking spaces reserved for vehicles bearing special license plates or placards indicating a handicapped driver or passenger. These spaces are marked by a wheelchair symbol and sometimes the words HANDICAPPED PARKING ONLY. It is illegal and extremely rude to use these spaces if you have not been issued the proper tags. Drivers (or their caregivers) who have a permanent disability can get license plates bearing the wheelchair symbol; those with a temporary disability, such as a broken leg, can get temporary placards to display in the window of a vehicle. Check with your state's department of motor vehicles for details.

READING

Many businesses and nonprofit organizations provide audiobooks (books on tape or CD) for the blind and visually impaired—or for people who simply prefer to listen to a book rather than read one. **Recording for the Blind**, 202-244-8900, provides a large selection that includes academic textbooks. Most large bookstores have a good selection of current titles and classics.

HOUSING

A local or regional **Center for Independent Living** can help you find accessible housing or contractors who specialize in making homes accessible. The **National Council on Independent Living** provides links to these regional agencies and more information about accessible housing, public spaces, and technology. Contact www.ncil.org. Also check out **The Disability Resource**, www.disabilityresource.com, an online store specializing in books and accessories for independent living.

If you lived here, you'd be home now.

> — *Advertising banner often seen on*
> *apartment buildings*

I f you're moving to the United States because of a transfer or promotion, your employer may offer relocation assistance to employees. Your company might even keep apartments or houses in your new city for employees to use temporarily, or at least offer you a housing allowance and recommend a good local real estate broker to help you find a suitable home. But if you're working for a smaller company, or you don't have a job lined up yet, you may be on your own—and even for Americans, finding a new home can involve many hours of research and legwork, often over several months.

Usually the most important resources are the real estate listings in the main local newspaper and the advice of a real estate broker. Also, houses on the market *for sale* or *for rent* are usually marked with a sign in front showing the phone number of the owner's real estate agent.

TYPES OF HOUSING

Most people in large cities live in **apartment** buildings or **townhouses**—tall, narrow houses adjoining similar houses on either side, also known as *rowhouses*. Apartments (flats) may be large or small; some are as spacious as a house. In some buildings, apartments are rented out by the owner of the

SOME IMPORTANT TERMS

Real estate means buildings or land owned as property. A real estate **agent** is any person who represents others in a real estate transaction; a real estate **broker** is specifically a buyer's agent. A **Realtor**® is an agent who belongs to a respected professional organization, the National Association of Realtors; this is such a standard credential that many Americans say "Realtor" when they mean *real estate agent*.

A **lease** is a contract to rent property—to occupy a piece of property for a specified time. The tenant may be said to *lease* the property; the owner, or **landlord,** is said to *rent out* a property (to *let* it, in British terminology); but, confusingly, the *renter* is the tenant. (In legal papers, the landlord is called the *lessor* and the tenant is called the *lessee*.) A **property manager** is a person or company hired by a landlord to handle tenant relations and building maintenance.

building; in **condominium** buildings, each apartment (*condo*) is owned individually. Detached **houses**, often called *single-family homes,* are more common in the suburbs and in the outer sections of a city. (A **duplex** is a detached house divided into two separate homes.) There are apartment buildings in suburban areas too—including **garden apartments** in long, low buildings of two or three stories—and townhouses in self-contained complexes. In outlying areas, you will also see residential **trailers**, in some regions also known as *manufactured homes* or *mobile homes,* clustered in *trailer parks.*

The size of a home can be quoted in square feet, but homes are more commonly classified by the number of bedrooms. A **studio apartment** includes a living space, small kitchen, and bathroom; a small one-room apartment is called an **efficiency**. And a **loft** is an apartment built in a converted old industrial building; the unit may be large or small, and usually features exposed brick and pipe (which some people prize as decor) and perhaps an open-sided sleeping platform, *also* called a loft, above the main floor.

Houses and apartments are available in a wide variety of styles, sizes, and levels of luxury and prestige. It may be worthwhile to make temporary housing arrangements as soon as you arrive in the country, but before you settle on long-term housing, you should take the time to visit lots of different homes.

RENTING VS. BUYING

Renting a home is a simple and speedy process compared to buying, and the initial costs are much lower. Most leases (rental agreements) are made for one year at a time; renting gives you a chance to explore a neighborhood and city in depth before you settle on long-term housing arrangements. In a rental home, the landlord is responsible for most repairs and maintenance, and in an apartment building, you won't even have a yard (garden) to maintain.

In the long term, however, it is often cheaper to buy a home than to rent one—the initial costs are high, but monthly mortgage payments can be lower than monthly rent for a similar home. (To help with the initial expense, many cities and counties offer significant tax breaks to people buying a home there for the first time.) But owning a home is a major commitment, and newcomers to a particular area should consider renting for a year or two in order to get acquainted with a community. And international newcomers are not likely to have a sufficient credit history, initially, to borrow enough money to buy a home. (See Chapter 4.)

Buying a home is a complicated matter. You will need to work closely with a real estate agent or lawyer. Many books are available to help you understand the process, and in most cities, government agencies or real estate companies offer helpful classes or workshops for prospective homebuyers. *Because very few new immigrants will be able (or be well advised) to buy a home right away, this book presents only a brief overview of the process in order to help you determine whether home ownership should be part of your long-term plans.* If you decide to buy a home, educate yourself thoroughly—read books and current articles about homebuying, take a class, and talk to lots of people who have been through the process—in the jurisdiction where you want to live.

Bearing that in mind, however, the advantages of owning a home are significant: your wealth is invested in an asset that will grow more valuable over time, and it's *yours* to alter and improve as you please. Home ownership reflects so much financial responsibility, planning, and personal accomplishment that it is sometimes called "the American Dream," a practical and valuable reward for years of work and savings.

FINDING HOUSING

Most homes available for rent or sale are advertised in the **classified ads** in the local newspaper, and that's a good place to start your search. Some advertisers indicate a certain time and date when they will hold an **open house**—anyone is welcome to drop by, without an appointment, to see the property and ask questions about it. Other ads simply list a phone number, and it's up to you to call and schedule a mutually convenient time to visit.

As you explore a neighborhood, you might see **yard signs** in front of some homes that say FOR RENT or FOR SALE along with the agent's name and phone number. Call and arrange for a tour. In the suburbs, similar signs on along major roads point the way to homes available for sale or rent. And if you're interested in a particular apartment complex, don't hesitate to call the rental office or condo association and ask whether there are any vacancies. You might see ads or signs that say **rent with option**; this means the tenant will have the option to *buy* the home at the end of the lease period, and rent paid under the lease will be applied toward the purchase.

If you have friends or relatives in the area, ask them to look out for any suitable homes. If you or your spouse attended a major university, perhaps an alumni office can put you in touch with fellow alumni in your new city. Look for notices posted on bulletin boards at coffeehouses and other gathering places, or on college campuses. And study the local **Newcomer's Handbook®** or the resources in the local Welcome Package available from First Books (see page 114).

Finally, in most cities, there are **apartment search firms**—agencies paid by property owners to find tenants to fill their buildings. Look in the Yellow Pages under APARTMENT FINDING & RENTAL SERVICE. Most search agencies are local or regional in focus, but one has 65 offices nationwide: **RelocationCentral Apartment Search**, www.apartmentsearch.com.

REAL ESTATE BROKERS

A broker, or buyer's agent, is a trained and licensed professional who keeps a close eye on the neighborhood he or she serves. A knowledgeable broker can probably recite the average test scores at the local high school, the crime rate in the local police precinct, how many minutes it takes to drive to the nearest major highway, and—most important, if you're buying a home—the long-term and recent trends in property values right down to a specific street. To help you find a home that suits your needs, a good broker will ask you many personal questions: Are you planning to have more children? Do you have hobbies that require a lot of space or special equipment? Do you want to plant a garden, or would you prefer an ivy-covered lawn that needs no maintenance? Would you prefer to ride a bike to work, or drive, or take public transportation? What factors are most important to you? The more information you provide, the better your broker can serve you.

You can find a broker through any of the real estate firms listed in the Yellow Pages under REAL ESTATE, but it's also a good idea to browse the ads in a neighborhood newspaper (one serving just the immediate area, not the whole city). These publications are most likely to carry advertising from brokers who have lots of experience helping people move into a particular neighborhood. To find a broker online, visit the STATE & LOCAL ASSOCIATIONS page at www.realtor.com.

Real estate agents usually do not charge fees for their services; instead, they get a **commission,** a percentage of the value of the sale or lease. (As a result, naturally, agents are much more interested in representing buyers and sellers than people seeking to rent. If you want help finding a home to rent, look for a broker who specifically advertises such services.) Note: Some agents know a given community better than others, but they all have the same central list of homes available for sale or rent. Also, a broker will only show you homes being sold or rented through a seller's agent or leasing agent; since many rental homes are leased directly by the owner or property manager, you will want to look at classified ads and "FOR RENT" signs on your own as well.

ABBREVIATIONS

Here are some specialized abbreviations (in addition to the standard ones listed in Appendix B) that you might see in real estate ads and listings:

A/C	air conditioning
BA	bathroom
BR	bedroom
CAC	central air conditioning
D/W	dishwasher
FPL	fireplace
FURN	furnished
HWF	hardwood floors
OSP	off-street parking
SF	square feet
SFH	single-family home (detached house)
UTILS	utilities
W/	with
W/D	washer/dryer
YD	yard

CHOOSING A HOME

Before selecting a home, even to rent, try to get acquainted with the neighborhood and several others for comparison. Probably the most important characteristics of a neighborhood are the location (especially in relation to your place of work) and, if you have children, the quality of the local schools (see Chapter 11). Here are some additional things to consider:

- **Transportation.** In some cities—most notoriously, Los Angeles and Washington, D.C.—traffic congestion is a serious problem. Millions of Americans spend an hour or more just traveling to and from work each business day, and a long and crowded daily commute can be very stressful. If you already have a job lined up, try to find a home nearby; if the streets don't seem too hazardous, you could walk or bike to work. Explore **public transportation** services—in some cities, they're convenient and reliable and go just about everywhere, and in other cities, they're practically nonexistent. Many cities have public or nonprofit agencies for people interested in **carpooling** (ride-sharing) arrangements—look in the consumer information section of the phone book, or on the bulletin board at the public library. Or ask a co-worker; in some workplaces, employees who live near each other might set up their own carpools. But explore these options *before* you settle on a place to live; after just a few weeks of tedious commuting, you might regret signing a lease.

HAZARDS AROUND THE HOME

Many homes in the United States contain potentially toxic materials that were used in construction before their health effects were known. Homes can also be infested with pests, some of them dangerous. Watch out for:

- **Lead.** Federal law requires the owners of rental housing to disclose any hazards due to lead-based paint and to provide an approved pamphlet informing tenants about such hazards. Lead-based house paint was banned in 1978, but the dust and chips from old layers can cause serious health problems, especially in young children. In many jurisdictions, if your child is found to have signs of lead poisoning and an inspection finds lead paint in your home, the landlord must pay for *abatement* (measures to minimize hazards). For more information, contact your local housing department or the Alliance to End Childhood Lead Poisoning, 202-543-1147 or www.aeclp.org. (Lead is also found sometimes in **tap water**—see Chapter 7.)

- **Radon.** Radon is an odorless gas that occurs naturally in harmless concentrations, but it can accumulate indoors—especially in basements lined with cinder block walls. The gas is radioactive and, over years of exposure, can cause lung cancer. Before you buy a home, you should have it tested for

- **Parking.** If you choose to own a car, keep in mind that parking space is a scarce and precious commodity in many urban neighborhoods. In the suburbs, most houses have driveways or garages (carports); if you live in a house in the city, you'll be lucky if you can park on the street in front of it. Some homes in the city have off-street parking in the rear, accessible through an alley.
- **Atmosphere.** Do you want to live in a neighborhood that is quiet at night, or do you prefer to be close to nightlife? Do you want to live in a predominantly ethnic neighborhood with lots of other expatriates from your native country, or in a diverse neighborhood? Is it important to you to live near parks or outdoor recreation areas? Do you want to be able to walk to a nearby grocery store and other convenient shops, or do you prefer to drive to shopping centers?
- **Safety and stability.** Local newspapers carry crime reports, typically once a week, that list the time and location of crimes investigated by the police. Don't expect

• •

HAZARDS AROUND THE HOME, CONT.

dangerous levels of radon; test kits are available at hardware stores for about $10. If there's a high level of radon, consult a radon abatement specialist to find out how it can be corrected. Before you rent a home, find out whether radon has been detected in the past and what has been done about it. The Office of Indoor Air Quality at the U.S. Environmental Protection Agency (EPA) provides background information about radon and a list of state agencies that can help you find radon abatement services in your area. Call 800-767-7236 or visit www.epa.gov/radon.
- **Asbestos.** Asbestos is a family of mineral fibers that were widely used in construction until the 1970s. Asbestos-based materials are strong and resistant to fire, but as they become old and worn, the microscopic fibers can break and become dust particles; inhaled asbestos dust can cause lung cancer. Most asbestos products were banned in the United States in 1989, but many buildings still contain asbestos—especially in floor tiles or attic insulation. It does not necessarily need to be removed; in some cases, it is safer to leave asbestos undisturbed. But, as with radon, you should find out whether this toxic substance is in your home and what can be done

• •

to find a neighborhood where there's *never* any crime, but use these reports to compare one area to another—and be wary of neighborhoods where violent crime is known to occur during daylight hours. Look for signs of residents making a personal commitment to the neighborhood: ask locals whether there is a lot of turnover (people moving in and out of the area) or a high proportion of settled, long-term residents. An active civic association or PTA (parents & teachers association), or robust (even heated) local politics, indicates that residents care about the community and devote time to its improvement.

HAZARDS AROUND THE HOME, CONT.

about it. Asbestos is regulated by the EPA under the Toxic Substances Control Act (TSCA); information for homebuyers and renters is available from the TSCA Assistance Information Service at 202-554-1404 or from the EPA web site at www.epa.gov/asbestos.

- **Termites.** These wood-boring insects live in many climates throughout North America, and a large termite colony can do serious structural damage to a building. It is standard procedure to have a house inspected for signs of termites before it is sold; in some jurisdictions, a termite inspection is required by law. It takes a trained professional to detect hidden termites and to get rid of them, but there are many precautions you can take to reduce the chances of an infestation. Ask a local termite inspector—who knows the local climate and construction practices—for more detailed advice. Look in the Yellow Pages under PEST CONTROL.

- **Vermin.** Local housing codes generally require the landlord to provide a clean home that is free of rats, mice, and roaches—all of which live in every U.S. climate and every kind of neighborhood, rich and poor, old and new. Hardware stores and drugstores sell a variety of products to trap or poison these unwelcome guests. If you're inclined to be more humane, or you don't want to bring strong chemicals into your home, nonlethal rodent traps and nontoxic pesticides are available by mail from Gaiam, 800-869-3446 or www.gaiam.com, and Real Goods, 800-762-7325 or www.realgoods.com. At the other extreme, you can always call a professional exterminator listed in the Yellow Pages under PEST CONTROL.

- **Tap water** (drinking water) can also contain hazardous chemicals or microbes in some areas. See Chapter 7.

- **Noise.** If you live within several miles of an airport, the roar of low-flying jets can be a constant annoyance. If there are railroad tracks nearby, ask the locals how often the trains pass through—some rail lines carry only a few trains a day, while others may carry several trains an hour. Also inquire locally about traffic noise from nearby highways—is the roar of traffic generally limited to certain peak hours, or is it constant?
- **Services.** Where is the nearest library? Hospital? Police station? Fire station? (Some insurance companies offer lower rates if you live within a mile of a fire station. Of course, with the added measure of safety, there's added noise.) Most houses and apartment buildings have laundry machines, but many don't; is there a laundromat (a shop with coin-operated washers and dryers) nearby? Are grocery stores, drugstores, hardware stores, banks, and other essentials conveniently located?
- **Pets.** Many landlords do not allow pets, or allow only small animals up to a certain weight. And most landlords who do allow pets require an extra deposit of $50 to $200 (in addition to the regular security deposit). Of course, you will also be held responsible for the cost of any damages caused by your pet. Your local Humane Society or animal shelter can provide a list of pet-friendly apartments. (See Chapter 8.)
- **Environment.** Check www.scorecard.org to find out whether there are any major sources of pollution in the area. This web site, sponsored by the nonprofit Environmental Defense Fund, is a database of polluters by zip code. Keep in mind, too, that exposure to *nonpoint sources* of pollution—such as highway traffic—can be irritating or harmful over long periods. And, though expert opinions vary, there is growing concern about the health risks of living near high-voltage power lines or radio towers (including wireless phone towers). If you have small children or you plan to have children, you might want to take an especially thorough look at nearby environmental hazards.

Finally, take a detailed tour of the vacant home and make sure everything is in good condition, it's an appropriate size, there's enough storage space, and all your questions have been answered to your satisfaction. Visit more than once if you feel you need to. *The Savvy Renter's Kit* by Ed Sacks (Dearborn Publishing, 1998) offers a detailed checklist of things to consider in your search for the perfect rental home.

RENTAL APPLICATIONS

In many cities, competition for good rental housing is fierce. As soon as you find a place you like, and you've given it a thorough inspection, it's time to fill out a rental application. Information typically required on an application includes:

- your employer, position, and income;
- the address and owner of the last home you rented—or perhaps of every home you've rented in the past few years;
- the name and address of your bank, and perhaps the amount of money you have on deposit;
- the names and ages of everyone in the household, and their relationship to the head of the household;
- the make, model, and license plate number of your vehicle(s); and
- the names and phone numbers of up to three people who will provide personal references (attest to your good character).

Be honest! Any information you provide in a rental application can be checked, and if any of it is found to be false or deceptive, your application will be denied—or, if you sign a lease and it is determined later that you made false statements on your application, you can be *evicted* (forcibly removed) from the property. If you've just arrived and you don't have anyone in the area who can provide a reference, explain the situation—it's not unusual. A letter from your employer might be helpful. References must come from people who are not related to you, but a relative in the United States who has good references could offer to provide a *guarantee*—to take responsibility for your debts to the landlord if you lose your job or immigration status.

The application process is often more informal and flexible with landlords who are not primarily in the business of owning rental property—for instance, military or diplomatic families who are moving away on a temporary assignment and renting their own house out while they're gone. The property management firm at a large apartment complex is likely to have much more objective—and simpler—criteria: you'll just have to show that the rent is no more than a certain percentage of your income, usually 1/3. Some landlords charge an application fee of $10 to $25 to discourage frivolous applicants.

LEASES

A lease is usually a one-year contract that the landlord and tenant can agree to renew. In some jurisdictions, it is the law or the prevailing custom for a lease to remain in effect on a month-to-month basis after the original term expires, until the landlord or tenant decides to terminate the agreement—with at least 30 days' notice. A lease should clearly state:

- the address to which rent payments should be mailed or delivered, and at what time of the month (usually the beginning);
- any penalties the landlord may charge if the rent is late;
- who is responsible for utilities (water and energy services);
- under what circumstances the landlord, or contractors employed by the landlord, may enter

PROTECTION FROM DISCRIMINATION

It is against federal law for any landlord, real estate agency, mortgage lender, or insurance company to discriminate on the basis of national origin—or on the basis of race, color, religion, sex, marital status, or disability. In other words, you cannot be denied a home, a mortgage, or insurance just because you are an immigrant, and your nationality or citizenship status cannot be held against you in a housing transaction. You cannot be charged higher rent or a larger security deposit than a U.S. citizen or be subjected to any other special requirements. The **Fair Housing Act** protects you from discrimination in the rental or sale of property and the **Equal Credit Opportunity Act** protects you from discrimination in lending. The **U.S. Department of Housing & Urban Development (HUD)** enforces these laws in the case of individual violations; the **U.S. Department of Justice** enforces them when a landlord or business is accused of a *pattern* of discrimination against a *category* of people.

If you think you have been the victim of discrimination in these matters, you can file a complaint with HUD at 800-669-9777 or www.hud.gov/complaints. Or you can sue the offender in civil court (see Chapter 6). But you must file a complaint within a year after the incident, or a lawsuit within two years.

the home to make inspections or repairs;

- rules regarding pets;
- under what circumstances the tenant may sublet the property (see SHARING & SUBLETS below), and how many people may live in the property;
- whether the tenant is required to buy renter's insurance (see INSURANCE below);
- who is responsible for minor repairs and maintenance, including lawn care;
- when the landlord may increase the rent, and by how much, and how much notice (warning) the tenant must receive; and
- under what circumstances the lease may be renewed, terminated, or continued on a month-to-month basis.

Many of these points may be addressed by local law, but a lease can impose further restrictions on the landlord or tenant by mutual agreement. You must usually pay your first month's rent at the time you sign the lease. In addition, almost all leases require the tenant to pay a **security deposit**, usually equal to a month's rent; the deposit is retained by the landlord until

REQUIRED MAINTENANCE

American homeowners pay close attention to changes in the average **property values** in their neighborhood. A home is a significant investment, and many families plan to sell their house when the children graduate from school or the parents retire. The aging parents can move into a smaller home, perhaps an apartment, and live on interest from the invested profits from the sale of a house they owned and maintained for many years. Property values reflect the overall desirability of a neighborhood—high housing prices usually indicate good schools; clean, quiet streets; low crime rates; reliable services from the local government, such as recycling and trash collection; and tidy, well-maintained lawns and exteriors.

To help maintain property values, many towns and counties have laws that require the occupants—whether owners or tenants—of each house to keep the grass cut to a certain height. And many jurisdictions send trucks around to collect fallen leaves; residents must rake leaves from their lawn into a pile at the curb for collection. (There are businesses that will do these chores for you—look in the Yellow Pages under LAWN CARE. You can also find neighborhood kids to do yardwork for cash.) In most places, you are required to clear snow from the sidewalk in front of your house within 24 hours after a snowstorm. For this chore, too, you can usually hire an enterprising young person in the neighborhood.

REQUIRED MAINTENANCE, CONT.

Every jurisdiction has **housing codes,** or regulations, that establish safety standards for residential buildings. For example, electrical wiring must be properly installed and kept in good condition; homes must have at least two exits, in case of fire; chimneys and rain gutters must be kept clear of debris; and every home must have at least one smoke alarm. In some cities and towns, rental homes are inspected once a year by a **building inspector** from the local government, to enforce these codes and protect the tenant's right to safe and decent housing.

There may be more elaborate rules in a **subdivision,** a neighborhood built by a real estate developer. This type of residential neighborhood is common in the outer suburbs of many cities. The homes in a subdivision are sold only to buyers who agree to abide by the rules of a local **homeowners association.** These policies, called **restrictive covenants,** usually require owners to get their neighbors' approval (or the association's approval) before altering the external appearance of their own home. There may be rules governing the planting and removal of trees; the size and placement of tool sheds, swimming pools, and ornamental fountains or bird feeders; the storage of motor vehicles, especially disabled ones in need of repairs; and the hours during which noisy activity is permitted in the yard.

you move out, when it is returned to you with interest minus the cost of any damages you have caused. (A certain amount of minor damage is considered *normal wear and tear;* in most jurisdictions, you cannot be billed for a few stains on the carpet or a few nails in the wall. But the cost of other damages, such as broken windows or severely unclean conditions, will be deducted.) The interest rate a landlord must pay on security deposits, and the deadline by which the landlord must return your deposit or prove damages after you move out, is usually specified by local law; if not, it should be specified in the lease. Before you move in, you and the landlord should inspect the property together and make a list of any existing damages so they cannot be blamed on you later. You and the landlord should both keep a signed copy.

Most leases allow the owner to increase the rent at least once a year (though not without advance notice, usually 30 or 60 days). Some cities—notably New York—have **rent control** laws that restrict the amount by which landlords may raise the rent each year. Ask the local *landlord-tenant agency* or *housing department* listed in the Blue Pages—but make sure you get all the details. Most rent control laws apply only to large buildings or apartment complexes. And if the law permits the landlord to raise the rent significantly when the unit is vacant, the landlord might have an incentive to avoid settling disputes with tenants and, instead, look for the slightest excuse to terminate a lease.

Note that many landlords use a standard lease copied from a law book or web site; you and your landlord can make any changes you agree to. Just be sure you both initial any handwritten changes and you both possess signed copies of exactly the same agreement.

SHARING & SUBLETS

In cities, it is increasingly common for unmarried adults to share a house or large apartment, especially in areas near a large university. You will see classified ads in the newspaper listing "room for rent" or "housing to share." In some communities, a neighborhood coffee-house or bookstore is also a good place to look for notices, pinned to a bulletin board, advertising rooms for rent in a shared home. (Note about confusing terminology: a *group house* is a house shared by several adults who are not related to each other, but a *group home* is an institution for mentally ill or disabled persons.)

Sharing a house or apartment might be an excellent way to learn about the country and the area where you live—and to meet lots of people, if each of your housemates has a different circle of friends. It's a popular arrangement among young adults because it's usually much cheaper than living alone—you and your housemates share the cost of rent and utilities; you can share furniture and cookware; and you might even decide to prepare meals together.

Choose housemates carefully. It is perfectly appropriate to ask your prospective housemates questions about their financial stability, their work, their personal habits, and their long-term plans—and you should be prepared to answer such questions too. Remember: not only will these people have keys to your house, but if they turn out to be unable or unwilling to pay their bills, you could be held responsible for the full cost of a big house! But they must be able to trust you as well, and if you follow your instincts and find the right partners, a group house can be a welcoming, reassuring, and inexpensive arrangement for a newcomer alone in an unfamiliar city.

Sometimes it is possible to rent a home for just a few months from someone who is going away for the summer or for a temporary assignment in another city. This arrangement is called a **short-term rental** if the regular occupant is the owner; if the occupant is a tenant, it's called a **sublet**—the tenant is *your* landlord, but is still responsible to the owner for rent and maintenance. Usually the tenant must get the owner's permission to sublet, so you may have to satisfy both the tenant and the owner that you are trustworthy and financially capable of renting (see RENTAL APPLICATIONS above). Sublets are listed in the classified ads in the newspaper, either under SHORT-TERM RENTALS or in their own category.

If you move into a group house, the contractual arrangement is usually a sublet—you will probably be renting a bedroom (and shared use of the rest of the house) from someone who is already living there as a tenant. In some group houses, however, each resident is named on the lease and is separately responsible to the landlord.

LANDLORD-TENANT DISPUTES

Almost every city and county has a **landlord-tenant commission** or a housing agency* that enforces local housing codes and tenants' rights under the law. These agencies can step in to mediate disputes between a landlord and tenant; in fact, many leases include a clause in which the tenant agrees to try mediation before filing a lawsuit against the landlord in the event of a serious dispute. You can also get pamphlets and advice from these agencies informing you of your rights as a renter, which vary from one jurisdiction to another. And if a dispute cannot be settled through mediation or arbitration services, there's always court—see Chapter 6.

Generally, local laws require a landlord to respond to complaints within a reasonable time ("reasonable" given the nature of the problem—a broken furnace during the winter is an emergency, but a broken dishwasher isn't). If your landlord fails to address a serious problem within a certain amount of time established by local law, you may fix the problem at your own expense and subtract the costs from your next scheduled rent payment. If a problem is so serious that the apartment or house is in violation of housing codes and is not legally considered **habitable**, you may withhold your rent payments completely until the problem is fixed. (This drastic measure is called a *rent strike,* and many jurisdictions require you to pay the money into an *escrow account*—a fund overseen by the courts and released to the appropriate party after the dispute is resolved.)

Some leases contain clauses that are illegal and unenforceable. For instance, you cannot sign away your right to sue your landlord,

---

* The term *housing authority,* however, usually refers to a local agency that provides subsidized housing for the poor.

and you cannot be required to pay the legal expenses incurred by your landlord in a claim against you that the courts do not uphold. But, under the principles of U.S. contract law, if one clause of a lease or contract is found to be illegal or invalid, the rest of the contract is still binding. Likewise, if one party violates a clause of a contract and the other party does not exercise its rights to seek a remedy, that does not mean the offending party has permission to violate the same clause again in the future. (In other words: you might be able to make a late payment once in a while, but that doesn't mean the landlord has to tolerate it the next time.)

If a tenant is in serious violation of the lease, the landlord can get a court order to **evict** the tenant and reclaim possession of the property. In most jurisdictions, eviction is a last resort available to landlords who have issued clear warnings and demands over a specified period of time, usually at least 30 days; however, if a court grants an eviction order because of failure to pay rent, the only way to stop the forcible eviction is to pay the full amount due in cash. Sadly, you will occasionally see a family's belongings piled on the curb outside an apartment building—a household has been evicted.

For detailed information about landlord and tenant rights and responsibilities, visit the online legal resources www.nolo.com or www.rentlaw.com. These sites include laws from every state and the District of Columbia, and Nolo sells several legal handbooks for tenants—notably *Every Tenant's Legal Guide* and *Renter's Rights: The Basics,* both by Janet Portman & Marcia Stewart.

If you must move out before a lease expires, it's not necessarily a disaster—but it will be costly. (In theory, a landlord could sue you for the total amount of rent you would have paid over the remaining term of the lease plus the costs of advertising the vacancy. Most landlords won't bother unless it's clear that they've treated you fairly and you've treated them unfairly.) Remember, though, your next rental application will ask for a reference from your previous landlord—so you will be much better off if you can negotiate an amicable deal. At www.nolo.com, there are helpful legal kits you can download for a small fee, such as "Break Your Lease Without Breaking the Law."

INSURANCE

As soon as you sign a lease, your next step should be to get **renter's insurance** to compensate for the loss of your possessions due to fire, theft, or natural disaster. (**Flood insurance** is separate and is advisable if you live in a house or basement apartment in a low-lying area.) Renter's insurance also covers any medical and legal expenses for which you might be held responsible if a visitor is injured on the premises of your home—for example, if a postal worker delivering the mail falls on a patch of ice outside your door. Depending on the total value of your possessions, renter's insurance won't likely cost more than $150 a year. Expensive jewelry, electronics, or other special items may require additional coverage. Structural damage to the property is usually not covered by a renter's policy—only by **homeowner's insurance**.

The ideal renter's or homeowner's policy provides *replacement value coverage,* paying the current market value of any items you need to replace. Inflation has made these policies less common in recent years; instead, many insurance companies cover 120% or 125% of the purchase price or standard value of your belongings. Shop around for a replacement value policy—if disaster strikes, you'll be glad you did.

Visit **www.insure.com** for an overview of different kinds of insurance policies, advice about filing a claim, and records of complaints filed against insurance companies. **Quotesmith**, www.quotesmith.com, and **QuickenInsurance**, www.insuremarket.com, offer quick rate quotes from hundreds of insurance companies. If you belong to a warehouse club or credit union, ask about insurance discounts for members.

To find an insurance agent in your neighborhood, check the Yellow Pages (where agencies are listed by town) or an insurance company web site. Here are some major companies with agents in most cities:

- **Allstate**, www.allstate.com
- **Hartford**, www.thehartford.com
- **Nationwide**, www.nationwide.com
- **State Farm**, www.statefarm.com
- **Travelers**, www.travelerspc.com

TEMPORARY HOUSING

Most cities have a few **extended-stay hotels** or **corporate apartments**—furnished apartments that you can rent by the week or the month, sometimes with a minimum stay of several weeks and a maximum stay of a year. These are listed in the Yellow Pages under APARTMENTS and they're advertised in business-oriented newspapers. This kind of short-term housing can provide an excellent "base camp" while you explore your new city and find a good home. And, like hotel rooms, extended-stay suites can be booked by phone or internet before you even leave your home country.

Here are some extended-stay hotel chains with locations in many U.S. cities:

- **BridgeStreet Corporate Housing,** 800 278-7338, www.bridgestreet.com
- **Charles E. Smith Corporate Living,** 888-234-7829, www.smithliving.com
- **Homestead Studio Suites,** 888-782-9473, www.homesteadhotels.com
- **Residence Inn by Marriott,** 800-331-3131, www.residenceinn.com

BUYING A HOME

Buying a house, condo, or co-op* is a time-consuming process and can be confusing, even mysterious. But the resources listed here—and professionals in the community—can help you determine your price range, find the right home in the right neighborhood, get a mortgage, move in, and make repairs and improvements.

CALCULATING COSTS

Finding the perfect home is just the beginning of the process. Your purchase will cost more than the price of the home. Related expenses (collectively known as **closing costs**) include:

- **Title search.** A real estate agent or lawyer must check the records of the local courthouse to make sure the seller has an undisputed, exclusive right to sell the property. You will need to pay for this service and for **title insurance** to compensate others who are found to have a fair claim to the property—such as any creditors (lenders) with a collateral interest.
- **Inspection.** For your protection, a house must be examined by a licensed building inspector before it is sold. If problems are found, you might be able to renegotiate

---

* Co-op apartments are popular in some cities, especially New York. Buying into a co-op means purchasing a share in the ownership of an apartment building; the share allows you to live in a unit, but you do not own the unit outright. You must be approved by the existing shareholders in order to join a co-op, and so does anyone to whom you later sell or rent your unit.

the price. Also, if you are buying a house, a **land survey** may be required in order to determine the exact boundaries of the property.

- **Recording tax.** The *deed,* or ownership papers, must be transferred by the Recorder of Deeds, an officer of the local government. There is a fee for this transaction.

- **Mortgage points.** As a fee for making the loan, your mortgage lender will charge you several percentage points of the amount you are borrowing. (This is also called *origination.*)

- **Escrow payments.** You will have to put money into an escrow account (a fund in care of a neutral trustee) that will be used to compensate the seller for declining other offers if you change your mind about the sale, and to pay property taxes and homeowner's insurance premiums.

These costs usually make the transaction cost 5% to 8% more than the purchase price (not counting interest on your mortgage). If you have a good credit history, you can usually qualify for a mortgage of 3 to 4 times your annual income—but be prepared for a thorough examination of your personal finances and employment status. The lender will also want to verify that you have enough savings to pay 10% to 20% of the purchase price outright. (This is called the **down payment**, the biggest single expense in the housing transaction. Generally, a lender will want a larger down payment if you pay low origination fees, or mortgage *points,* and a smaller down payment if you pay higher origination fees.)

• •

"FOR SALE BY OWNER"

This may seem like an obvious point—after all, who else would sell a home but its owner? However, the phrase means that the home is being marketed to buyers by the owner personally, not by a real estate agent. A buyer's agent will have to do extra work to identify these homes, as they are not included in the listings that agents compile and share. It may be worth the effort: because the seller is not paying a commission to a sales agent, you can negotiate a lower price than the home would otherwise command. Homes for sale by owner are listed in their own section of the classified ads and on the internet—for example, at www.4salebyowner.com, www.fisbos.com, www.homesbyowner.com, and www.owners.com.

• •

You can usually claim a **tax deduction** for interest paid on a mortgage. In other words, you may subtract the amount of interest you've paid in a given year from the income figures used to calculate your tax obligation for that year. See the current IRS instruction booklet or www.irs.gov for details.

CHOOSING (AND GETTING) A MORTGAGE

Mortgage lenders usually charge interest of 5% to 10% over a 30-year period. It is possible to **refinance** your mortgage (renegotiate the terms of payment) later if prevailing interest rates decrease. Lenders' rates are reported in local newspapers and on a number of web sites (see Chapter 4), but to get the best possible terms, you might benefit from the advice of a professional **mortgage broker**. These financial advisors work on commission (at no direct cost to you). Ask your real estate broker to recommend a mortgage broker.

Lenders recommend that you *pre-qualify* for a loan—that you meet with a prospective lender to determine a realistic range of financing. Go prepared with documentation of your finances, and contact the three major credit bureaus (see Chapter 4) to make sure your credit history is accurate.

HELPFUL RESOURCES

The **Fannie Mae Foundation**, a nonprofit educational extension of the Federal National Mortgage Association (FNMA), publishes a series of free booklets for first-time homebuyers: *Knowing and Understanding Your Credit; Opening the Door to a Home of Your Own; Borrowing Basics; Choosing the Mortgage That's Right For You* and, for 20 major cities, the *Directory of Home-Buyer Resources*. To order these resources by mail, call 800-611-9566; to download them, visit their website at www.fanniemaefoundation.org.

The **U.S. Department of Housing & Urban Development** provides extensive information about renting and buying homes, obtaining a mortgage, and local **housing counseling agencies** that can help guide you through the process. Look in the federal section of the Blue Pages to find the closest HUD field office, or contact the agency at 800-569-4287 or www.hud.gov.

These web sites list homes for sale nationwide and offer advice about mortgages, real estate agents, relocation, neighborhoods, home improvement, and more:

- www.homefair.com
- www.homeseekers.com
- www.homestore.com / www.realtor.com
- http://houseandhome.msn.com
- www.realtylocator.com

And these sites provide detailed advice about mortgages—including tips for choosing a mortgage lender and avoiding unfair lending practices:

- **BankRate**, www.bankrate.com
- **Freddie Mac** (Federal Home Mortgage Corporation), www.freddiemac.com
- **The Mortgage Professor**, www.mtgprofessor.com
- **www.owners.com**

UTILITIES

There are no government-owned energy companies in the United States. Until the late 1990s, however, electricity and natural gas were supplied to homes mainly by licensed monopolies—corporations called **public utilities** that charged prices regulated by a local **public service commission** in exchange for an exception to the federal laws that ban monopolies. In recent years, electric and gas services have been opened up to competitive markets in most states. Public utilities (and the public service commissions that oversee them) are listed in the consumer information section of local phone books. The state public service commission also keeps a list of all private companies licensed to sell energy. And many state government web sites offer advice about choosing energy services.

Practically all homes are wired for electricity. Some homes are fitted with gas lines and some aren't, depending on the preferences of the builder or original owner and on prevailing local practices. Some homes use gas for cooking and electricity for heating; others are heated by oil, which is sold by private companies and delivered by truck to a storage tank on the property as needed. Few homes are heated entirely by wood or other biofuels, but many homes in the cold northern parts of the country have wood-burning stoves for supplemental heat, and a few environmentally conscious homeowners have been experimenting with corn as a heating fuel in recent years. Whatever form of energy is burned in your furnace, in a modern home (built after World War II), your heat will probably be distributed through air ducts with an electric fan; many older homes have steam radiators. Some homes are equipped with a **heat pump** (also called a heat exchanger), an energy-saving device that helps keep heated air inside during the winter.

Water and sewer service is supplied by public utilities. In most cities and towns, the local government provides **solid waste** (sanitation) service—the curbside collection of trash and recyclable materials once a week. (Whether the waste is collected by government workers or a private company under contract to the government, the service is funded by property taxes or annual fees.) In rural areas and some small towns, there is no curbside waste pickup, and residents must haul their own solid waste to a dump or **transfer station** for recycling or disposal.

Fuel oil dealers are listed in the Yellow Pages under OILS, and fuelwood dealers are listed under FIREWOOD. For information about **renewable energy** systems—including solar heating, generation of electricity through solar cells and windmills, and geothermal systems that harness the Earth's natural heat—check out the *National Green Pages* published by Co-op America at www.greenpages.org (also available in print by calling 800-584-7336). Or browse the ECO Services *International Green Pages* at www.eco-web.com. Many states offer tax credits or utility rebates to help homeowners invest in energy-saving technology.

Most utilities and private energy companies will require you to pay a **deposit**, typically around $50, if you do not have a credit history and have not had similar utility accounts in your name before. The amount will be refunded with interest or credited to your account after you've made timely payments for a year. And many offer you the option of paying for your **actual** measured energy consumption each month—which means paying very large bills during seasonal

ENERGY IN THE UNITED STATES

According to U.S. Department of Energy statistics for 2001, most of the nation's energy comes from fossil fuels: 32% from coal, 28% from natural gas, and 17% from oil. Another 11% comes from nuclear fission, and 4% from biofuels and waste incineration; 4% is geothermal, 3% is hydro-electric, and solar and wind power each contribute just under 1%. The United States consumes about 24% of the world's energy, far more than any other country; for comparison, the entire continent of Europe consumes 31%, and Asia 28%.

extremes and very small bills in temperate months—or paying a flat monthly amount based on your **estimated** annual consumption. (The amount may be adjusted as needed if the estimate turns out to be wrong.)

If you don't have your health, you don't have anything.

— Old American saying

The United States has an exceptionally advanced, comprehensive, reliable health care system—and it's also exceptionally expensive. There is no national health insurance except for the elderly and disabled, though some public assistance is available on the basis of low income or extraordinary medical need. You will need to obtain some kind of private health insurance for yourself and your family.

Most health care in the United States is **allopathic** (aimed at treating problems); preventive care is usually limited to an annual checkup, and many types of preventive treatment are not covered by the typical health insurance plan.

There are several reasons why the cost of medical care is so high—many doctors have to borrow money for medical school and pay interest on it; medicines and medical equipment reflect years of scientific research and clinical testing, and the manufacturers hope to profit from those investments; and hospitals must treat anybody who needs emergency care, but 41 million people in the United States have no health insurance and cannot afford to pay medical bills, so hospitals must socialize those costs. But perhaps the biggest factor in the cost of health care is the American tendency to sue somebody in court whenever something goes wrong. Doctors and hospitals have to buy special insurance in case they have to compensate a patient for damages caused by *malpractice* or medical errors. And to help avoid malpractice claims, a doctor will often send a patient to a specialist for tests to *rule out* serious medical problems that are not actually suspected, but just possible—the American expression is "better safe than sorry."

HEALTH INSURANCE

Private insurance is based on the concept of shared risk. You and the other people enrolled in an insurance fund (called an insurance *plan* or *policy*) each pay a monthly fee, called a **premium**, and the insurance company (sometimes called a *carrier*) invests the funds it collects; from the interest earned by its investments, the company pays the costs of medical care for those members who need it.

Naturally, older people are more likely to have costly medical problems than younger people; smokers are more likely to have costly medical problems than nonsmokers; and insurance industry research shows other demographic patterns. Unmarried males under age 25, for example, are statistically more likely to be injured than married males over age 25, and people who live in cities are more likely to have asthma than rural people. Insurance premiums reflect these statistics—so a 70-year-old who smokes and lives in a city will pay a higher insurance premium than a 30-year-old nonsmoker who lives on a farm.

Most insurance plans require you to pay certain minimal medical expenses each year and only cover expenses in excess of that amount. In other words, your insurance might not cover the first $200 in medical bills you get each year. That amount is called a **deductible**, and generally, the lower your deductible, the higher your insurance premium. (Most plans allow you to choose a low premium and high deductible, which makes sense for young people in good health, or a high premium and low deductible, which makes sense for people with chronic medical conditions.) Also, in order to discourage unnecessary *claims* (requests for insurance payments), most insurance plans require you to make a small token payment, perhaps $25 or 10%, for each visit to a doctor or hospital. This is called a **copayment** and, like the deductible, is generally lower for those who pay higher premiums.

When you enroll in a health insurance plan, you will be asked to take a physical examination or submit recent medical records. Insurance companies may limit their coverage of pre-existing medical conditions (except pregnancy) during your first year of membership.

KINDS OF HEALTH INSURANCE

There are two broad categories of health insurance plans: **fee-for-service** plans, which cover actual medical expenses as they occur, and **managed care** plans, which provide members with prepaid medical services. Managed care plans usually have no deductibles and very low copayments, but members must get their medical services from doctors and hospitals selected by the insurance company, except in an emergency; fee-for-service plans allow you to visit any doctor you choose, but your out-of-pocket costs will usually be higher.

There are several types of managed care plans. The most common is the **HMO**, or health maintenance organization, which provides all of your medical care or makes referrals to specialists whose fees the HMO has agreed to cover. You may also encounter a **PPO** (preferred provider organization) or **POS** (point-of-service) plan. These offer the low costs of an HMO if you choose to visit the plan's own doctors, and the freedom of a fee-for-service plan if you choose to visit outside doctors and pay the extra cost. An industry association, America's Health Insurance Plans, explains: "HMOs and PPOs have contracts with doctors, hospitals, and other providers. They have negotiated certain fees with these providers—and, as long as you get your care from these providers, they should not ask you for additional payment."

A relatively new kind of health insurance is the **health savings account**, an individual bank account that offers certain tax advantages as long as the money in it is dedicated to medical expenses. HSAs can only be used to pay for routine medical expenses; people with HSAs still need some health insurance for major medical bills in case of serious illness or injury, but they can select a plan with a very low premium and high deductible. This arrangement is intended for self-employed individuals, small business owners, and their employees.

CHOOSING AN INSURANCE PLAN

Health insurance is often an *employee benefit* provided by an employer, along with salary or wages, as part of a compensation package (see Chapter 12). Your health insurance usually covers your spouse and dependent children (children under age 18 or who live with you and rely on you for financial support). All large employers and many small businesses have group health insurance plans that employees may join. Make sure you know what specific services are covered by your insurance plan—for example, many insurance plans do not cover eyeglasses, hearing aids, or dental care, and you may want to buy supplemental insurance for such expenses.

If you do not get health insurance through your employer, or your spouse's, you will need to do some shopping: decide what kinds of coverage you need, look at a variety of insurance plans, ask a lot of questions, and make a careful decision. **Insurance agents**, listed in the Yellow Pages, are salespeople who market insurance plans. Agents know all the details of the plans they sell and can answer all your questions, but their motive is to sell you an insurance plan and earn a sales commission or fee from the insurance company. So listen to several different agents before you make a decision, and read each insurance company's promotional materials very carefully—especially the *fine print,* the blocks of tiny lettering where important details of the legal contract are often buried. If you have any doubt about the meaning of the legal jargon, ask someone to translate.

The **Center for the Study of Services** is a nonprofit organization that evaluates thousands of companies in dozens of industries. The group publishes, among other resources, the *Consumer's Guide to Health Plans,* and the latest edition of this guide will be a good investment if you have to choose your own insurance company. To order, or to see a sample of the information provided, call 202-347-7283 or visit www.checkbook.org. Also check out *Consumer Reports* magazine at www.consumerreports.org.

CONFUSED?

So are most Americans. Health insurance is a complex industry, and many people are confused by the variety of insurance programs and the esoteric jargon. With your health and your family's health at stake, it's important to keep asking questions until you feel comfortable with the amount and scope of insurance coverage you're getting, whether it's through an employer or on your own—or through another group, such as a union or professional association, that might have its own group insurance plan.

Probably the best overview of the general concept of health insurance, the types of insurance plans, and related issues is the consumer information page on the web site of **America's Health Insurance Plans** at www.aahp.org. Resources available there include the *Guide to Managed Care; Glossary of Insurance Terms; Guide to Disability Income Insurance* (which replaces lost income if you become unable to work due to a serious injury or illness); *Health Care Costs and Your Insurance Premium;* and *Guide to Medical Savings Accounts.* The consumer information or reference section of any public library also has general information about health insurance; also, for information about insurance rates and risk factors, contact the state **insurance commission** listed in the Blue Pages of the phone book.

MEDICARE

Medicare is a limited national health insurance program for persons over the age of 65 and certain younger persons with permanent medical conditions. Medicare coverage of hospital expenses is generally free for U.S. citizens and permanent residents; aliens who are not eligible for free hospital coverage can buy it for a premium if they have lived in the United States for at least five years. For details, call 800-633-4227 or visit www.medicare.gov and request a free pamphlet called *Understanding Your Medicare Choices.* You can also get help with Medicare from the Social Security Administration (see Chapter 4), because Medicare enrollment is handled through Social Security field offices.

MEDICAID

Medicaid is an insurance program funded by the federal government and administered by the states to pay for health care for low-income individuals and families. Eligibility varies from state to state and is based on income, assets, and medical needs. Under the 1996 welfare reform law, aliens are normally eligible for Medicaid benefits only if admitted for permanent residence or under certain policies providing for refugees, battered women, or conditional amnesty for illegal immigration. However, all aliens—even undocumented or illegal immigrants—are eligible for Medicaid coverage of *emergency* medical care if they meet the income limits and other criteria set by the state. For details, and links to state Medicaid agencies, contact the **Centers for Medicare & Medicaid Services** at 877-267-2323 or visit www.cms.gov/medicaid.

MEDICAL EMERGENCIES

Most hospitals have an **emergency room** staffed at all times with doctors and nurses specializing in emergency treatment of life-threatening injuries and acute illness. Emergency rooms cannot refuse to treat a patient in immediate medical need. You will eventually get a bill for emergency treatment and be asked to provide insurance information, but *first* you will get any urgent medical care.

In major cities, emergency rooms are almost always crowded. Many uninsured people go to the emergency room for routine medical care because they can't afford it anywhere else. But the most urgent cases get treatment first—emergency rooms do not favor the rich, the insured, the natural-born citizen, the old or the young, or patients of a particular race, gender, ethnicity or religion. *Triage* (sequencing of patients) is based on medical urgency and available resources, and all doctors, nurses, and other health care workers are required to follow that basic principle. (In many communities, there are walk-in medical clinics that can treat urgent problems that aren't quite emergencies, such as a broken arm.)

Every community in the United States has emergency **ambulance** service, and in most areas, the phone number is **911**. Nobody on the phone or the ambulance crew will ask you any questions about money or insurance or demand to see your papers (except relevant medical documents). If you have difficulty communicating in English in a stressful situation, medical personnel might ask to see your ID just to be sure they recorded your name and age correctly.

Ambulance and hospital personnel will, however, ask you many personal questions, some of which may be embarrassing or deal with subjects you do not usually discuss with strangers. This is to ensure that you get the correct medical treatment; if you do not answer their questions—correctly and completely—you could get the wrong treatment and make your condition worse. *Any information you give a health care worker is confidential.* Medical personnel cannot give anyone (except other medical personnel) any information about you without your consent—not the police, not your family, not your employer, nobody. There are only two exceptions:

- If you are charged with a crime or sued in court, a judge can order medical information to be submitted as evidence; as in all court proceedings, you would have a lawyer to speak up for your rights.

- Medical personnel can and must give information about a sick or injured child (under age 18) to the child's parents or legal guardians, unless the child is legally "emancipated" from adult guardianship by reason of pregnancy, marriage, or a court order.

It's a good idea to carry, at all times, a list of any chronic medical conditions or allergies you have; any medications you take regularly; and any major illnesses or injuries

THE AMERICAN RED CROSS

In many countries, the Red Cross (or Red Crescent or Magen David Adom) is the agency that provides emergency medical care and ambulance service. *The American Red Cross is not a medical care provider. Emergency medical services are provided by the local government*—usually by the fire department or a private company under contract to the government. The Red Cross provides **disaster relief** services; for example, if a home burns down or a low-lying neighborhood is flooded, the Red Cross will provide residents with temporary shelter and emergency food and clothing. The Red Cross also provides first aid training and collects donations of blood, organs, and tissues. For more information, visit www.redcross.org.

● ●

MEDICAL SPECIALISTS

DOCTORS	AREAS
allergists	allergies
cardiologists	heart and circulation
dentists	teeth
dermatologists	skin
endocrinologists	glands and hormones
gastroenterologists	digestive system
gynecologists	female reproductive system
internists	internal medicine
nephrologists	kidneys
neurologists	nervous system
obstetricians	pregnancy and childbirth
oncologists	cancer
ophthalmologists*	eyes
orthopedics	bones
otolaryngologists	ear, nose and throat
pediatricians	children
podiatrists	feet
proctologists	colon and prostate
psychiatrists	psychological well-being
surgeons	operations
urologists	urinary tract

Note: **M.D.** means *medical doctor*, the academic degree held by most of these professionals; dentists have **D.D.S.** degrees. Some physicians have a **D.O.** degree, *doctor of osteopathy*, an alternative approach to medicine that emphasizes body structures as a key to healing.

* Not to be confused with *optometrists*, who test vision and prescribe corrective eyeglasses or contact lenses, and *opticians*, who make corrective lenses

● ●

you have had in the past. You may be unable to communicate this information in an emergency, especially if you are just learning English. If you have a potentially serious condition such as diabetes or a severe allergy, consider wearing a "Medic Alert" bracelet or necklace to inform medical personnel. These are available from the Medic Alert Foundation, an international nonprofit organization—call 800-432-5378 or visit www.medicalert.org.

FINDING A DOCTOR

Most communities have services that will refer you to a doctor or dentist who suits your needs, and there may be a local publication or agency that rates doctors on their performance or peer evaluations.

Except in an emergency, your **family doctor** or **general practitioner** is the doctor you see when you have any medical problem or need a routine checkup—in other words, your *primary care physician*. This doctor will refer you to an appropriate **specialist** or hospital if he or she thinks you need further care (or a more detailed diagnosis).

Of course, if your insurance plan specifies a doctor who will serve as your primary care physician, then that's the person you call for any medical attention except in an emergency. (You can always ask to be seen by a doctor of your gender, and you don't have to give a reason.) Otherwise, start looking for a general practitioner as soon as you arrive—don't wait until you get sick or injured.

In many cities, you can find an appropriate doctor for your needs by calling 800-DOCTORS (800-362-8677), a private referral service. The Center for the Study of Services—the same group that publishes the *Consumer's Guide to Health Plans* mentioned above—publishes the *Consumer's Guide to Top Doctors* and the *Consumer's Guide to Hospitals*. These are based on peer surveys—the organization asked more than a quarter million doctors to list the doctors, other than themselves, they would recommend to their own friends and relatives. The book and online database list more than 20,000 doctors nationwide. Call 202-347-7283 or visit www.checkbook.org.

Several web sites can help you find a doctor and get advice about general health care online: **www.healthfinder.gov**, sponsored by the federal government; **www.webmd.com**; **www.healthyideas.com**; and **www.drkoop.com** (whose proprietor, Dr. C. Everett Koop, was the head of the U.S. Public Health Service during the early years of the AIDS epidemic and remains a popular and influential leader in the field of disease prevention).

Before you visit a new doctor, unless you need immediate medical attention, you should check the doctor's professional record. The **state medical board** can tell you whether a doctor has ever been disciplined for medical or ethical misconduct. For links to the web sites of every state medical board an online list of every state medical board, visit www.fsmb.org/statehome.htm. (This site, provided by the Federation of State Medical Boards, also includes links to the medical licensing agencies of the District of Columbia, Guam, the Northern Marianas, Puerto Rico, and the U.S. Virgin Islands.) Or look for "Medicine, board of," in the state government section of the Blue Pages of the local phone book.

Also, check with the **American Board of Medical Specialties** to find out what specialties a doctor is *board certified* (approved by peers) to practice—call 800-776-2378 or visit www.certifieddoctor.org/verify. And if you want to be extremely thorough, check with the **Public Citizen Health Research Group** to find out whether the state medical board itself has a good reputation, and whether a particular doctor has been named to this nonprofit group's national list of "Questionable Doctors." Call 202-588-1000 or visit www.citizen.org/hrg.

PRESCRIPTIONS

If a doctor prescribes medication, you take the *prescription* (the doctor's written orders) to a **pharmacy** to obtain the preparation. The pharmacist will also give you precise instructions for taking the medicine correctly. *If you do not understand the instructions, ask someone to interpret.* Prescription medicines are dispensed in labeled containers that include your name, the name of the doctor who prescribed the medicine, the pharmacist's instructions and the expiration date. It is illegal (and may be dangerous) to give your prescription medicine to anyone else. If you run out of medicine and you have not fully recovered, call your doctor—perhaps it will be necessary to renew your prescription (the doctor can call the pharmacy to authorize a *refill*) or adjust the prescribed dose.

A pharmacist can also advise you in the correct use of "over-the-counter" medications available without a prescription. Be sure to let the pharmacist know what other medications you take, to avoid harmful interactions.

DENTAL CARE

A German journalist living in Washington, D.C. claims that the United States has the best dental care in the world, and many British immigrants agree. But, like other kinds of medical care, it's expensive—and some health insurance plans don't cover it. As a result, many Americans are lazy about preventive care and develop gum disease at some point in their lives.

Dentistry has its own specialties, such as **orthodontics**, or the corrective treatment of growing teeth, and **periodontics**, the treatment of gum disease. According to the American Association of Orthodontists, roughly 40% to 60% of children need some corrective care as their adult teeth begin to grow, and many children are fitted with prescription braces or a removable retainer to correct the angle and spacing of their teeth.

Children are generally given routine dental checkups every six months for cleaning and fluoride treatment to prevent tooth decay. Teens and adults should have a dental checkup once a year. Drugstores and grocery stores sell a huge variety of dental care products, including dozens of competing brands of toothpaste; they all advertise different features, such as ingredients to make your teeth whiter or make your breath smell good, but basically any toothpaste used properly will keep your teeth clean. American children are taught to brush their teeth after every meal and to clean between their teeth with dental floss.

To find a dentist, an orthodontist, a periodontist, an *oral surgeon* to treat serious injuries of the mouth, or other dental specialist, call 800-DENTIST (800-336-8478) or visit www.usadentaldirectory.com, www.dentaldocshop.com, or www.dentists.com, all private referral services. For an overview of American dentistry, visit www.go2dental.com.

ALTERNATIVE MEDICINE

A common complaint (among newcomers and native-born citizens alike) is that medical care tends to be rushed—a doctor might spend only a few minutes with a patient before prescribing medications or making a referral. This can be disconcerting if you come from a culture where a doctor spends time talking with you about every aspect of your lifestyle. There is a growing interest in alternative health care disciplines in the United States, and you can probably find services like those you had in your home country—but your insurance might not pay for them.

Here are some web sites that offer links to a variety of alternative health care providers around the country and background information about alternative medicine:

- **Alternative Medicine Foundation:** www.amfoundation.org
- **Natural Health and Longevity Resource Center:** www.all-natural.com
- **HealthWorld Online Alternative Medicine Center:** www.healthy.net
- **Healthwell:** www.healthwell.com
- **WholeHealthMD:** www.wholehealthmd.com

You can also find alternative health care providers by contacting a professional association representing skilled practitioners in a specific discipline. Here are just a few:

Acupuncture: American Association of Oriental Medicine, 888-500-7999, www.aaom.org; American Academy of Medical Acupuncture, 323-937-5514, www.medicalacupuncture.org

Aromatherapy: National Association for Holistic Aromatherapy, 888-275-6242, www.naha.org

Chiropractic: American Chiropractic Association, 800-986-4636, www.amerchiro.org

Herbal medicine: American Association of Naturopathic Physicians, 866-538-2267, www.naturopathic.org

Feldenkrais: Feldenkrais Guild of North America, 800-775-2118, www.feldenkrais.com

Reflexology: Reflexology Association of America, 508-364-4234, www.reflexology-usa.org

Reiki: International Association of Reiki Professionals, 603-881-8838, www.iarp.org

Yoga: American Yoga Association, 941-927-4977, www.americanyogaassociation.org; Yoga Directory (online), www.yogadirectory.com

MENTAL HEALTH & EMOTIONAL SUPPORT

Most health insurance plans recognize mental health conditions as medical problems warranting medical attention. For instance, anyone suffering from **chronic anxiety, eating disorders,** or **clinical depression** (a general lack of enthusiasm that doesn't go away and that results in loss of appetite or sleep, changes in work habits, interpersonal tension, or drug abuse) should ask a doctor for a referral to a psychiatrist or psychologist (counselor). The doctor will first want to rule out underlying medical problems affecting mood and behavior, but will then recommend mental health care. If you just want to talk confidentially to a neutral professional, on a strictly confidential basis, about fears, relationships, habits, or culture shock and adjustment, you can go to any psychologist or counselor at your own expense. It's still a good idea to get a referral, however—if not from your doctor, then from an employee assistance program, school counselor, or place of worship.

Almost every community has a **crisis hotline** staffed by trained volunteers to help people deal with drug addiction, unintended pregnancy, domestic violence (spouse or child abuse), or other overwhelming problems, and to assist teens and children who run away from home. Look in the front pages of the local phone book to find the crisis hotlines serving your area. If someone is planning or threatening to commit suicide and you do not know the phone number of a local **suicide prevention hotline**, call 800-999-9999, a nationwide hotline run by Covenant House.

If you face a long-term illness, a physical disability, grief from a death in the family, or any kind of addiction or drug abuse, there are **support groups** in which people with similar problems gather to help each other, pledging discretion and confidentiality. A doctor can refer you to a support group for victims of a particular disease or physical condition. Any place of worship, whether you belong to it or not, can provide information about support groups for emotional distress and addiction; so can a public library. And on many university campuses and in communities with a large proportion of immigrants, you might even find support groups for newcomers who are having difficulty adjusting to life in the United States.

RED CROSS

Although a red cross on a square white background is a registered trademark of the International Red Cross (relief organization), the symbol is often used informally to indicate **first aid**. If you see this symbol in a public place, it often shows the location of a first aid kit.

STAR OF LIFE

The six-pointed Star of Life is the symbol approved by the U.S. Department of Transportation for **emergency medical services**—ambulances and personnel involved in transportation of the sick and injured.

CADUCEUS

Based on ancient Greek mythology, the Caduceus, a staff entwined by two snakes, is the symbol of the **medical profession**.

RX SYMBOL

This symbol indicates a medical **prescription** or a **pharmacy** that sells prescription medications. (It combines the letters Rx as a shorthand mark for the word *recipe*.)

CHAPTER ELEVEN

EDUCATION

A mind is a terrible thing to waste.

— *Fundraising slogan of the United
Negro College Fund**

New immigrants are often surprised and confused by the American approach to education. American schools try to promote critical thinking, debate, and curiosity—not just correct answers. A student's education is expected to last at least 12 to 16 years, and most of that time is devoted to broad-based study of varied subjects and disciplines; specialized training for a career does not usually begin until college, and even then, it is not the focus or purpose of American education. Professional training will begin in earnest when an educated young adult enters the workforce or advances to graduate school after college. These are some of the main themes presented by Dr. Anne Copeland and Georgia Bennett in their outstanding book, *Understanding American Schools: The Answers to Newcomers' Most Frequently Asked Questions.*

In most states, the law requires that children attend school at least until age 16. Parents and students have a wide range of choices, however, to meet that requirement:

- local *public schools;*
- public *magnet schools* offering a specialized curriculum;
- religious or secular *private schools;*
- experimental *charter schools* run by independent organizations with public funding and oversight; and
- approved *homeschooling* programs taught by parents.

The academic requirements for a **high school diploma**, a certificate of academic readiness for general work or college, are set by each state and are the same for all students, regardless of the type of school they attend.

PUBLIC SCHOOLS

Every child in the United States is entitled to attend public school for free.

---

*This organization was founded in 1944. The term *Negro* is no longer used to describe African-Americans.

That's worth repeating: *Every child in the United States is entitled to attend public school for free.* That does not mean you can choose just any public school and enroll your child; ordinarily, children attend the closest school that offers classes at their **grade** level, determined by placement tests and past academic record. Consequently, the quality of local schools may be the most important factor a family will consider in choosing where to live, and you may want to visit local schools and arrange to meet with school officials *before* you select housing for your family.

Public schools are governed mainly at the local level (city or county **school district**), with some basic policies set by the state. Almost all jurisdictions have an elected local school board that sets the budget and employment policies and hires a **superintendent** to serve as the director of the school system. Within state government guidelines, the local school district can set its own curriculum and choose its own textbooks.

Most school districts have three levels of schools:

- **elementary school** (grades K-5 or K-6);
- **middle school** (grades 6-8) or **junior high school** (grades 7-8 or 7-9); and
- **high school** (grades 9-12 or 10-12).

You may also hear the terms *primary school* and *secondary school.* The primary grades are K-8; secondary school is high school. College or university courses, vocational (trade) school, and other advanced options beyond high school are collectively known as *higher education.* Older Americans might speak of *grammar school,* an archaic term for elementary school.

Most parents enroll young children in **preschool** programs for a year or two before they are old enough to start primary school. These programs, public and private, cultivate basic social skills and good learning habits. Children usually start **kindergarten** in September of the year they reach their fifth birthday, although this varies somewhat depending on the individual school district.

In elementary school, everyone studies the same broad curriculum, though the pace of instruction—especially in math and reading—can be adjusted to provide extra help for students having difficulty or extra challenge for students showing rapid mastery. Not until seventh or eighth grade do students begin to choose specialized programs, and even then, only to a limited degree—for example, a

● ● ● ● ● ● ● ● ● ● ● ● ● ● ●

SOME IMPORTANT TERMS

In high school, the following terms are sometimes used to refer to grade levels:

Grade 12: *senior*
Grade 11: *junior*
Grade 10: *sophomore*
Grade 9: *freshman*

An *upperclassman* is a junior or senior; an *underclassman* is a freshman or sophomore. (Some schools discourage the use of these somewhat archaic terms, and refer to freshmen as first-year students, reflecting the idea that words ending with "-man" implicitly exclude female students. The use of masculine words to refer to persons of unspecified gender has been replaced, since the 1980s, with more inclusive—and accurate—language.)

The same terms are used to describe students in their first, second, third, and fourth years of college; anyone beyond that, seeking an advanced degree from a university, is called a *graduate student* ("grad student" for short). A student in college seeking a four-year degree is an *undergraduate*.

All of the students scheduled to graduate in a particular year are known collectively as the "class of" that year; for example, students entering ninth grade in the fall of 2008 are expected to finish high school in the spring of 2012. They will always be known as *the Class of 2012*.

● ● ● ● ● ● ● ● ● ● ● ● ● ● ●

student might be required to study one of the fine arts, but may choose among music, visual arts, or theater; or a student might be required to study a second language, but may choose which one (usually Spanish or French).

There is some specialization available in public schools, however. A growing number of school districts have one or more **magnet schools** that emphasize certain subjects, such as science or the arts. (They're called "magnet" schools because they *attract* talented students from all over the city or county, whereas regular public schools serve only the surrounding neighborhood.) There is usually a competitive process to be admitted to a magnet school—applicants take special tests and submit letters of recommendation from teachers, and might be interviewed. For a performing arts or visual arts magnet, an audition or portfolio might be required. Magnet high schools are more common than magnet primary schools. (For students who excel in one or two subjects, most high schools offer some **advanced placement** courses that allow students to begin college-level studies early.) School districts also operate **special education** schools or programs for students with physical or developmental disabilities, because public schools *must* accommodate all students in their geographic area. (If a child with special needs cannot be served by the local public schools, the school district may pay for appropriate private schooling—including transportation to and from school.)

Some school districts are experimenting with **charter schools**—public schools run by an approved committee that is independent of the local school board, but still accountable to the performance standards and curriculum requirements of regular schools. Charter schools are sometimes founded to offer a specialized curriculum, but they may also be set up by parents and teachers who are dissatisfied with the local public schools. Many urban schools are overcrowded and insufficiently funded, and there aren't enough teachers to provide the level of attention to each student that parents demand. So if there are a lot of charter schools in your community, be sure to find out whether their purpose is to provide specialized options or to address some basic need that the regular schools are not meeting.

Charter schools, like magnets, usually limit enrollment to a certain number of students at a time and may have a competitive admissions process. But they *are* public schools, and students, once admitted, do not have to pay to attend them.

ENROLLMENT

To enroll (register) your child in public school, simply contact the appropriate school nearest your home. (Public schools are listed in the Blue Pages of the phone book under SCHOOLS, PUBLIC. If you are not sure which school serves your neighborhood, ask a neighbor or a real estate agent, or call the superintendent's office—also listed in the Blue Pages.) Although enrollment in public school is automatic, not competitive, you will need to show certain documents to help the school officials make sure your child is placed in the correct school and grade:

- child's passport or birth certificate, for proof of age;
- your lease, a current utility bill, a state driver's license, or other official document showing your current address; and
- academic records.

Your child might be required to take several **placement tests**. These are not to exclude anybody (again, public schools *must* accommodate *all* students who live in the area they serve), but to ensure correct grade placement and identify any special educational needs your child has. Sometimes academic records alone can provide school officials with enough information to determine a student's grade level, but if your home country's educational system is very different from the U.S. system, placement tests may be necessary.

You will also need to show proof of certain **immunizations**. Every state requires children to be immunized against several communicable diseases before starting school. Specific requirements vary—check with school officials or your doctor. *Keep your child's immunization records in a safe place—* you will need them every time your child changes schools. (Many school districts set up immunization clinics in the later weeks of summer break. Also, if you arrive in the country during the school year and you do not yet have a local family doctor, school officials will work with you to get your child any needed immunizations.)

Some states also require children to be tested for **lead poisoning**. Children who live in old houses with lead-based paint often have elevated levels of lead in their blood, and developmental difficulties can result. For more information, including preventive measures, contact the **Alliance to End Childhood Lead Poisoning** at 202-543-1147 or www.aeclp.org.

PRIVATE SCHOOLS

Roughly 10% of the schoolchildren in the United States attend some kind of private school. Some private schools are **day schools**—students live at home and commute to school just as they would if attending the local public school. Others are **boarding schools** (residential schools) where students live in dormitories on campus. Types of private schools include:
- religious schools (especially Roman Catholic and Jewish);
- specialized schools catering to students with physical or developmental disabilities, or students with advanced talents or interests in a particular field;

- international schools, serving the children of foreign nationals from a particular country or region; and
- military schools, teaching military discipline (often, but not exclusively, to students who have a history of discipline problems).

Most private schools are expensive—often more than $10,000 per year—but many offer **scholarships** (grants of money for educational expenses) based on talent or financial need. Some jurisdictions offer a limited number of government **vouchers** to help pay private school tuition.

Private schools are inspected every few years by a council of their peers who issue a seal of approval or **accreditation** to schools meeting rigorous standards of academic performance and general management. Some very small private schools might not have facilities that meet accreditation requirements, but parents should be very cautious and skeptical about unaccredited schools—find out exactly why the school is not accredited and exactly what plans the school has made to gain accreditation. Some accreditation boards evaluate schools in a particular region of the country; others evaluate a certain type of school nationwide. Major accreditation boards include:

- **National Association of Independent Schools:** 202-973-9700, www.nais.org
- **European Council of International Schools:** Office of the Americas, 908-903-0552, www.ecis.org
- **International Baccalaureate Organization:** North America regional office, 202-696-4464, www.ibo.org
- **Association of Christian Schools International:** 800-367-0798, www.acsi.org (serving evangelical Protestant schools)
- **Jewish Educational Services of North America:** 212-284-6950, www.jesna.org (lists local Central Agencies for Jewish Education)
- **Middle States Association of Schools and Colleges:** Commission on Secondary Schools, 215-622-5603, www.css-msa.org; Commission on Elementary Schools, 610 617-1100, www.ces-msa.org (both serving Delaware, Maryland, New Jersey, New York, Pennsylvania, the District of Columbia, Puerto Rico, and the U.S. Virgin Islands)
- **New England Association of Colleges and Schools:** 781-271-0022, www.neasc.org (serving Connecticut, Maine,

Massachusetts, New Hampshire, Rhode Island, and Vermont)

- **North Central Association Commission on Accreditation and School Improvement**, 800-525-9517, www.ncacasi.org (serving Arkansas, Arizona, Colorado, Iowa, Illinois, Indiana, Kansas, Michigan, Minnesota, Missouri, North Dakota, Nebraska, Ohio, Oklahoma, New Mexico, South Dakota, Wisconsin, West Virginia, and Wyoming)
- **Northwest Association of Accredited Schools and Colleges:** 208-426-5727, www2.boisestate.edu/nasc (serving Alaska, Idaho, Montana, Nevada, Oregon, Utah, and Washington)
- **Southern Association of Colleges and Schools:** 404-679-4501, www.sacs.org (serving Alabama, Florida, Georgia, Kentucky, Louisiana, Mississippi, North Carolina, South Carolina, Tennessee, Texas, and Virginia)
- **Western Association of Schools and Colleges:** 650-696-1060, www.wascweb.org (serving California, Hawaii, American Samoa, Guam, and the Northern Marianas)

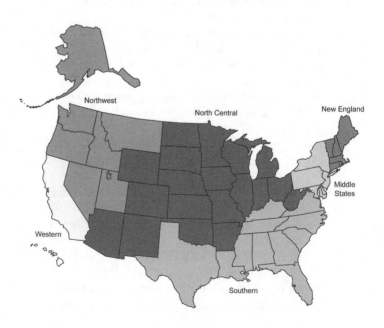

CHOOSING A PRIVATE SCHOOL

The major nationwide directories of private schools are those published by **Peterson's, Porter Sargent,** and **Princeton Review.** Any public library or bookstore should have these in the reference section; in addition, in major cities, you there may be a more detailed regional directory. The regional and specialty accreditation boards listed above also have directories of accredited schools on their web sites—along with helpful advice about choosing a school. And, once again, Copeland and Bennett's *Understanding American Schools* offers valuable tips.

SCHOOL RULES & CUSTOMS

Many schools issue a **student handbook** explaining what to do if your child is sick and cannot attend school, how to find out whether the school will be closed due to snow, what supplies your child will need to purchase, what the dress code is, when you can meet with teachers to discuss your child's performance, and how you can get involved in your child's school through the local **Parents & Teachers Association** (PTA). If this information isn't provided in a handbook, ask the principal or your child's teacher for it. Also, many schools provide an **orientation** program for new students, usually a week or two before the fall term begins. These programs are always useful and sometimes compulsory, and will acquaint incoming students with the school's policies on everything from restroom breaks and chewing gum to internships and summer employment.

ATTENDANCE & SCHEDULES

In general, students must attend school every day it is in session and must arrive on time. In most school districts, the academic year is 180 days—Monday through Friday from early September to mid-June. Elementary schools are typically in session from 9 a.m. to 3 p.m.; secondary schools often convene earlier, perhaps as early as 8:15. Elementary school students get a half-hour break for lunch and a half-hour of *recess* or free play; secondary school students may get a longer lunch break, typically an hour.

If a child is sick or has some other legitimate reason to miss a day of school, the student must present a note from a parent or legal guardian explaining the reason; otherwise, the student may face disciplinary action for *truancy,* unauthorized absence from school. Whether the cause of a student's absence meets local criteria for *excused* (permissible) absence or not, the student is expected to make up any missed lessons or tests as soon as possible.

COUNSELORS

Almost all high schools, and many primary schools, have staff members called **guidance counselors** who are trained in education and child psychology, and whose job is to help students adjust to their new school, choose elective (optional) courses, apply for admission to college, identify scholarships and other sources of funding for higher education, and consider career paths. A counselor can also help resolve any difficulties your child may be having with teachers or other students.

DISCIPLINE

Students who violate school rules may be required to stay at school for an hour or so after classes are dismissed and perform extra academic work or light chores; this form of punishment, called *detention,* does not require a formal hearing or parental approval. More serious violations can result in *suspension* from school for several days, but usually the student has an opportunity to present his or her case to school officials before such a drastic punishment is imposed. In extreme cases—for example, involving violent acts or drug-related crimes on school property—a student can be *expelled* and must enroll in private school or a special public school for students with a history of behavioral problems.

DRESS

In most public schools, the official **dress code** is fairly informal and, some parents feel, permissive. Students are generally free to dress as they please as long as they meet the community's standards of decency and as long as they do not wear apparel bearing obscene words or images. Some schools do not allow students to wear hats indoors (except for religious reasons), because it is traditionally considered disrespectful and because some urban street gangs identify themselves by certain hats. A few public schools (and many private schools) require uniforms or have a specific dress code in order to cut down on social divisions that sometimes develop between groups of young people who dress differently.

GRADES AND ACADEMIC PROGRESS

Most school districts and private schools measure and report academic performance using a system of letter grades (marks). These are based on the number of points earned for good work on tests, quizzes (smaller, less rigorous tests), and other assigned work. Some teachers calculate grades as a percentage of possible point totals:

A = 90% to 100% (excellent)
B = 80% to 90% (good)
C = 70% to 80% (satisfactory)
D = 60% to 70% (minimal)
F = below 60% (failing)

Some teachers, instead, calculate grades "on a curve," meaning the highest number of points actually earned by anyone in the class is considered the best grade, and letter grades reflect a percentage of that total:

A = top 10% (excellent)
B = top 11%–20% (above average)
C = top 21%–30% (average)
D = top 31%–40% (below average)
F = failing

Beyond this level of comparison, students in primary schools are not ranked relative to each other. U.S. educators do not promote such a competitive climate among children. (Some schools do not even start awarding letter grades until the second or third grade; younger students receive, instead, written evaluations.) High school students are ranked when they graduate, but colleges and employers understand that schools can vary so much from one community to another that class rank alone is not taken as seriously as an individual's grades and academic honors.

In most schools, grades are calculated officially twice each semester (term), once at midterm and once at the end. At those times, the school issues a **report card** for each student, showing grades earned in each course or subject. Some schools give report cards directly to the student and others mail it to the parents; many require the student to return the report card with a parent's signature to show that the parent has seen it.

Some schools issue *interim progress reports* to students who are in danger of receiving a low grade if their performance does not improve, and most schools schedule at least one evening each semester when parents are invited to meet with teachers to discuss their children's progress. (But you can always call the school and ask to schedule a meeting if you have concerns about your child's performance.)

Colleges take an interest in a high school student's **grade point average** (GPA). This is calculated by adding four points for every A earned on a report card, three points for every B, two for every C, and one for every D, and dividing the total by the number of courses or subjects in which the student earned a grade. Thus, a student who earned a B in math, an A in literature, a B in history, a C in chemistry, an A in music, and an A in Spanish would have a GPA of 3.3 out of a possible 4.0.

HOMEWORK

Students are expected to continue their studies at home in the afternoon or evening and on weekends. Teachers give specific reading assignments, writing exercises, or math problems to be completed at home. Young children in grades 1-3 might have little or no homework, but the amount and importance of homework increases each year; high school students can expect to spend up to three hours each night completing assignments that must be submitted the next day, or studying for quizzes, or working on substantial research papers.

RESPECT

Children are usually expected to address teachers and other adults in school by title and last name (Mr. Smith, Ms. Jones). In most schools, the teacher will address students by their given name. In some private schools and just a few public schools, teachers address students by their family names (surnames), with or without the title *Mr.* or *Miss.* In either case, students should not take offense if a teacher seems to have difficulty remembering names at the beginning of the school year—after all, the teacher has to learn a lot of new names all at once.

Teachers are supposed to show respect for children, too, and avoid harsh criticism of a child in front of a whole class. Most American educators believe that the child's **self-esteem** and confidence is vital to academic success, so they try to inspire and coach rather than scold and drill.

Just as in the workplace, sexual harassment and bigotry are not supposed to be tolerated in public schools, even among young children.

Talk to school officials and find out what they do to prevent bullying and hazing and to encourage conflict resolution.

In some schools, students start the day by reciting the Pledge of Allegiance (Appendix C), a patriotic ritual that is not expected of foreign nationals. A guest in the country may stand quietly while Americans rise to recite the pledge—much as a courteous American would show respect when another country's national anthem is played.

Copeland and Bennett, in *Understanding American Schools,* report that many immigrant parents are surprised by the amount of debate and discussion that goes on in an American classroom: "Your children will be encouraged to speak their opinions aloud, to challenge or respectfully disagree with the teacher's opinions, and to speak in front of the group about their ideas and activities." A good teacher *hopes and strives* to be questioned; it is not considered disrespectful to show keen interest and independent thought. Schools try to inspire critical reasoning and skeptical inquiry—because a democratic nation requires a citizenry endowed with these skills.

SCHOOL SUPPLIES

Elementary schools may provide all of the paper, pencils, and other materials your child will need; often the only item you will need to purchase is a *binder* or looseleaf notebook. Students in middle school or junior high school might be expected to supply their own paper and pens, and perhaps a different notebook for each class. In high school, students might be expected to own a calculator, athletic clothes, and perhaps other specialized supplies, and will usually need a small backpack to carry their books. In many communities, school supplies are available from local charities for students whose families are unable to pay for them; you can ask your child's teacher or guidance counselor where you might obtain free supplies.

Textbooks are issued by the school at the primary and secondary levels, and they remain school property and must be returned at the end of the year or semester. College students must buy the books required for their courses, but can usually obtain used copies at a low cost. A few colleges and universities require students to own a computer, but most provide well-equipped computer labs.

In August, many stores advertise "back-to-school" sales with discounts on school supplies, clothing, and electronics. In some states, a week in August is declared a sales tax holiday, and the sales tax is

● ● ● ● ● ● ● ● ● ● ● ● ● ● ● ● ● ● ●

CONTROVERSIAL TRENDS

In the late 20th and early 21st centuries, there has been increasing emphasis on **standardized tests**—tests of general academic progress that are administered to every student at the same grade level throughout the state, to compare the overall performance of an entire school to other schools. This kind of testing is intended to evaluate teachers and help refine school district budgets, so teachers have a strong incentive to make sure their students do well on standardized tests—and parents and educational scholars worry that teachers may be coaching students to pass a test rather than cultivating the critical thinking skills that will serve young people in future endeavors. Also, some schools use individual students' standardized test scores to determine whether the student needs to be placed in a faster or slower class, and critics argue that one test on one day does not provide enough information to guide such an important decision.

One of the policies determined by the local school board (governing a public school district) is the availability and depth of **sex education**. Most school districts, in an effort to discourage teen pregnancy and the spread of sexually transmitted diseases, present basic factual information about human reproduction and sexuality as part of a science class or *physical education* (fitness) class. Some American parents prefer that their children learn about sex at home, but any child who watches American TV or movies—or who sees advertising posters, magazine covers, and people dressed to show off their bodies—will already know (or imagine or assume) quite a lot about sex at an early age. Some school districts provide "abstinence only" sex education, and some schools discuss contraception in the context of disease prevention as

● ● ● ● ● ● ● ● ● ● ● ● ● ● ● ● ● ● ●

waived on everyday goods and clothing (but not on fine jewelry, major appliances, or other expensive items).

EDUCATIONAL PHILOSOPHY

Primary schools in the United States aim to teach every student to read, write, make mathematical computations, gather information through research and experimentation, and apply critical thinking and reasoning skills to a variety of practical and abstract problems. From this broad foundation, instruction begins to focus more specifically on subject matter in the higher grades, but American schools do not attempt to direct students toward particular careers or trades.

The criteria for letter grades are generally objective, but teachers do have some leeway. For example, if a student is very close to the threshold of a higher grade, the teacher may consider whether the student's work has been improving or declining and make a judgment call based on the trend. And some teachers award points for *class participation*—favoring students who take part in discussions and volunteer to answer questions put to the class. Teachers should explain their expectations and grading criteria up front, on the first day of class, at least in secondary school (younger students are not presumed to be so concerned about grades), and if you or your child has any questions about academic policies, it's always OK to ask. (Note: American teachers do *not* respond favorably to bribes or ostentatious gifts.)

ENGLISH AS A SECOND LANGUAGE

At every grade level, public schools are required to provide ESL instruction to students who need it. Except in bilingual magnet schools, classes are conducted in English only, and the school's ESL classes are designed to enable the student to benefit from **mainstream** (regular) classes. Some bilingual schools aim to teach two languages, while others offer bilingual classes only to help students become fluent in English. Private schools are not required to offer ESL, so be sure to find out how a particular private school helps students who are not fluent in English at their age-appropriate level of reading, writing, and verbal communication.

CONTROVERSIAL TRENDS, CONT.

well as pregnancy prevention. Sex education may start in elementary school and continue into high school; most schools give parents an opportunity to ask that their children *not* be included in sex education class.

In *a few very conservative places,* school boards do not allow science teachers to present as fact any scientific information that seems inconsistent with Christian doctrine. A classic film, *Inherit the Wind,* depicts the true story of the 1925 trial of schoolteacher John Scopes, who violated a local law against teaching Charles Darwin's theory of evolution. Now evolution is taught in all U.S. biology classes. However, some school districts require that it be presented as a "theory" alongside other competing theories—such as **creation science**, which seeks to reconcile modern science with the chronology outlined in the Bible.

There is also a long-running debate about organized religious rituals in public schools. Teachers and school officials are not allowed to lead compulsory **prayer**. Some school districts allow teachers to ask the class to observe a moment of silence together at the start of the day, and students may pray quietly if they wish. Many athletic teams pray before a game, but the adults in a public school are secular authority figures and cannot encourage any student to join in a group prayer. Some parents and religious leaders want to change that, but the First Amendment allows "no law respecting an establishment of religion." If you want a dose of religion in the classroom, you have to send your child to a private school.

TUTORING

If your child seems to need extra help in a particular subject, or general help developing good study habits, there is no shame in asking for it—and you need not be offended if your child's teacher recommends such assistance. Everyone involved in your child's education wants your child to learn and succeed. A **tutor** is a teacher or mentor who works one-on-one with a student after school hours, or during summer vacation, focusing on skills or subjects in which the student would especially benefit from extra practice. (Some tutors are older students—for example, an 11th-grade student who is particularly talented in math might tutor a fifth-grader whose math scores have not always met expectations.) Your child's teacher should be able to recommend a good tutor in the area.

SPORTS AND EXTRACURRICULAR ACTIVITIES

A young adult graduating from the U.S. educational system is expected to be well-rounded—to have a wide variety of interests and creative talents. Students are strongly encouraged to take part in one or more optional school-sponsored clubs, projects, or athletic teams. Some students school join a school football, basketball, swimming, or gymnastics team that competes against other schools; some join a school choir or orchestra, write for a school newspaper, or act in a school play; some join a student-run organization that addresses political issues or a student club devoted to a hobby, such as photography or chess. Many students are involved in a variety of such *extracurricular activities* over the course of their 12 years in school, and more in college. Many schools have international clubs where students from a particular country or region can meet each other and help interested American students learn about their culture. Most schools also have an elected student "government" that coordinates the activities of all of the recognized student organizations and plans major school events such as dances or talent shows.

Student organizations generally meet one day a week, after school is dismissed for the day, but an athletic team—and the cheerleaders and marching band who accompany it—might practice several afternoons a week and compete on weekends.

Some school districts require high school students to perform some **community service**—for example, spending a few hours a week reading to the blind or collecting clothes to send to victims of a natural disaster. Educators expect these to be deeply rewarding experiences and hope that young people will be inspired to continue to do volunteer work throughout their lives—and many do. (See Chapter 16.) Colleges and universities tend to look favorably on a record of involvement in various extracurricular activities and community service projects—plus, a club or community project is a great way to meet people with similar interests and make new friends.

GETTING TO SCHOOL

School districts provide free transportation to public school for students who live more than a certain distance away or who would have to cross large or busy streets to walk there. Students who live within a short distance—typically half a mile—are expected to walk. Some parents drive their children to school—and many high school students have cars of their own.

In the suburbs or rural areas, the school district usually operates its own buses, and a sturdy yellow **schoolbus** with flashing safety lights will pick your child up within a few blocks of your home. In cities with ample public transportation, the school district might instead provide tokens or passes for students.

YOUTH SPORTS

Most American boys and girls play some organized sport at some point in their childhood or teen years. Some join community leagues organized by a local government's recreation department, but most youth sports are extracurricular activities offered by public and private schools. Exceptionally talented athletes might earn an athletic *scholarship,* a grant of money to help pay for college. Most schools offer two levels of athletic programs: **varsity** sports, in which schools compete against other schools, and **intramural** sports, in which several teams from the same school compete on a less rigorous basis.

HOMESCHOOLING

You have the right to educate your own children at home; they can earn a diploma through testing. Many parents believe that they are best suited to design an educational program that will engage and challenge their children, responding to each child's unique traits. Homeschooling is especially popular among strongly religious parents who object to the secular nature of public schools, and among liberal parents who object to the public schools' increasing reliance on educational materials provided by corporate sponsors with a possible bias or hidden agenda. Many cities have homeschooling networks to provide group activities for homeschooled children.

If you decide to educate your own children, you'll need all the help you can get from resources listed in **Homeschooling Today** magazine, at www.homeschooltoday.com.

HIGHER EDUCATION

Approximately one in four adults in the United States has graduated from college, and there are more than 3,000 peer-accredited colleges and universities in the United States. Some are very expensive, some more affordable; some are more generous than others with financial aid for needy students. Academic philosophies and competitiveness vary, too, and American students are just as diverse as the range of institutions that serve them—some rush through college in three years, while others attend school part-time throughout their adult lives. It is not at all unusual to see Americans of all ages going back to college after years in the workforce—to seek an advanced degree or a second bachelor's degree in a new area of study, or to learn new skills or a new language. It is not even necessary for young adults to proceed directly from high school to college; some take a year or two off to work, travel, or volunteer (see Chapter 16). But most people who intend to go to college begin making plans in their second year of high school to choose a college, get admitted in a competitive process, and attend for four years immediately after high school.

COMMON ACADEMIC DEGREES

B.A.	bachelor of arts
B.S.	bachelor of sciences
D.D.S.	doctor of dental science
D.O.	doctor of osteopathy
D.V.M.	doctor of veterinary medicine
J.D.	juris doctor (a graduate of law school)
LL.B., LL.D.	bachelor of laws, doctor of laws
M.A.	master of arts
M.B.A.	master of business administration
M.D.	medical doctor
M.Ed.	master of education
M.F.A.	master of fine arts
M.Lit.	master of literature
M.L.S.	master of library sciences
M.S.	master of sciences
Ph.D.	doctor of philosophy

Types of higher education institutions include:

- **Universities.** Public and private universities grant **bachelor's degrees** (four-year degrees in a field of the arts or sciences) and advanced **master's degrees** and **doctorates**. A master's degree typically reflects two or three years of study after graduation from college. A doctor of philosophy (Ph.D.) is an advanced scholar who has completed three to five years of specialized study after graduation from college and a *dissertation*—a work of research reviewed by a committee of respected scholars and making a fundamentally new contribution to human knowledge. A university consists of several *colleges* or *schools* sharing the same campus; these may include specialized advanced institutions such as a law school or medical school.
- **Colleges.** Public and private colleges grant bachelor's degrees. Many also offer **continuing education** programs for adults who are not full-time students, but wish to pursue studies to expand their career options or just out of intellectual curiosity. (*College* is also an informal generic term for post-secondary education between the levels of high school diploma and bachelor's degree—whether the student attends a four-year college or a university.)
- **Community colleges.** Also called *junior colleges,* community colleges are public two-year institutions that prepare students for more specialized education at a four-year college or in an internship or entry-level job. Tuition is much less expensive at a community college than a four-year college, and enrollment is not competitive. Some award two-year **associate degrees** or other certificates of academic achievement in a particular field. They also offer continuing education opportunities.
- **Vocational schools.** Trade schools, business schools, and other private institutions cater to high school graduates who want to develop specific job skills that are prized by employers—for example, accounting or computer programming—without seeking a four-year degree. Many offer classes at night or on weekends to accommodate students who already have jobs.
- **Service academies.** U.S. citizens of exceptional academic talent can ask their Representative or one of their

Senators to nominate them to the U.S. Military Academy in West Point, NY; the U.S. Naval Academy in Annapolis, MD; the U.S. Air Force Academy in Colorado Springs, CO; or the U.S. Coast Guard Academy in New London, CT. There is no tuition—it's a free four-year education with a guaranteed (and compulsory) job awaiting every graduate: as an officer in the military for a minimum of four years.

As Copeland and Bennett point out, "any reasonably good student who wants a university education (and can afford it) can get one" at one of the 3,400 schools of higher education in the United States. And almost any student whose family cannot easily afford college tuition can get some form of **financial aid** to help pay for higher education. But a college-bound student, along with his or her family and the school guidance counselor, needs to do a lot of work—research, planning, and discussion—to identify the most appropriate colleges and universities where he or she is likely to be admitted and be happy, and to find and pursue every possible source of financial aid.

CHOOSING A COLLEGE OR UNIVERSITY

Teenagers who plan to go to college face a momentous decision that can have a huge impact on the course of their lives. (Fortunately, it can always be changed—almost all colleges and universities accept **transfer** students from other colleges.) A student who chooses a school on the basis of its reputation alone is not likely to be happy or successful there. Important considerations include:

- **Size.** At a small college with 1,500 students, you will probably know most of your professors (instructors) by their first names and they will work closely with you as mentors. At a huge university with 30,000 students, you will have a much greater variety of academic programs and extracurricular activities to choose from—but larger classes and less access to faculty members.
- **Location.** Do you want to go to college in the city or in a quiet, secluded area? What part of the country do you want to live in? How often do you plan to visit your family?
- **Cost.** If you're a permanent resident, you can attend your home state's public university at relatively low cost. On

the other hand, an expensive private school might be endowed with funds for generous scholarships, especially for students with exceptional talent or a minority ethnic background.

- **Philosophy.** Are students expected to pursue a broad interdisciplinary curriculum or to focus heavily on one or two subjects? Does the school have a religious affiliation, and if so, how does that affect daily life on campus? Is the atmosphere competitive once you're admitted, or does the school foster personalized learning at an individual pace?

- **Academics.** Yes, a school's reputation matters—but it depends on your field of interest. One university might have a respected journalism program, but a lackluster school of engineering; another might be considered an outstanding school for computer science, but not for the study of dance and theater. Even more important: does a school place a lot of students in meaningful or prestigious internships? Do undergraduate students assist faculty members with significant research? Does a school offer merit-based scholarships in recognition of academic excellence?

- **Athletics.** Many students who perform well in high school sports—especially football or basketball—can get athletic scholarships that help cover college expenses if they commit to the rigorous practice schedule of a competitive college team.

High schools have many resources to help students gather and consider such information. The guidance counselor's office or school library should have all of the major **college guides**—Barron's, Fiske, Peterson's, and Princeton Review, to name just some of the most popular—and **viewbooks**, or recruiting pamphlets, from hundreds of schools. The school or the public library might even have the **catalogs** (complete course listings and faculty directories) from many schools. If not, you can always call or e-mail a school's admissions office and request a free viewbook and catalog. Check out the **U.S. Journal of Academics** at www.usjournal.com, intended specifically to help international students choose higher education programs in the United States and gain admission (both to the school and the country).

ADMISSIONS TESTING

Most colleges require applicants to take the **Scholastic Aptitude Test**, a standardized test of critical skills. The SAT is administered several times a year, and students may take it as often as they wish—for a fee. (Some colleges place the most emphasis on your most recent scores; others look at your previous scores as well.) High schools help students prepare for the test, but many students benefit from outside tutoring or a book of practice tests. ESL students may also be required to take the **Test of English as a Foreign Language** (TOEFL). Ask the guidance office at your child's school to recommend good ways to prepare for these tests.

The SAT and TOEFL are administered by a private organization, the **Educational Testing Service**; for more information, call 609-921-9000 or visit www.ets.org. Here are some other standardized tests you might need to take—all administered by ETS unless otherwise noted:

ACT
> **American College Test**—accepted by some colleges as an alternative to the SAT (administered by ACT, Inc., 319/337-1000 or www.act.org)

CLEP
> **College Level Examination Program**—placement test for older students returning to school after several years of work

GMAT
> **Graduate Management Admission Test**—entrance exam for advanced programs in business administration

GRE
> **Graduate Record Exam**—entrance exam for advanced programs in a particular field

LSAT
> **Law School Admission Test** (administered by the Law School Admission Council, 215-968-1001 or www.lsac.org)

MCAT
> **Medical College Admission Test** (administered by the Association of American Medical Colleges, 319-337-1357 or www.aamc.org/students)

PSAT/NMSQT
> **Preliminary SAT/National Merit Scholarship Qualifying Test**—short version of the SAT administered for

practice purposes and as a basis for prestigious scholarship awards

TOEIC

Test of English for International Communication—
proficiency test required by many employers

Study guides for each of these tests are available at libraries and
bookstores, but the best source of information about admissions testing
is a guidance counselor or academic advisor.

Another test sometimes given to high schools is the **Armed Services Vocational Aptitude Battery** (ASVAB), which is designed to
help students identify their talents and suitability for various careers.
It was designed by the U.S. Department of Defense to place military
recruits in appropriate training programs, but some schools encourage all students to take the test whether they plan to enter the military or not.

APPLICATIONS

Every college has its own admissions policies, and evaluation of applicants can be very subjective. Grades and standardized test scores
are important, but so are extracurricular activities that demonstrate
varied interests, initiative, and independent learning. Almost all schools
require one or more essays by the student and letters of recommendation from several teachers. Applicants must usually make arrangements to be interviewed by a representative of the school—prefer-
ably during a visit to the campus, but if a student lives far away, the
school might arrange for a traveling recruiter or a member of the
local alumni network to meet with the student.

Most students apply to about half a dozen schools: one or two
very selective schools that reject a large percentage of their applicants;
one or two schools that admit most of their applicants; and several
schools that seem like an ideal fit. Note that most colleges charge an
application fee, typically $25 to $75, to discourage frivolous applications; fee waivers are sometimes available for students from low-
income households, and some schools reduce or waive the fee for
applications submitted electronically.

There is no shame in being rejected by any private college or
university—competition for limited space in each year's freshman class
is so tough, and the factors that go into each school's effort to assemble a diverse and talented freshman class are so complex, that a

rejection letter is not necessarily a comment on the student's merit. The school might simply be full.

FINANCIAL AID

College tuition is expensive, and growing more expensive every year. And most students also have to pay for *room and board* (housing and meals), textbooks (which can cost several hundred dollars per semester), and travel to and from school. In 2002, the average cost of higher education (not counting travel) was about $23,000 per year at private institutions and about $9,200 per year at four-year public institututions. Many students need help paying these expenses; there is no shame in asking for financial aid—indeed, a family would be foolish not to apply.

The **U.S. Department of Education** provides roughly $67 billion a year in financial aid to students who have been admitted to a degree program at a college or university and who cannot pay the cost of tuition. Federal aid includes **grants** of money that the student does not have to repay; low-interest **loans** that must be repaid after the student leaves school; and **work-study** programs, in which the student is placed in a part-time job on campus.

You do not apply separately for specific grants, loans, and work-study opportunities. You file one comprehensive financial disclosure form, the **Free Application for Federal Student Aid** (FAFSA), providing information about your family's income, assets (property and bank accounts), and expenses; the Department of Education reviews the form and determines how much money your family can reasonably contribute toward your education. Then the agency looks at your college expenses and assembles an aid package to cover the difference. The FAFSA is available online at www.fafsa.ed.gov, along with lots of information and advice to help you file it properly. You can also get a copy at a public library or from your high school.

Information about federal student aid programs is available at 800-433-3243 or www.studentaid.ed.gov—for example, you can order or download a free booklet called *Funding Your Education* that provides details about the types of financial aid available. (It also includes advice about choosing a college and avoiding financial aid scams and ripoffs, and it lists the phone numbers of every state's office of higher education—another potential source of financial aid.) You *do not* have to be a U.S. citizen to receive federal financial aid. You do need a Social Security number (see Chapter 4) and a high school diploma or equivalent certificate; also, if you are a male between ages 18 and 26 and not exempt, you must be registered with Selective Service (see Chapter 2). Persons convicted of drug-related crimes may lose eligibility.

The federal government provides about 70% of the student financial aid available in the United States. Other scholarships and grants are available from colleges and universities themselves; businesses that sponsor high school science competitions or essay contests; private employers (many offer small scholarships to the children of employees); and unions, civic organizations, and other nonprofit groups. The FAFSA will *not* connect you to these private scholarships—you will need to find them and apply for them yourself, with the help of your guidance counselor. But be suspicious of letters or e-mail messages offering you a scholarship you did not apply for, or "exclusive" information or services pertaining to scholarships—there are a lot of scam artists who collect fees from students and offer nothing of value in return.

Finally, most families of college students are eligible for an **income tax credit** to offset tuition expenses. Check the IRS tax instruction booklet or www.irs.gov for the tax year in which you made a tuition payment.

SCHEDULES, CREDITS AND MAJORS

The academic year for most colleges and universities is late August through mid-May, with a break at the end of the calendar year (just before Christmas until mid-January) and a one-week *spring break* in March or April. And there are optional summer sessions for students who want to complete their degrees at an accelerated pace. Some colleges also take a one-week midterm break in the fall semester.

Most full-time students enroll in four classes each semester, and each class meets for approximately four hours a week—for example, twice a week for two hours or three times a week for 90 minutes. The bulk of college coursework is homework, including substantial reading assignments, library research, or lab work. For each course completed with a passing grade, the student earns a number of **credits** equal to the number of hours per week the class convened throughout the semester—so a course meeting for four hours would be worth four credits, and a typical courseload would be worth 16 credits per semester. (A bachelor's degree usually reflects 128 credits, or eight semesters of a "full" courseload.)

In their third or fourth semester of a four-year degree program, students declare a **major**—a field of study in which they will concentrate at least ¼ of their coursework (32 credits). Even then, at most colleges, it is expected or required that a student will continue to take a broad-based courseload and pursue a well-rounded education in the sciences and humanities—a *liberal arts* curriculum. Many colleges also require or allow students to declare a **minor**, a secondary field in which they will earn 16 to 32 credits. Students select a major in close consultation with an **academic advisor**, a faculty member whose role is similar to that of a high school counselor.

A major is still not as specialized an educational track as many international students might expect. A student who wishes to become a psychiatrist, for example, might choose an undergraduate major in biology or psychology and then go to medical school—and then choose psychiatric medicine as a specialty at an advanced level of medical school. A student planning to become a lawyer might *major* in English or political science at the undergraduate level and pursue more specialized studies in graduate school. One law school admissions officer advises college students interested in the law to major in math as undergraduates—to develop logical reasoning skills that will serve them well as they advance to more specialized studies.

*Is there anything you expected about the United States that
turned out not to be true?*
"That it would be easy to make money."

— *Felipe Ramirez, auto mechanic, from
El Salvador*

E very workplace has its own customs and expectations—some
are more formal than others, and some bosses like to supervise
their employees in detail while others just set goals and leave
employees to their own devices to meet them. But all employers must
abide by certain laws regulating wages and working conditions, and
in order to recruit and retain good workers, employers must offer a
broader range of benefits than just money.

HOURS, WAGES, AND BENEFITS

The standard work week is usually 40 hours, typically 9 a.m. to 5 p.m.
Monday through Friday. However, in many businesses, one is expected
to arrive early and stay late if there is urgent work to do, and many
end up working far more than 40 hours a week—even on weekends,
at least occasionally. A job where you are expected to work less than
35 hours a week is considered *part-time,* though the term usually refers to a job of 20 hours a week or less.

Almost everyone working in the United States must be paid at
least the federal **minimum wage**, an amount adjusted periodically
by Congress. Some states and localities have a higher minimum wage
or "living wage" law. State and local wage laws sometimes apply only
to companies that trade with the government; the federal minimum
wage applies to practically all employers. (Wages are discussed in more
detail in the section on EMPLOYMENT LAW below.)

Health insurance, paid **vacation** time, paid **sick leave**, and other
employee benefits (sometimes called *fringe benefits*) are considered
part of a compensation package along with salary or wages and are
negotiable. There may be a probationary period for new employees—
typically 90 days or six months—before such benefits are provided.

The benefits offered by a large company, especially to senior
employees, may be extensive. Many companies have **profit-sharing**
plans, in which all employees get an annual bonus based on the company's
profits, or **stock options**, allowing employees to buy shares of the

185

• • • • • • • • • • • • • •

GETTING THE JOB YOU WANT

If you are applying for a job in the United States for the first time, you may need to consult one (better yet, several) of the many reference books that explain how to prepare a **résumé** and **cover letter**. These documents offer a prospective employer the first impression of your accomplishments and your professional demeanor. You might want to get advice from a friend or business mentor, but be wary of advertised résumé services—some just take your money and throw together a standard résumé that could describe almost anyone. Before you agree to pay for résumé services, get references from satisfied clients. You should also get lots of advice—from friends and from books—about the job interview process. Some good resources include:

- **Résumés and Cover Letters That Have Worked** by Anne McKinney (Prep Publishing, 1997)
- **The Résumé Handbook** by Arthur D. Rosenberg & David V. Hizer (Adams Media Corp., 1996)
- **Cover Letter Magic** by Wendy S. Enelow & Louise Kursmark (Jist Works, 2000)
- **Winning Cover Letters** by Robin Ryan (John Wiley & Sons, 2002)
- **Power Interviews: Job-Winning Tactics from Fortune 500 Recruiters** by Neil M. Yeager & Lee Hough (John Wiley & Sons, 1998)

• • • • • • • • • • • • • •

company's stock at a fixed price. Other benefits may include **family leave,** a policy that allows employees to take time off (with pay) to care for a newborn child or sick relative; a **commuting** allowance for parking expenses or public transportation fares; and a **retirement** plan, in which a small percentage of your paycheck is invested in a pension fund (stock portfolio) to provide you with income after you retire. Some employers will match your own deposits to an IRA (see Chapter 4) or a **401(k)** plan, a retirement fund in which you can set aside a portion of your income to earn interest *before* it is subject to taxes. Large companies often have an **employee assistance program** or counseling service, offering free and confidential advice about a variety of personal problems— drug and alcohol habits, interpersonal conflict in the workplace, even legal issues. These services can help you adjust to a new culture and address any problems that arise as you make the transition.

If a valuable employee or job applicant is known to be considering offers from other employers, a company might offer extra benefits, called *perquisites* or simply *perks,* to "sweeten the deal." A reserved parking space, for example, is a prized perk in downtown areas. So is the use of a company-owned car, or money and services to help with relocation. Some employers, especially in cities with traffic problems, are experimenting with **flextime** programs that allow you to work any schedule you choose as long as it adds up to 40 hours a week, and **telework** programs that allow you to work from home several days a week.

Some businesses or large office buildings have their own gym. Some buy expensive tickets to cultural and sporting events to give to employees to reward good performance. Almost all workplaces provide free coffee and tea, and many have a kitchen (or at least a refrigerator and a microwave oven) for employees to use.

Some employers offer "cafeteria-style" benefits. (A *cafeteria* is a restaurant in which prepared food is set out on a counter; you select the items you want and place them on your tray.) In a cafeteria benefits system, the company offers a menu of different health insurance plans, profit-sharing and stock purchase plans, paid time off, commuter allowances, and other benefits, and you select those most desirable in your situation—up to the total value of benefits allowed for your job. For example, if you don't have children or elders to look after, you don't need family leave, and you might want to direct a greater percentage of your salary to your retirement fund. And if you walk to work, you might decline a commuting allowance and instead take an extra week of vacation every year.

Most companies have a **benefits administrator** or **personnel manager**—or, in larger businesses, a **human resources** department—in charge of employee benefits, especially health insurance. This person or department will process your immigration paperwork and tax documents when you are hired, and will help you set up your insurance plan.

PAYROLL DEDUCTIONS

Your paycheck will show automatic deductions for federal and state taxes and the Social Security fund. The portion of your pay that is withheld for taxes is based on the amount of income tax you are likely to owe the government at the end of the year. If your tax return shows that you actually owe less, the government will send you a refund; if you owe more, you will have to pay it. (See Chapter 4.) You can also arrange to have a portion of each paycheck given to charity if you wish. And many employers offer **direct deposit**—an arrangement where your pay is automatically deposited in your bank account instead of being issued by check.

EMPLOYMENT LAW

Federal law prohibits **discrimination** in hiring or promotion on the basis of race, color, religion, disability, national origin, sex, military record, or advanced age. Some states also prohibit discrimination on the basis of marital status or sexual orientation. In other words, an employer cannot deny you a job or a promotion on the basis of these conditions without a compelling reason. (An employer *could* state a compelling reason why, for example, a blind person would not be hired as an air traffic controller or a female actor would not be hired to play a cowboy in a movie, and anti-discrimination laws would not apply in those cases.) It is illegal to discriminate against a job applicant because he or she is a resident alien, a temporary resident, a refugee, or an alien receiving asylum—*unless* the applicant is eligible to apply for naturalization and has chosen not to.

The **Equal Employment Opportunity Commission** enforces federal anti-discrimination law; to find the field office nearest you, call 202-663-4900 or visit www.eeoc.gov. Most states have a **human rights commission** or similar agency to enforce state anti-discrimination law—check the Blue Pages or the state government web site.

Sexual harassment is not supposed to be tolerated in the modern American workplace, and unwelcome sexual advances by a supervisor toward a subordinate can get the entire company in legal trouble. An employee can sue an employer in court if a co-worker engages in conduct that results in a "hostile work environment" or if a manager suggests that promotion or performance evaluation might be linked to sexual favors. Most employers try to resolve employees' complaints before they result in a lawsuit, and all but the smallest companies are adopting written policies on sexual harassment—trying to define precisely what constitutes inappropriate behavior and how complaints should be handled.*

Other federal and state laws govern eligibility to work in the United States (based on residence and age); the minimum wage an

---

* Although sexual harassment in the workplace is a centuries-old problem chronicled by Victor Hugo in the 1862 novel *Les Misérables,* the American public and government began to acknowledge it in 1991: a high-ranking federal judge, Clarence Thomas, was nominated to the Supreme Court and his former assistant, Anita Hill, accused him of making repeated, vulgar sexual advances. The Senate did confirm Thomas to the highest court, but claims of sexual harassment have been taken very seriously ever since.

employer must pay; the maximum hours an employee can be required to work each week; compensation for job-related medical problems; and medical leave if an employee or close relative is sick or injured.

EMPLOYMENT AUTHORIZATION DOCUMENTS

If you are not a permanent resident (with a green card) or a U.S. citizen, you will need an Employment Authorization Document (EAD, also called a *work permit*) from the **U.S. Citizenship & Immigration Service** in order to work and earn wages in the United States. (Certain categories of alien workers, such as employees of foreign governments, are exempt.) If you plan to work, you should file USCIS **Form I-765 (Application for Employment Authorization)** as soon as you arrive in the country.

Most aliens are eligible to file this form online at www.uscis.gov (exceptions are listed on the site), but you will still need to visit a government office near you to provide a signature, fingerprint, and photo; also, you must have a bank account (or a representative who has one) to pay the filing fee. (Fee waivers are available for applicants who can prove inability to pay.) If you are not eligible to file electronically, or you prefer to use the paper form, you can download one from the USCIS site or order one by calling 800-870-3676. The fee is the same either way.

Employment eligibility is governed by Section 274(a) of the Immigration & Nationality Act and policies in the Code of Federal Regulations, 8 CFR 274(a); the reference desk at any public library can help you find these documents, and if you have any questions, ask an immigration lawyer or call the nearest USCIS field office listed in the Blue Pages. The USCIS office can also refer you to local nonprofit organizations that help immigrants apply for work permits and other documentation.

FAIR LABOR STANDARDS ACT AND THE MINIMUM WAGE

The Fair Labor Standards Act (FLSA) is a federal law that sets the minimum wage most workers must be paid in the United States. For a free guide to the law, contact the **Wage & Hour Division** of the Department of Labor at 888-487-9243 or www.wagehour.dol.gov. This is the agency that enforces federal law regulating wages and hours, and regional offices are listed in the Blue Pages of the phone book under LABOR DEPARTMENT.

Only the smallest businesses are exempt from the FLSA, and only if their gross receipts are less than $500,000 per year and they do not engage in interstate commerce. Since almost any activity— buying office supplies, for example, or sending and receiving mail— involves some interstate commerce, it's just a slight exaggeration to say the FLSA applies to all jobs in the United States.

The FLSA also defines **overtime** as an excess of 40 hours of work in a single week; employers must pay 1½ times the regular hourly rate ("time and a half") to most wage-earning employees working overtime. (Employers are exempt from paying the overtime rate to some categories of skilled workers above a certain income threshold determined by Congress.)

Certain workers can legally be paid less than the minimum wage:

- Some restaurant workers and others who routinely receive tips can be paid less—provided their average tips make up the difference.
- Workers under 20 years of age can be paid a lower "training wage" for their first three months on the job.
- A college student who takes a part-time job or seasonal job can be paid 85% of the minimum wage and cannot work more than 20 hours per week while school is in session or 40 hours per week during school vacations.
- A high school student in a vocational education program can be employed as an apprentice for 75% of the minimum wage.
- Disabled workers can be paid less than minimum wage if the employer gets authorization from the U.S. Department of Labor.

In most states, and in Guam and Puerto Rico, the **state minimum wage** is the same as the federal minimum. Here are the exceptions:

- State minimum wage *higher* than the federal minimum: Alaska, California, Connecticut, Hawaii, Maine, Massachusetts, Oregon, Rhode Island, Vermont, Washington; also the District of Columbia
- State minimum wage *lower* than the federal minimum (for workers not covered by the FLSA): Kansas, New Mexico, Oklahoma; also the U.S. Virgin Islands
- *No* state minimum wage (for workers not covered by the FLSA): Alabama, Arizona, Florida, Louisiana, Mississippi, South Carolina, Tennessee

- Minimum wage *varies* by industry: American Samoa

WORKING CONDITIONS

The federal **Occupational Safety & Health Administration** (OSHA) sets and enforces rules to prevent injuries and illness in the workplace. OSHA sends inspectors to workplaces—especially, but not only, industrial sites—and can order companies with safety violations to pay a fine. For information about the agency, including resources to help you keep yourself and others safe at work, visit www.osha.gov.

The importance of workplace safety is obvious with regard to factories, mines, railroads, and other industrial operations, but even office workers can develop serious health problems. According to the **Bureau of Labor Statistics**, a Labor Department agency, an estimated 300,000 U.S. workers each year report carpal tunnel syndrome or other chronic pain resulting from repetitive motion—for example, typing on a keyboard all day. Office workers can also develop respiratory problems due to indoor air pollution (also called "sick building syndrome") in buildings with poor ventilation. The **National Institute of Occupational Safety & Health**, www.cdc.gov/niosh, educates workers and employers about the latest government and private research in injury prevention and health.

If you are injured on the job, or develop an illness, or aggravate an existing injury or illness, you will be eligible for **workers' compensation** benefits (usually just called "workers' comp"). Every state has workers' comp laws that require employers to carry insurance and pay for medical care and lost income resulting from work-related injury or illness. So do the District of Columbia, Puerto Rico and the U.S. Virgin Islands. You must be able to prove that your medical problem originated at work and that you weren't violating any safety rules, and you must report the

SOME IMPORTANT SLANG

You may hear the expressions **blue collar** and **white collar**, though they are not as commonly used as they once were. Blue-collar workers are hands-on industrial workers and tradespeople; white-collar workers are office workers and executives. The terms date from an era when tradespeople usually wore blue shirts and bosses wore white. The expression *white-collar crime* refers to acts of embezzlement, fraud, and other kinds of theft committed by moving numbers around on paper (as opposed to theft by armed robbery or burglary).

problem as soon as it appears, even if it does not seem like a serious problem at first. (Your employer should have a designated *claims administrator* for workers' comp cases; this person can explain your rights and responsibilities and the procedure for making a claim.) For links to **state workers' comp agencies** and laws, visit their website at www.workerscompensation.com or you can also go to www.workerscompensationinsurance.com. You can also find your state workers' comp office in the Blue Pages of the phone book.

In addition to workplace safety, other working conditions are regulated at the state level. Most states set a minimum length and frequency of rest periods ("coffee breaks") and meal periods, and require that wages or salary be paid on a certain schedule—usually twice a month. Some states have so-called *right-to-work* laws, which block trade unions from controlling entry to a trade.

States also regulate **child labor**. In most states, a person under the age of 18 must obtain a **work permit** from the government and cannot be required to work more than a certain number of hours per day or week. In some states, a person under a certain age—usually 14 or 16—cannot be employed at all except in the performing arts. (Many children under 16 who work for pay—babysitting, mowing a neighbor's lawn, washing cars or delivering newspapers—are technically self-employed contractors.)

For specific information about state labor laws, follow links from www.dol.gov/esa, the web site of the **Employment Standards Administration** at the U.S. Department of Labor.

If you lose your job through no fault of your own—for example, if your employer reduces staffing or goes out of business—you may be eligible for **unemployment** benefits from the state, from an unemployment insurance fund set up with taxes paid by employers. Unemployment benefits are intended to provide temporary aid—typically for no more than six months—while you are actively seeking a new job.

Under the **Immigration & Nationality Act,** foreign employees of U.S. businesses must be paid wages or salary comparable to their American counterparts. The Labor Department monitors the prevailing wage in hundreds of industries and occupations in order to enforce this law. The policy is intended both to prevent U.S. employers from taking unfair advantage of foreign workers and to protect U.S. workers from being replaced by foreign workers who might accept lower wages. You can look up the prevailing wage for your profession and skill level at www.flcdatacenter.com, the web site of the Labor Department's **Foreign Labor Certification Data Center**. The Immigration & Nationality Act also regulates temporary employment of aliens in the United States; details are available at www.dol.gov/esa under "Compliance Assistance."

FAMILY & MEDICAL LEAVE ACT

If you work for a large business (generally, one with at least 50 employees) and you or a close family member develops a serious medical problem, federal law requires your employer to give you leave from your job and to let you return to the same position, or an equivalent position, up to three months later. You may take *medical leave* if you yourself have a medical problem and *family leave* if your spouse, child, or parent has a medical problem requiring your care—but you will have to show medical documentation. And if a medical condition is foreseeable—for example, if you are scheduled for surgery and you know you will need to stay in bed for a week afterward—you must give your employer 30 days' advance notice if possible. There are some restrictions; for details, contact the Wage & Hour Division of the Labor Department, 888-487-9243 or www.wagehour.dol.gov.

UNIONS

U.S. workers in most industries and trades have the right to organize unions, and many do. Individual employers try hard to discourage their employees from joining unions, sometimes resorting to illegal threats against union organizers, but certain unions are influential in their industries and in American politics. Self-employed professionals such as plumbers, carpenters, and even writers and musicians may join a union that can help them obtain health insurance and legal services. Unions rarely go on strike anymore; usually, labor and management settle their disputes with the help of a neutral mediator.

Approximately 16 million U.S. workers belong to labor unions—13% of the workforce—but union membership is much higher among government workers than in the private sector. (Almost 38% of government workers belong to a union, but fewer than 9% of private-sector workers do.) Most unions, in turn, belong to the **AFL-CIO**—the American Federation of Labor and Congress of Industrial Organizations. Through delegates from each of its 65 member unions, the AFL-CIO represents more than 13 million workers. For more information about union membership and benefits, visit www.afl-cio.org.

THE WORKPLACE

Some workplaces are very hierarchical places where you are expected to address subordinates by their first name and address superiors by title and surname. But in most workplaces, everyone is on a first-name basis. In some offices, the high-ranking people tend to dress more formally than their subordinates, but in others everyone wears flannel shirts and khaki trousers. Some workplaces allow casual attire on Friday or whenever the staff won't be interacting directly with clients. There are usually plenty of other signs of hierarchy: executives and senior managers tend to have the biggest offices, the most windows, and the most comfortable chairs. A corner office is almost always a badge of high rank.

You should always dress conservatively when applying for a job, and once you start work in your new position, take your cues from the people you work with. Conservative business attire means, for men, a suit and necktie, and for women, either a mid-calf skirt and blouse or a pantsuit. The salespeople at any department store can advise you in selecting business apparel, including appropriate "business casual" attire for companies that do not expect employees to dress formally.

Likewise, take your cues from co-workers about the proper way to address superiors and peers, or pay attention to the way people invite you to address them. It is always acceptable to behave a bit more formally when you're new to a workplace than the seasoned employees do; after all, they know each other and have earned each other's trust and confidence, and a new employee still has to impress people—subordinates and peers as well as superiors—in order to gain that level of trust.

Some people socialize with co-workers, eating lunch together or going out for drinks or dinner after work; some people prefer to keep their professional and personal circles separate. A workplace may have certain customs or occasions when people gather and socialize together, such as *happy hour* (drinks and snacks after work, usually at a bar) once a week or once a month. Some bosses buy lunch for their staff occasionally, while others consider it inappropriate to fraternize with subordinates. These customs are so varied from one office to another that new American employees probably don't know what to expect either; you may have a lot to discover, but it's not because you're in a new country—it's because you're in a new job.

SOME IMPORTANT TERMS

Aside from key terms defined in this chapter, here is some other jargon you might hear in the job market:

advancement
    promotions or steps toward increased authority and responsibility

entry level
    describes a junior position, suitable for recent graduates or students

glass ceiling
    unofficial (and often unacknowledged) level in a company's hierarchy beyond which women or minorities are likely to encounter discrimination

headhunter
    an OUTPLACEMENT consultant who matches job seekers with companies that are recruiting

help wanted
    means a position is available; "help wanteds" are another name for WANT ADS

human resources (HR)
    the division of a company that handles personnel matters, including hiring and benefits

internship
    a short-term job held by a student earning academic credit for work-related learning

layoffs
    dismissal of employees whose jobs are being eliminated—not supposed to reflect adversely on those employees

networking
    the informal, but often systematic, process of meeting people and exchanging business cards on general principle—because the more people you know, the more likely you are to know the right person to help you in any situation that may arise

outplacement
    services to assist job seekers

performance review
    a scheduled or occasional evaluation of an employee's strengths and weaknesses; often a factor in ADVANCEMENT, pay raises, and benefits

• •

SOME IMPORTANT TERMS, CONT.

probationary
describes a period during which a new employee is evaluated to determine whether a conditional job offer will be made permanent, and at what level of compensation

references
persons who can vouch for the factual accuracy of statements in a résumé, cover letter, or job interview; usually representatives of former employers or schools

want ads
classified advertisements in a newspaper listing jobs available

ABBREVIATIONS

Here are some specialized abbreviations (in addition to the standard ones listed in Appendix B) that you might see in WANT ADS and job notices:

BENES	benefits
CL	cover letter
CV	curriculum vitae (academic résumé)
FT	full-time (at least 35 hours per week)
HIST	history, as in salary history
OP, OPPTY	opportunity
PRINS ONLY	principals only (job seekers, not OUTPLACEMENT consultants)
PT	part-time (usually 16-24 hours per week)
REFS	references
REQS	requirements, as in salary requirements
RES	résumé
SAL	salary

• •

ETIQUETTE & SOCIETY

In this building there lived a young American woman whose beauty was renowned. One day, in a gesture we had seen only in films, her husband pulled out of their garage, interrupting our football match as he slowly drove by, and kissed the tips of his fingers, sending a kiss to the beautiful woman wearing a nightgown and waving her hand on the balcony. We were overcome with silence. No matter how much love the adults we knew shared, they never revealed their happiness and privacy in front of others with such ease.

> — *Orhan Pamuk, Turkish novelist; from "What We Think of America," a collection of essays in the British magazine* Granta, *Spring 2002*

Manners and social customs vary from one region of the United States to another, among Americans of different social and economic backgrounds, between older and younger generations, and especially between urban and rural areas. And, of course, some individuals are simply more polite than others. In any new social setting, look and listen for a sense of the formality or intimacy with which locals address each other. At the same time, keep in mind a few stereotypes about U.S. manners that have a kernel of truth at the center:

Americans are informal. There are plenty of exceptions, but often, visitors or newcomers—especially from Europe or Asia—say they find Americans to be more casual, direct, and "forward" with each other than is customary back home. Americans address each other by first name, without title, in a broader range of situations than would be acceptable in most countries, and rarely call anybody "sir" or "ma'am" except strangers. In the United Kingdom, it is considered impolite to ask a new acquaintance what he or she does for a living; in the United States, it is usually one of the first things a new acquaintance will ask as a way to start a conversation.

Americans value their privacy. Despite the informal tone of social interaction, many people are hesitant to discuss personal matters such as religion, politics, or money—and some people consider it rude to bring such topics up in conversation except among close friends. And even though movies, television, magazines, and advertising posters are full of images of sexuality, and many American ads would be unfit for public display in a country with a conservative religious government, many Europeans report that Americans are individually shy and reserved about sexuality and the human body. (At a gathering of international youth volunteers in Washington, D.C., some students visited a public swimming pool; one visitor from Morocco was amazed to see how much skin the men's and women's swimsuits revealed, and one from France was amazed to see how much they covered.) It is especially important for men to understand that American women are not necessarily interested in being approached for sex just because they are wearing revealing clothing. Rape and *stalking* (a pattern of unwelcome sexual advances) are serious crimes.

Some Americans welcome unannounced visitors at home, but many prefer visitors to phone before dropping by. And telemarketers—people who call you on the phone to peddle goods or services—are often greeted with angry grumbling about an "invasion of privacy," especially if they happen to call during the evening meal. And you'll find that many Americans are reluctant to have conversations with strangers on a crowded bus or subway, in an elevator, or at a bus stop. (Generally, Americans in big cities are more often reserved or cautious around strangers; in smaller towns, people are more likely to offer a friendly greeting and strike up a conversation.)

Americans are very conscious of time. Punctuality is expected in the workplace, and the lunch hour should not routinely last longer than an hour. Social engagements at a restaurant or other gathering place are expected to start at the appointed time, though the advent of the wireless phone has made it easier to adjust plans if someone is delayed by traffic or other obstacles. A dinner party at a private home, likewise, will begin at the stated time; for other types of parties, however, it is customary to arrive anytime within the first hour or so after the stated time. Many city dwellers seem to be in a hurry most of the time, and indeed, a person living in a major city and trying to devote time to a job, a family, friends, hobbies, entertainment, and household chores might have little time to spare. As a result, Americans are likely to be irritable and perhaps rude if compelled to wait in line (queue) for a long time at a store or government office, or if stuck in slow-moving traffic.

Americans are competitive. You won't see soccer (football) riots in the United States, but that's surprising, given the passion with which many Americans vie to be the best or the first in any endeavor. Drivers cut each other off in traffic to avoid being passed; junior executives compete to curry favor with the boss; fans of rival sports teams wager on the outcome of games. State and local governments, too, worry about "staying competitive" and attracting the biggest corporations and the most jobs. Men, especially, tend to spend hours comparing the new stereo or computer or car to the neighbor's or coworker's, hoping to boast the model with the most features or capabilities. In a game of baseball or soccer between two youth teams, often the parents are more fiercely competitive than the 12-year-old players. As long as it's friendly and good-natured, a competitive streak will be greeted with respect, especially in business.

INTRODUCTIONS & GREETINGS

Except in the most formal situations, modern Americans have little sense of social precedence. In many countries, and traditionally in the United States, there is a strict and complicated order of precedence that determines who is introduced to whom—a young person to an elder, a subordinate to a superior, a man to a woman, a party guest to the guest of honor. Today, introductions are much more casual and many Americans are not even schooled in the traditional protocols. No offense should be taken by an apparent reversal of rank or precedence. (The same applies to seating at a table.) It is also acceptable to introduce yourself to a stranger at a party or business function—just say "Hello, I'm..." and say your first and last name. A typical reply to an introduction is "It's a pleasure to meet you."

Whether you introduce yourself or you are introduced by a third party, and regardless of gender, it is always appropriate to offer your right hand for a friendly handshake. Declining a handshake, unless one's hand is messy with food, is a rare and emphatic gesture of disapproval. A businesslike handshake is firm and brief; you might see old friends clasp hands more elaborately, along with a pat on the shoulder or back, or even a hug. Regardless of gender, this is not to be mistaken for a sexual gesture.

Americans do not normally kiss each other on the cheek in greeting unless they're related. Americans also rarely bow to anyone unless on a stage in a theater. If someone returns a bow of greeting or thanks, it probably indicates a sincere desire to show respect for a visitor's culture.

It is always OK to offer a business card except at purely social gatherings, and it's acceptable even then if a conversation has led to extended talk of business. It is unusual, though, to exchange business cards at the *beginning* of a conversation or upon introduction; you offer your card to indicate that you wish to continue a conversation at a later date.

NAMES & TITLES

Most Americans have a *first name* given by their parents and a *last name* or *surname* inherited from the father's family. Traditionally, a married woman takes her husband's surname, but it's increasingly common for married women to keep their own surnames. Most Americans also have one or more *middle names,* secondary given names used mainly in formal situations.

Sometimes a son is given his father's name and is distinguished by the suffix *Jr.,* meaning *junior,* and the father takes the suffix *Sr.,* meaning *senior.* If the name is handed down to a third generation or beyond, the individuals are distinguished by Roman numerals: Martin Luther King Sr.; Martin Luther King Jr.; Martin Luther King III.

For many official purposes, including business paperwork and academic records, names are written in reverse—last name and then first name separated by a comma, then middle initial and any suffixes. For example: King, Martin L., Jr.

Many Americans are commonly addressed by a **nickname** (sobriquet), usually either a shortened or diminutive form of their first name or an affectionate name made up by friends reflecting some aspect of the individual's background, character, or physical features.

It is always acceptable to address a new acquaintance by a title and surname, using either a **courtesy title**—usually Mister (Mr.) or Miz (Ms.)—or a title reflecting the person's professional, academic or political stature, such as Reverend, Doctor, or Senator. Some married women prefer to be addressed as Missus (Mrs.), and some unmarried women prefer to be addressed as Miss; take your cues from the way your host introduces a person or the way people introduce themselves. Children are usually addressed by their first names.

Most often, upon being introduced, a new acquaintance will immediately let you know how he or she wishes to be addressed—and it will often be a less formal way than you might expect. If someone introduces you to a high-ranking corporate executive by saying "This is Dr. Adams, the vice president of the research division," the executive might shake your hand and say "Please call me Anne." You can acknowledge this invitation by saying something like, "It's a pleasure to meet you, Anne."

The appropriate written and verbal forms of address for public officials, religious leaders, military personnel, and persons of academic or professional distinction are listed in etiquette books and almanacs available in any public library or bookstore. But if you're not sure how to address someone, the easiest and most reliable solution is to ask. It is understood that personal preferences and variations can be tricky, so that there is no cause for shame or embarrassment if a new acquaintance politely corrects you in these matters.

HOSPITALITY & MEALS

In some countries, an honored guest is always taken to a restaurant, in the belief that home cooking is too ordinary. In the United States, though it is certainly a friendly gesture to take a guest out for a meal, it is a sign of special warmth and hospitality to invite a guest to dine in one's own home. Dinner in a private home may be very informal, but you are expected to arrive at the stated time. It is polite to bring a small gift, such as a bottle of wine or a souvenir from your country, and to write a brief note of thanks the next day. (Though a handwritten thank-you note is traditional, among close friends a phone call or e-mail message is acceptable.) Seating arrangements and serving customs vary, but tend to be informal. At the end of the meal, a polite guest will offer to help clear the table and wash the dishes, and a polite host or hostess will refuse the offer—unless the guest is a relative or very close friend, or is staying overnight.

Americans typically eat three meals a day: breakfast, in the morning before work or school, usually the most informal meal; lunch, around noon, often shared with business associates to talk business or with co-workers to socialize; and dinner, after work, usually the largest and most elaborate meal of the day. Americans also tend to eat lots of snacks between meals. On weekends, some people have a single large meal around noon (brunch) instead of breakfast and lunch.

Many Europeans say Americans dine in a hurried manner and leave the table too soon after the meal, but lingering conversation after a meal is in fact welcome in most social circles. Working people might not have time for a leisurely lunch during the business day, but the evening meal is another matter. (If a restaurant is crowded, however, and customers are waiting for a table, then it may be considered rude to linger.) Europeans are sometimes surprised by American table manners, too—for example, we tend to switch a fork from one hand to the other when cutting a piece of meat, and in some countries that would be considered ungraceful. In general, Americans behave formally in formal settings (such as an elegant restaurant) and casually in casual settings (such as a downtown lunchroom).

If someone invites you to a restaurant, it usually means he or she expects to pay for the meal. It's polite to offer to "pick up the check" (pay for the meal), but your host is supposed to decline and insist on paying, usually with a remark like "It's my treat" or "Dinner is on me." There is no need to feel uncomfortable—your host invited you to dine because he or she wanted to spend time with you, whether for business or social reasons. However, you should return the invitation in the near future—take your host out to lunch or dinner, and it will be your turn to pick up the check.

RESTAURANTS

In most restaurants, you will be asked to wait just inside the front door until the host or hostess escorts you to a table. This is not a matter of social precedence or prestige; rather, the manager is trying to ensure that customers (and tips) are distributed evenly among the waiters and waitresses assigned to different tables. In very casual restaurants, you may walk in and sit at any available table you choose. And in very formal restaurants, it is customary and sometimes obligatory to phone in advance to make **reservations** (request a table for a certain number of people at a certain time on a certain date). If you show up at a fancy restaurant without reservations—or if you make reservations but you arrive more than 15 minutes late—you might be turned away or have to wait a long time to get a table.

In most restaurants, you are expected to order from the printed or posted menu; some chefs are happy to accommodate special requests, while others feel insulted if you do not want something from the menu they have prepared. Restaurants are required to serve drinking water for free if you ask for it, and some serve a basket of bread or small appetizers as soon as you are seated. A few restaurants offer *prix fixe* menus—the French term for "fixed price"—from which you order a full meal composed by the chef, but most have *à la carte* menus from which you order exactly what you want.

MARRIAGE & COUPLES

Most married Americans, male and female, wear a wedding ring—often a simple, unadorned gold band—on the third finger of the left hand. Women who are *engaged* (betrothed) often wear a diamond engagement ring on that finger. But a ring may also be merely ornamental, and there are married people who don't wear rings. So there is no way to know whether someone is married without asking—and in a business situation, it might be considered an inappropriate question. A man and a woman dining together, attending a movie or play together, or shopping together might be a married couple; they might be on a *date,* a romantic liaison; or they might simply be friends or even business associates. Unless they're kissing or behaving very affectionately, you can't tell by looking whether any two people are a couple or not.

Divorce is much more common than it was a few generations ago, and many divorced people remarry. Sometimes the result is a nontraditional household—for example, with one "biological" parent and one step-parent (spouse of a biological parent), or with half-siblings who have one parent in common. In most areas, and certainly in big cities, these situations are no longer considered unusual.

In very formal situations (for example, on an engraved invitation to a special social function) or in conservative social circles, it is still customary to address a married couple as "Mr. and Mrs." followed by just the husband's name—Mr. and Mrs. John Smith. Some Americans consider this practice a relic of a bygone era in which women were accorded little respect and were legally treated as their husbands' subordinates. But, as practically all American children have heard their elders say, "Old habits die hard."

Unmarried American teens and adults **date** a lot—in other words, we develop romantic relationships that might last for many years or for just a few days, and shared activities (including sex) with a romantic partner do not necessarily imply plans to get married. It is important for people who are dating to communicate openly and in detail about their desires and expectations—especially when different cultural influences are involved.

Gay and lesbian couples have become increasingly visible since the 1970s; although there is still some bigotry against gay, lesbian, bisexual and transgender individuals, this is another category of nontraditional families that is commonly accepted, at least in cosmopolitan areas. Certain cities—and in some cities, certain neighborhoods—are considered especially hospitable to same-sex couples. In most cities, there are guidebooks and newspapers catering to gay and lesbian interests. Only a few states allow same-sex couples to seek the same legal status as a married couple, but many large businesses allow their employees to designate a same-sex partner to receive the same insurance benefits as an employee's spouse.

SPECIAL OCCASIONS

In addition to the holidays listed in Chapter 14, many Americans celebrate the personal milestones in their own lives and those of friends and relatives. As you make friends in the United States, you will be invited to join in the celebration of people's birthdays, weddings, and various religious rituals.

BIRTHDAYS

Americans give presents and cards to friends and relatives on their birthdays, and may also mark the occasion with a party in the person's honor. In the workplace, coworkers might celebrate someone's birthday by taking a few minutes during the day to share a cake and sing "Happy Birthday." A birthday cake is presented with lit candles set in it—traditionally, but not necessarily, the same number of candles as the person's age in years—and the person is supposed to blow them out and make a secret wish. Parents often throw birthday parties for their children and invite the child's friends, who bring gifts and play games.

ANNIVERSARIES

Married couples celebrate their wedding anniversaries with romantic gifts, a special dinner, or a weekend getaway (short vacation). The couple's immediate family and closest friends might give them presents or cards, especially on "milestone" anniversaries (first, 10th, 25th). Couples reaching their 50th (or "golden") anniversary are usually honored with a large, festive gathering of extended family, and sometimes "renew" their wedding vows in a symbolic ceremony similar to a wedding.

WEDDINGS & SHOWERS

Weddings are the most elaborately planned rituals in most people's lives, and wedding invitations are often sent months in advance. The initials RSVP mean the same thing in the United States as throughout Europe: *répondez s'il vous plait,* French for "please respond." It is essential courtesy to accept or, with apologies, decline a wedding invitation no later than the specified RSVP date. (Actually, the same rule applies to any kind of written or e-mailed invitation, but it's especially important with such a lavish event as a wedding.)

Traditionally, a wedding is hosted by the parents of the bride, but in some modern marriages, both families serve as hosts and issue the invitations, or the couple may host their own wedding. The length, format, and formality of a wedding varies based on the couple's religious practices and personal preferences, but most weddings consist of a brief ceremony followed by a reception with dinner and dancing.

It is customary to give the couple a gift, which you may bring to the wedding or send to the couple's home soon afterward. (Sometimes friends of the bride will host a **shower**, a party at which the bride is "showered" with gifts. A shower might also be held for a woman expecting a baby.) Some couples open a **gift registry** at a favorite store: they make a list of items they need for their new home, and friends and relatives can consult the list to see what other wedding guests have already purchased. Traditionalists and true romantics say this practice eliminates the personal touch from gift-giving, while practical young newlyweds say it prevents the inevitable problem of getting lots of identical presents. (If your friends know you love fresh popcorn, you'll get 14 popcorn machines.) If you're invited to a wedding and you want advice about an appropriate gift, you're welcome to ask the couple's family, "Are they registered anywhere?" and then consult the gift registry—but you're also welcome to find your own thoughtful gift that's not listed on the registry.

If you are invited to be "in" a wedding, that means the bride or groom considers you a very special friend and would like you to be one of his or her attendants during the ceremony. This is also known as *standing up with* the groom or serving as a *bridesmaid*, a *groomsman*, or an *usher*. The leader of the groom's party is called the *best man* and the leader of the bride's party is called the *maid of honor*. There is usually a rehearsal of the ceremony a few days in advance.

The etiquette books listed below under RECOMMENDED READING describe various wedding traditions in detail. Wedding customs are evolving as new nontraditional family structures gain acceptance, and there are newspaper columns and entire magazines devoted to trends in wedding rituals. It's always okay to ask advice from somebody close to the couple.

RITES OF PASSAGE

In some religious traditions, a child's *confirmation* or *first communion* is a special occasion, but usually celebrated only among close relatives.

The Jewish rite of *bar mitzvah* (for males) or *bat mitzvah* (for females), at age 13, is often observed with a large and lavish birthday party as well as religious ceremonies.

When a young relative or the child of a close friend graduates from high school or college, you might send a card or a gift, depending on how well you know the graduate. Parents and grandparents give the graduate substantial gifts—perhaps a car or a computer. Immediate family and close friends attend the graduation ceremony, which usually features an inspirational speech by a person of great accomplishment. The graduates march in, wearing ceremonial caps and gowns, to the music of Elgar's "Pomp and Circumstance," and ritually turn the tassels of their caps from one side to the other when the head of the school pronounces them graduated.

An American saying reminds us, "The only sure things in life are death and taxes." When a person dies, usually anyone who knew the deceased or the family is welcome to attend the funeral or memorial service. Most newspapers have a page of *death notices* listing the time and place of services; at the family's preference, ceremonies may be held in a place of worship, in a funeral home (undertaker's), or at graveside. It is customary to wear conservative, dark attire and optional to send flowers; sometimes, the death notice will specify the family's request that friends and loved ones make contributions to a particular charity instead of sending flowers. It is always appropriate to send a card with a note of sympathy to the closest relatives of a person who has died.

OTHER MILESTONES

When a person moves into a new house or apartment, friends might send a card or a *housewarming* gift—perhaps something practical for the new home, or a bottle of champagne or basket of fruit. The person might invite friends to a housewarming party, and this is a good time to bring a gift.

A promotion, a significant business deal, or an award might warrant a note of congratulations or an invitation to dinner or lunch. It's not so much a question of expected recognition as a reflection of your genuine goodwill toward a friend or business associate.

An artist or author celebrating the completion of a major work, or a company or organization celebrating an important accomplishment, might hold a *reception*. Usually this is a gathering lasting just an hour or so, with wine and cheese or light snacks and a few speeches. This is also a customary way to welcome and introduce a distinguished visitor. Another kind of reception is an *open house,* which means you are welcome to drop in anytime during the stated hours.

Many personal milestones can be suitably observed by sending a gift of fresh flowers, and most florists (flower shops) make deliveries. (You can even arrange through a local florist to have a florist in another city make a delivery there.) Though it is far more common for a man to send flowers to a woman, there is no reason why a woman should not send flowers to a man or to another woman. But most heterosexual American men would feel uncomfortable receiving flowers from another man except in a time of mourning. Flowers are also a nice gift for an associate's birthday or to celebrate a major professional achievement. And if you end up dating Americans, you will quickly discover that flowers—especially roses, which are associated with romance—can work wonders.

BUSINESS ETIQUETTE

As noted in Chapter 12, some employers expect more formality than others, and the only way to get a feel for the appropriate conduct is to observe others, ask questions when in doubt, and behave rather formally until you and your coworkers get to know each other. Respect other people's time by being punctual, by answering phone messages and e-mail promptly, and by keeping presentations and meetings on schedule so they can be completed in the time allotted. Here are some other points to keep in mind:

- Americans do engage in *small talk*—conversation about the weather, sports, television or movies, and (among acquaintances) hobbies or mutual interests. However, many international newcomers find American businesspeople much quicker to end or even skip the small talk and "get down to business." It depends on the situation and how well two people know each other—and on how busy everyone is. No offense should be taken if someone wishes to avoid small talk, perhaps simply due to a pressing schedule or unrelated concerns.

- "Who are you with?" is a tricky question. At business-oriented gathering, it probably refers to your employer (meaning "what firm are you affiliated with?"), but at a purely social party or in a bar or nightclub, "Are you with somebody?" usually means "Did you come here with a date?"

- In business, at the end of a phone conversation or a small meeting, one party will usually indicate plans to *follow up*; within a day or two, that party will write a memorandum (often by e-mail) summarizing the main points of the conversation and any decisions that were reached or commitments made. This gives both parties a chance to make sure they understood each other and left the meeting with the same expectations.

- To some newcomers, especially from cultures where a business is typically run by the same family for generations, it may be disturbing to hear Americans say "it's nothing personal, it's business." If you make a proposition or a sales pitch to a U.S. company and the company isn't interested, the company's representative will say so, simply and directly. You may or may not be given a reason—"Another bidder offered us a lower price" or "Our government contract requires us to give preference to local firms"—but it is important to understand that, in U.S. culture, business decisions are motivated solely by business interests and do not reflect on you or your company. The same company that rejects one proposition from your firm might well be interested in working with your firm in some other situation later on.

PARDON OUR SUPERSTITION

Chapter 13 would upset some Americans—not because of its content, but just by being the 13th chapter. An old folk superstition holds that 13 is an unlucky number—and many high-rise buildings in the United States do not have a 13th floor, but skip from the 12th to the 14th. If the 13th day of the month happens to be a Friday, many Americans believe it will be a day of bad luck.

COMMON PLEASANTRIES

The phrases *please, thank you* and *you're welcome* are basic cornerstones of any conversational English course you may have taken; but Americans have many idiomatic ways to express these and similar sentiments.

You'll hear people say:	When they mean:
HEY	hello, hi
HAVE A NICE DAY; SO LONG; LATER; SEE YOU LATER; BYE	goodbye

You'll hear people say:	When they mean:
HOW ARE YOU? HOW ARE YOU DOING?	a vague expression of good wishes; the expected reply is "fine, thanks, and you?"
WHAT'S UP? WHAT'S NEW? WHAT'S HAPPENING?	do you have any news?
THANKS	thank you
IT'S NOTHING; NO PROBLEM; NOT AT ALL; DON'T MENTION IT	you're welcome
EXCUSE ME	pardon me for interrupting; or, please move out of the way

And you'll hear people say *bless you* (or *God bless you*) when a person sneezes. (Some people say *gesundheit*, a German and Yiddish word wishing someone good health.)

Americans also say *goodbye* in various languages almost as a kind of slang—you'll hear people say *adios* our *au revoir* or *ciao* even if they don't know another word of Spanish, French, or Italian. In the indigenous language of Hawaii, *aloha* is an all-purpose term of hospitality that means both hello and goodbye. You might also hear people say *gracias* or *merci*, the Spanish and French words for *thank you*.

RECOMMENDED READING

The two most complete, authoritative, respected etiquette manuals that cover every aspect of American life are **Emily Post's Etiquette** (published by HarperCollins, with recent editions written by Peggy Post) and **The Amy Vanderbilt Complete Book of Etiquette** (published by Doubleday, with recent editions by Letitia Baldrige). These are 800-page reference books that address any social situation you can imagine and plenty that you probably can't. And they're revised from time to time as customs and manners evolve—as the pace of life gets faster, especially in business, and as new technology changes the way we communicate. You'll find it very helpful to spend some time with one of these books.

Probably easier to read, however, is **Miss Manners' Guide to Excruciatingly Correct Behavior** by Judith Martin (published by Atheneum). Martin writes an etiquette advice column that is featured in many U.S. newspapers, and this book—like the others in the Miss

Manners series—is a collection of replies she has written to hundreds of requests for her advice.

All three of these distinguished authorities also publish a series of smaller, more specialized etiquette books—for example, books focusing on business etiquette, dining and entertaining, weddings, or etiquette for children. And another specialized etiquette book that might be useful is ***How to Be a Perfect Stranger: A Guide to Etiquette in Other People's Religious Ceremonies,*** edited by Arthur J. Magida (published by Jewish Lights Publishing). It covers everyday and special occasions in more than a dozen different faith traditions.

CHAPTER FOURTEEN

A YEAR IN THE UNITED STATES

Life would just pass in a blur if it wasn't for times like these.

— *Kermit the Frog, from* A Muppet Family Christmas

In the course of a year, you'll see Americans celebrate dozens of national, religious, and traditional holidays; follow different spectator sports every season and participate in different seasonal recreation themselves; take vacations at certain times; debate politics at certain times; worry about the weather at different times; and, in short, mark the passage of time by a dazzling variety of natural and artificial seasons.

HOLIDAYS

There are ten **national holidays** recognized by the federal government. On these days, federal buildings are closed, and so are most places of business other than stores and restaurants. States may decide individually whether state and local government facilities—including schools and libraries—will be closed, but most states observe all federal holidays. There is no mail delivery on these days, and most people who do have to work on these days get paid at 1½ times the regular rate (see Chapter 12). Some states also celebrate their own official holidays that are not observed nationally.

Americans celebrate many other **religious and secular holidays** that aren't government holidays, but they don't get a paid day off work to do so. You can usually arrange to take leave from work, and arrange to have your children excused from school, on holy days of a religion you are known to practice.

If you're ever unsure what holiday Americans are looking forward to, just step into any greeting card shop or drugstore. These merchants are always one or two festivals ahead of the calendar—for example, peddling Christmas decorations in early November; Valentine's Day cards right after New Year's Day; Easter candy in February; patriotic Fourth of July decorations in May; and Halloween candy in September.

• • • • • • • • • • • • • • • • • •

NATIONAL HOLIDAYS

- New Year's Day: January 1
- Martin Luther King Jr. Day: third Monday in January
- Presidents Day: third Monday in February
- Memorial Day: last Monday in May
- Independence Day: July 4
- Labor Day: first Monday in September
- Columbus Day: second Monday in October
- Veterans Day: November 11
- Thanksgiving: fourth Thursday in November
- Christmas: December 25

OTHER MAJOR HOLIDAYS

- Valentine's Day: February 14
- St. Patrick's Day: March 17
- Easter: first Sunday after the first full moon of spring
- Passover: usually in April; lasts eight days*
- Mother's Day: second Sunday in May
- Father's Day: third Sunday in June
- Rosh Hashanah: late September or early October; lasts two days*
- Yom Kippur: 9 days after Rosh Hashanah*
- Halloween: October 31
- Election Day: Tuesday after the first Monday in November
- Hanukkah: in December; lasts eight days*
- Kwanzaa: December 26 to January 1
- New Year's Eve: December 31

* Jewish holidays with fixed dates in the Jewish calendar. These observances begin at sunset the evening before the first day and end at sunset on the last day.

JANUARY

The year begins with parties in homes, restaurants, and bars, lasting from the evening of December 31 to the early morning of January 1. Traditionally, the last ten seconds of the year are counted down, and at the stroke of midnight, you kiss your loved ones and raise a glass of champagne for a toast. If there's a band, it usually plays the Scottish fiddle tune "Auld Lang Syne," written to accompany the words of poet Robert Burns about old friends and fond memories. On the East Coast, at midnight, people might gather around a TV to watch a giant ball of lights slide down a pole above Times Square in New York City. In some communities, families with young children go out for a First Night celebration—an evening of music, games, fireworks, and (in striking contrast to more common New Year's Eve festivities) no alcohol. **New Year's Day** traditions include college football games, parades, and black-eyed peas (a kind of beans eaten for good luck).

The first week of January marks the gradual end

• • • • • • • • • • • • • • • • •

of the holiday season and return to normal work schedules. Children return to school after a winter break; college and university students might remain on vacation until mid-January. Festive holiday decorations often remain on display until January 6, celebrated in some religious traditions as **Twelfth Night** or the **Feast of the Epiphany**.

On the third Monday in January, Americans celebrate the life of **Dr. Martin Luther King Jr.**, who led a series of boycotts and marches in the South in the 1960s that revolutionized race relations in the United States. His efforts certainly did not bring racism and bigotry to an end, but did lead to legal reforms protecting African-Americans from various kinds of discrimination—especially at the voting booth. King was assassinated in 1968.

FEBRUARY

According to American folklore, on February 2, **Groundhog Day**, a mythical groundhog in Punxsutawney, Pennsylvania climbs out of his burrow after hibernating all winter. If he sees his shadow, he is frightened back down the hole and we have six more weeks of winter; if he doesn't see a shadow, he stays outside and we have an early spring. Some people figure this couldn't be any *less* reliable than the weather forecasters on TV.

Also in early February, on the first or second Sunday of the month, 130 million Americans gather around the TV to watch the biggest sporting event of the year: the **Super Bowl**, the championship game in the National Football League. People squeeze into sports bars with big-screen TVs or attend Super Bowl parties.

February 14 is **Valentine's Day**—a modern derivative of the feast day of St. Valentine, patron saint of lovers. Men and women exchange romantic gifts with their sweethearts—including a billion dollars' worth of chocolates, 150 million roses, and a million diamond rings. Schoolchildren might have Valentine's Day parties where they exchange cards or candy, without the romantic overtones (at least among young children).

The third Monday is a national holiday, **Presidents Day**, honoring all of the nation's former presidents. For most of the 20th century, the birthdays of Presidents George Washington and Abraham Lincoln, both in February, were celebrated as holidays; in recent years, the two beloved presidents have been honored together on a single holiday, but in some communities Washington's birthday is still marked with parades led by a fife-and-drum band reminiscent of the Colonial era.

February is recognized as **Black History Month** (also called African-American History Month), and schoolchildren pay extra attention to influential Americans of African heritage—not only civil rights leaders and those who helped to abolish slavery in the 19th century, but also distinguished scientists such as Benjamin Banneker (who built the first mechanical clock ever made in North America) and Charles Drew (the first physician to isolate blood plasma); writers such as Phillis Wheatley and Zora Neale Hurston; and modern heroes such as Guion Bluford, the first African-American astronaut, and Thurgood Marshall, first African-American member of the Supreme Court.

The **Chinese new year** begins on the second new Moon after the Winter Solstice, so it can occur anytime from January 21 to February 19. Parades and street festivals mark the occasion in communities with a large Chinese-American population.

MARCH

Only a handful of religious traditions practiced in the United States celebrate the **Vernal Equinox**, but the Christian calendar is full of special occasions in the weeks before **Easter**. In some parts of the country—especially New Orleans and other places along the Gulf of Mexico—**Mardi Gras** is the biggest festival of the year, a purely fun party offering a last dose of wild abandon before the somber season of **Lent**. On **Ash Wednesday**, seven weeks before Easter, many Catholics go to church to have a cross drawn on their foreheads with wood ash, and on **Palm Sunday**, a week before Easter, Catholic churchgoers carry palm fronds in a ritual procession. Five days later, **Good Friday** is observed as the most solemn holy day in the Catholic year, the anniversary of the crucifixion of Jesus; Easter Sunday commemorates the rebirth of the savior.

Easter is the first Sunday after the first full moon of spring, so it can occur anytime from March 22 to April 25. So Mardi Gras, the beginning of the Christian spring holiday season, can be any Tuesday between February 4 and March 9.

By some estimates, one out of four Americans has some Irish ancestry. Irish-Americans, along with anyone else who appreciates the Irish influence on U.S. culture, celebrate **St. Patrick's Day** on March 17 in honor of the patron saint of Ireland on March 17. The occasion is marked with Irish music and beer, and people dress in green clothing and sometimes put green dye in decidedly non-Irish food (such as bagels or American Pilsener-style beer). Cities with a large Irish-American population, such as Boston and New York, have parades.

Jewish Americans celebrate **Purim** in March on a date determined by the Hebrew calendar. The spring holiday commemorates the Hebrews' revolt in Persia around 400 years B.C.E.

To the nation's 40 million basketball fans, March is synonymous with **college basketball** finals—affectionately known as "March Madness." The best 64 basketball teams from large universities compete for a berth in the **Final Four** championship tournament.

APRIL

The first day of April is **April Fools' Day**, when it is customary to play practical jokes on one's friends and coworkers. April Fools' pranks may be creative or trite, elaborate or simple, blatant or subtle, but they are not supposed to be mean-spirited or harmful. And you should only play practical jokes on people you know well enough to be sure they will take it in good humor.

Easter usually falls in early April. Though it is even holier than Christmas in some branches of Christianity, Easter itself has cultural roots in religious traditions older than the Christian era, dating back to the pagan Eostar festival in ancient Europe. Many Americans observe Easter as a secular or spiritual time of renewal, a celebration of spring, and tell young children that the mythical Easter Bunny will visit while they sleep and leave them a basket of candy. Sometimes the Easter Bunny paints hard-boiled eggs with colorful dye and hides them for children to find; other times, it's hollow plastic eggs with candy inside. Parents who want to help the Easter Bunny make such deliveries will have no trouble finding all the necessary supplies—including chocolate bunnies and marshmallow eggs—at any drugstore.

The eight-day Jewish observance of **Passover**, usually around the same time as Easter, recalls the Old Testament story of the Exodus, the liberation of Hebrew slaves from ancient Egypt. The first two nights of Passover are marked with a ritual meal called a *seder*, and during the week, observant Jews abstain from eating leavened bread; as the story goes, the slaves fleeing across the desert did not

• • • • • • • • • • • • • •

CANDY CALENDAR

According to industry and government statistics compiled by the online newsletter *Candy USA*, Americans consume nearly $2 billion worth of candy at Halloween, $1.9 billion at Easter, $1.4 billion at Christmas, and just over $1 billion at Valentine's Day. That includes 36 million heart-shaped boxes of candy for Valentine's Day; 60 million chocolate bunnies and 15 billion jellybeans for Easter; 20 million pounds of candy corn for Halloween; and for Christmas, nearly 1.8 billion peppermint candy canes.

• • • • • • • • • • • • • •

have time to wait for bread to rise, so they ate only flat bread called *matzo*.

April 15 is, for most U.S. residents, the deadline for filing **income tax** papers disclosing income earned during the previous calendar year.

In 1970, Americans first observed **Earth Day**, a day set aside to honor the planet and reflect on our own impact on its limited resources. Many communities now mark April 22 (or the nearest Saturday) as a day to plant trees, clean up local parks and streams, or hold educational fairs where people can learn about environmental concerns.

Most public and private schools close for a week in early April—**spring break**. (Spring break is a bit earlier at colleges and universities, perhaps even late March.) In the days preceding spring break, many schools hold **midterm exams**.

Also in April, **baseball season** begins. In men's basketball, the regular season ends; the top teams in each conference advance to the playoffs held in May and early June.

MAY

At colleges and universities, the academic year ends in May, so a lot of rental housing becomes available in college towns and major cities—and the job market, especially at entry level, becomes crowded with ambitious young graduates. **Women's basketball season** starts in May. Students also flock to the beach, where seasonal jobs and short-term summer leases make a 10-week vacation (holiday) affordable. Many businesses in seaside towns—and many parks, campgrounds and other recreational sites—are open only from Memorial Day in May to Labor Day in September.

Memorial Day, a national holiday honoring U.S. military personnel killed or wounded in service, is also considered the unofficial and cultural beginning of summer. Many households and businesses fly the flag, and some communities have a parade or a memorial service, but—like many holidays of solemn origin—millions of Americans observe it mainly as a day off from work or school. The holiday originated during the American Civil War as Decoration Day, when mourners would decorate the graves of the Union (loyalist) dead.

On the second Sunday of the month, we honor our mothers. Adults might give their moms a gift or take them to dinner at a nice restaurant to celebrate **Mother's Day**; a family with several young children might give Mom the supreme gift of a day of rest and relaxation. It is also appropriate to give tokens of thanks to grandmothers and wives on Mother's Day. (Father's Day comes next month.)

May Day, a labor movement holiday in many countries, is not celebrated in the United States except by a few dedicated labor activists. It is generally considered a socialist holiday, and socialism is still unpopular in a nation whose adult population grew up during the Cold War. (The United States honors its working people in September, on Labor Day.)

American teenagers look forward to their **senior prom**, a formal dance near the end of the school year. Many high school seniors spend the preceding summer earning money for a fancy evening gown or tuxedo, a rented limousine, and a lavish dinner at a special restaurant for the big night.

JUNE

To schoolchildren, June means the end of the academic year and the beginning of **summer vacation**—usually around the time of the **Summer Solstice**, June 21. The word *vacation* can mean either a break from work and school or an actual travel holiday, and families often take a vacation—a journey—together soon after school closes for the summer. After a week or two of rest, some students begin **summer school**, either to review material they did not fully master during the school year or to get an early start on the next year's coursework. Other students, especially preteens (under age 13), might go away to **summer camp** for a few weeks.

June 14 is **Flag Day**, the anniversary of the day in 1777 when the revolutionary Congress adopted the first U.S. flag. (It was similar to the modern flag, but had 13 stars in a circle to represent the original 13 states. Every time a new state has been admitted to the nation, the flag has been redesigned with a new star.) Flag Day is not a government holiday; Americans celebrate by displaying the flag and perhaps wearing red, white, and blue.

• • • • • • • • • • • • • •

SUMMER CAMP

Many children and young teens spend a few weeks in the summer at a summer camp away from home—without their parents. At summer camp, groups of children live in cabins or dormitories under the supervision of adult counselors and trained, supervised older teenagers. These programs provide an opportunity to meet to make new friends from other communities and to learn a variety of sports, crafts, or special skills.

Traditional camp activities include swimming, horseback riding, hiking, canoeing, and gathering around a bonfire to sing silly songs. Many modern camps, however, offer intensive training in a particular sport or an academic subject, such as computer programming or a second language. There are chess camps, soccer camps, music camps, theater camps, camps for children with disabilities, and even camps designed to give teenagers an early taste of college. There are religious camps, secular camps, camps run by nonprofit youth organizations, camps run by schools, and camps run by sports celebrities to cultivate new talent in their sport. And if you're hesitant to send your child away for a few weeks, there are also **day camps** in many communities that offer the enriching activities of a summer camp, but the children commute from home each day.

• • • • • • • • • • • • • •

In men's professional basketball, the **NBA championship** tournament takes place in early June.

The third Sunday of the month is **Father's Day**, when we honor our fathers (and grandfathers and husbands) with gifts and special favors. Many men show up for work the next day wearing garish neckties that their young children picked out as gifts.

A growing number of cities celebrate their gay, lesbian, bisexual and transgender communities with a **Gay Pride Day** parade or festival, usually in late June. In some cities, it's a major event that features big-name entertainers and attracts a large general audience; in other communities, it might be the only day of the year that same-sex couples feel safe holding hands in public in their own hometown.

In many parts of the country, June is the beginning of storm season. Violent summer **thunderstorms** sweep across vast areas of the Plains, Midwest, and East Coast, sometimes producing hail that damages crops or tornadoes that can destroy an entire town. (See Chapter 15.)

The **Supreme Court** adjourns for its summer recess, reconvening in October, so many of the most controversial or complicated legal rulings are handed down in June. And even the TV industry goes on summer vacation—new programming is shown from late

September to May, and summer audiences watch **reruns** of programs that have been shown before.

JULY

July begins with the nation's birthday, **Independence Day**—on, and often simply called, the **Fourth of July**. It is actually *not* the anniversary of the day King George III of England recognized the United States as a new and independent nation; rather, it is the date when, in 1776, the Continental Congress announced that it had adopted a resolution claiming the colonies' independence from the British crown. That **Declaration of Independence** (see Appendix C) remains one of the most eloquent articulations of human rights in the history of the world—even though,

SUMMER CAMP, CONT.

The **National Camp Association** offers a free referral service called **CampQuest** to help you find specific summer camps that would suit your child's interests. Call 800-966-2267 or visit www.summercamp.org. You can also search listings of summer camps online at **http://camppage.com**, **www.campsearch.com**, or **www. kidscamps.com**, or in camp **directories**, such as *Peterson's Summer Camps & Jobs,* available at libraries and bookstores.

Note: *Camping,* or *camping out,* means sleeping outdoors or in a tent or temporary shelter, usually for recreational purposes; *camp* refers to an organized group retreat, whether participants camp out or sleep in cabins or dormitories. If you go on a rustic trip and sleep in a tent in the woods, you would say you're *going camping;* if you attend a summer camp, you would say you're *going to camp.*

ironically, it was understood at the time to refer only to the rights of aristocratic white men, and many of the men who signed it kept African slaves.

John Adams, one of the leaders of the American Revolution and later the second President of the United States, called for the Declaration to be celebrated with bells and cannon fire. Its anniversary has been celebrated ever since by making lots of noise, mainly with fireworks. All major cities and most smaller towns have displays of fireworks just after dark on the evening of "the Fourth," after a day of parades, concerts and **cookouts** (outdoor parties where food is cooked on a charcoal-burning grill).

Cookouts (also called barbecues) are not limited to the Fourth of July. A typical summertime social gathering might be a cookout with a softball or volleyball game. If there is any cuisine that is distinctly American, it's grilled hamburgers and hot dogs, corn on the cob, potato salad, watermelon, iced tea, and domestic beer. Some parts of the country—notably North Carolina, Tennessee, and Texas—are renowned for varieties of *barbecue*, pork ribs or chicken wings cooked over a fire in a brick barbecue pit and smothered in spicy sauce. And vegetarians, a growing minority in the United States, grill giant portobello mushrooms, Asian tempeh, corn, and Middle Eastern kebabs of summer vegetables.

Swimming pools are crowded in midsummer, at public recreation centers and private swimming clubs, and families with children flock to **amusement parks** with roller coasters and splashy water rides. Kids might play **soccer** or **baseball** in a youth league. The movie industry saves its action-and-adventure spectaculars and its fluffy comedies for the summer months when people gladly pay $8 to sit in an air-conditioned theater for two hours. Older children might earn spending money by mowing neighbors' lawns, and teenagers and college students often get **summer jobs** or do volunteer work (see Chapter 16).

AUGUST

To the chagrin of schoolchildren enjoying their summer vacation, stores in August begin to advertise **back-to-school** sales, offering discounts on school supplies and clothing. Some states, in order to ease the financial burden on families with children in school, declare a tax holiday in August and allow stores to sell merchandise for a week without charging sales tax.

Students who will be attending a new school in September—because they're advancing to a grade taught at a higher level of school or because they've moved to a new school district—might report to the new school for a few days in August for an **orientation** program to familiarize new students with the school (see Chapter 11).

In most of the country, August is the hottest month of the year, and city dwellers escape to the beach or the mountains if they can—or travel abroad. Accordingly, travel and lodgings tend to be most expensive and most crowded during the summer, both in the United States and in foreign resorts catering largely to Americans. Even some remote natural destinations, such as the Grand Canyon and Yosemite Valley, get crowded in the summer. If you live in a U.S. city that has popular museums and other tourist attractions, you might want to visit them in the "off season" (winter) and explore less-famous places during peak **tourist season**.

Along the southeastern coast, from Texas to North Carolina, late August through late October is **hurricane** season. Several of these huge storms strike the U.S. coast every year, causing extensive damage from wind and flooding. (See Chapter 15.)

August is the only month with no official or traditional holidays.

SEPTEMBER

The first Monday of September is **Labor Day**, a national holiday honoring working men and women—and, in cultural if not scientific terms, the end of summer. Most elementary and secondary schools convene for the new academic year on the day after Labor Day; colleges and universities tend to open a week earlier.

The 10-day Jewish *high holy days* usually fall in late September, beginning with the two-day observance of **Rosh Hashanah** (the new year of the Hebrew lunar calendar) and ending with the 24-hour fast of **Yom Kippur**, a day of atonement. Public schools in areas with a large Jewish population may be closed on the first day of Rosh Hashanah, and if not, Jewish students are excused from school on that day as well as on Yom Kippur. And five days after Yom Kippur, the Jewish harvest festival of **Sukkot** begins; you might see *sukkot*—huts made of wood and brush—on people's lawns.

The Muslim holy month of **Ramadan**, in the ninth month of the Muslim lunar calendar, celebrates the revelation of the Qu'ran and often occurs during the fall. Devout Muslims, during Ramadan, fast from dawn to sunset every day.

And it is in September that Congress finalizes the 13 separate annual **appropriations bills** that set the federal budget and authorize federal agencies to spend tax revenue in the following **fiscal year**, which begins on October 1 and ends on September 30.

Football season starts around Labor Day, as baseball season comes to an end in cities whose teams have not qualified for the playoffs leading to the **World Series** in October. And women's basketball season ends.

OCTOBER

Although **Halloween** isn't until the last day of the month, the United States in October can seem like a massive costume shop and candy store. More than 90% of the children in the country take part in this tradition, very loosely based on ancient pagan rites and on All Hallows Eve as it was observed in medieval Europe. On the evening of October 31, children dress up in scary or whimsical costumes and go around the neighborhood, knocking on doors and shouting "Trick or Treat!" The expression was, in earlier times, a threat: *give us a treat or we'll play tricks on you.* (In some communities, Halloween is still a time for good-natured practical jokes. Ask your neighbors what to expect.) Today, the phrase is a ritualized request for candy; if you live in a neighborhood with lots of children, make sure you have plenty of candy on hand.

It is also customary to make fanciful lanterns, called **jack-o'-lanterns**, by hollowing out a pumpkin and carving a face in it. The eyes, nose, and mouth serve as vents for the light of a candle placed inside. You'll see these in front of many homes in October, along with decorations in the image of things that are supposed to be scary (skeletons, bats, ghosts, and stereotypical "witches" with green skin and warts). In addition to "going trick-or-treat," children (and adults) attend **costume parties**.

Though you wouldn't know it from a drugstore or greeting card shop, Halloween is not the only notable occasion in October. The second Monday of the month is **Columbus Day**—a national holiday honoring Christopher Columbus, the Italian seafarer who is credited with "discovering" the Americas as far as European peoples are concerned. U.S. schoolchildren can recite the year of his first voyage to the Americas (1492) and the names of his ships (the *Niña, Pinta,* and *Santa Maria*), but many are also taught that Columbus introduced and proved the notion that the Earth is round; actually, the ancient Greeks had proven this and had even calculated the circumference of the globe. (Columbus *was* the first European to make a deliberate attempt to reach east Asia by sailing west around the world and to return to Europe with reports from the Americas.) In the late 20th century, many Americans began to reconsider Columbus' place in history, showing more sensitivity to the millions of indigenous people who lived here before any Europeans arrived. (Historians also debate whether Scandinavian and East Asian people visited North America centuries earlier.) Still, to millions of Americans of Italian ancestry, Columbus Day is a celebration of Italian-American culture.

The **Supreme Court** convenes on the first Monday in October to begin hearing cases it will decide during the winter. And the **basketball** court convenes too—the men's professional season begins.

NOVEMBER

November, to Americans, means **Thanksgiving**: the oldest traditional American holiday, the feast celebrating the harvest and prosperity and marking the beginning of the winter holiday season. First celebrated by European colonists in North America in 1621, and proclaimed a national holiday by President Abraham Lincoln in 1863, Thanksgiving is a time when extended families gather and share a feast. Schoolchildren learn a folkloric version of the history of the Puritan Pilgrims from England who settled in Massachusetts and survived their first winter there with the help of the natives, who taught them to hunt wild turkey and to cultivate corn and sweet potatoes. The **Macy's Thanksgiving Day Parade** in New York City, sponsored by Macy's department store, is famous for its giant balloons in the likeness of characters from children's comic books, film, and TV.

Thanksgiving Day is the fourth Thursday in November, and the only national holiday traditionally declared by Presidential proclamation. Schools and most businesses are closed the following day, making this the only annual four-day weekend. And the day after Thanksgiving is the busiest day of the year at shopping malls and other stores, as people begin to get ready for Christmas.

But the month begins with an even more momentous ritual: **Election Day**. On the Tuesday after the first Monday in November, U.S. voters choose their leaders at the national, state, and local levels. In many parts of the country, there is an election only in even-numbered years, in which the entire membership of the U.S. House of Representatives is elected. The President and Vice President are elected in alternate even-numbered years—2004, 2008, 2012, and so on. States and local jurisdictions each decide whether their governors, legislators, mayors, school boards, and other elected officials are chosen in the same year as the President or in "off" years.*

Veterans of the nation's armed forces are honored on **Veterans Day**, the November 11 anniversary of the Armistice of 1918 that ended World War I.

---

* There are also elections at other times of the year—**primary elections** to choose the candidates from each party who will appear on the ballot in November in the **general election**. In a presidential election year, there may be a presidential primary election in the spring and a separate primary election for other public offices later in the year.

DECEMBER

From the moment Santa Claus arrives at the local shopping mall on Thanksgiving weekend, it's Christmastime. Walk into any store and you'll see **Christmas** decorations glittering and hear Christmas music playing—mostly secular pop music that practically all Americans learned by the time they were old enough for school. By the first weekend of December, you'll see homes decorated with Christmas lights; you'll see seasonal concerts, movies, and *A Charlie Brown Christmas* on TV; and you'll see parking lots piled high with cut pine, spruce, and fir trees that people will take home and decorate. That's a **Winter Solstice** tradition even older than Christianity—and, even though it has been identified with Christmas for centuries in some countries, it reflects the fact that Christmas in America has secular and interfaith components as well as a strong Christian tradition. Simply put, the American interpretation of Christmas was best expressed by the British novelist Charles Dickens in 1843, in *A Christmas Carol:*

> I have always thought of Christmas time, when it comes round ... as a good time: a kind, forgiving, charitable, pleasant time: the only time I know of, in the long calendar of the year, when men and women seem by one consent to open their shut-up hearts freely, and to think of people below them as if they really were fellow-passengers to the grave, and not another race of creatures bound on other journeys.

At the same time, many (perhaps most) Americans say they feel pressure and stress as the Christmas holidays approach. There are travel plans to make as families gather from far corners of the country; there are children who want all the toys they've seen advertised on TV; there are cards to send to loved ones, decorations to hang out, cookies to bake, gifts to buy (or make)—and everyday work does not stop in the meantime. It's also a busy social season, as people attend parties with coworkers, parties with neighbors, and more parties with personal friends. The season is everything Dickens says it is—but it can also be a lot of work, however pleasant. If your first impression of Americans is that we're always in a hurry—always impatient, never relaxed—then just wait until December. Whatever we are, good and bad, we get more so.

But we're *not* all Christian, and Christmas isn't the only cause for celebration. The Jewish festival of light, **Hanukkah**, spans eight days in December, set by the Jewish calendar. Its roots are similar to this nation's: desperate acts in the struggle for religious freedom. Some 22 centuries ago, the Maccabee clan of Jewish rebels overthrew the Syrian army occupying their temple. The dregs of oil in the temple's *menorah* lamp miraculously burned for eight days, enough time to purify more oil for ritual use; the modern holiday celebrates those eight days of light.

From the day after Christmas to New Year's Day, some African-American families celebrate **Kwanzaa**, a festival of African heritage and the values reflected in strong African-American communities. One day of the seven-day observance is devoted to the contemplation of each of the seven

SANTA CLAUS

In secular and Christian households, American children are taught at an early age that Santa Claus (a corruption of the Dutch name for St. Nicholas) lives at the North Pole and visits every home on Christmas Eve—in a sleigh drawn by flying reindeer—to deliver toys and gifts to well-behaved children. It is difficult to dispute this. Santa visits most shopping malls in December and children can meet him and get photos taken. Moreover, children traditionally leave a plate of cookies for Santa when they go to sleep on Christmas Eve and find, in the morning, that the cookies have indeed been eaten.

Principles of Kwanzaa: *Umoja* (unity), *Kujichagulia* (self-determination), *Ujima* (collective work and responsibility), *Ujamaa* (cooperative economics), *Nia* (purpose), *Kuumba* (creativity), and *Imani* (faith).

Schools are closed during the last week of the year, and many people work a light week, but shops are busy with people exchanging items they received as gifts and that don't fit. (Many people also exchange items received as gifts that they just don't like—a practice that may be shocking to people from societies in which any gift is inherently cherished. Some Americans consider it rude, too, while others prefer to know that they've given you something you will enjoy. But it is generally considered tactless to *mention* the fact that you've exchanged a gift.) People also keep a busy social calendar through **New Year's Eve**.

SPORTS

A quarter of every evening news broadcast, a section of every major newspaper, and some $50 billion a year is devoted to sports. If you're trying to get acquainted with U.S. culture, you'll need to attend at least one **baseball** game, and ideally some **football** and **basketball** too. (Note that American football is not related to the globally popular sport known as football, which is called **soccer** in the United States.) Americans of all ages, male and female, follow their home teams in these sports with passion and loyalty—both in professional leagues and, in football and basketball, at the college level. Americans also watch soccer, tennis, hockey, lacrosse, golf, horse racing (practiced mainly for the sake of gambling), auto racing, boxing, and other sports that are essentially the same all over the world, but the most popular sports are uniquely American. (Okay, Americans grudgingly admit that Japan and Cuba have produced some excellent baseball.)

A basic familiarity with American football, baseball, and basketball is useful not only because many Americans like to chat about sports with coworkers or casual acquaintances, but mainly because a lot of terminology from these particular games creeps into everyday language, including the language of business and politics. You might hear an executive or a manager say "it's fourth and long" or "two outs in the bottom of the ninth," or that the firm's latest proposal was a "home run" or it "struck out," and most Americans know what these expressions mean. If you've never seen a single football game or baseball game, you might be at a disadvantage.

ATTENDING SPORTING EVENTS

Usually the easiest way to get tickets to a major sporting event is to call a **ticket agency** (see Chapter 8) or go to the **box office** of the venue. If a game is sold out in advance—as is common with football games, since each team might play only eight home games in a season—you might find someone selling tickets through the classified ads in the local newspaper. **Scalping**, or selling tickets on the street, is illegal but commonplace; if you buy tickets from a scalper, expect to pay very high prices and take the risk that the tickets may be counterfeit.

Traditionally, at the beginning of a sporting event, the **national anthem** is played (see Appendix C). Everyone is expected to stand and face the U.S. flag while the anthem is being performed, and American men remove their hats and place them over their hearts. Americans may or may not sing along, depending less on patriotism than on their ability to sing the difficult tune.

FOOTBALL

Football is a rough contact sport, often compared to English rugby; however, football players wear lots of padding and protective equipment. Almost any kind of hitting, grabbing, or shoving is OK when directed at the player carrying the ball. Amateurs playing a friendly game of football are more likely to play a watered-down version—such as *touch football*, in which the player with the ball can be stopped by a simple tap, or *flag football*, in which a player must stop running when an opponent snatches a colored handkerchief or "flag" from his or her belt.

Football is still generally a men's sport; a women's professional football league was founded in 2001, but does not draw nearly as much attention as the all-male **National Football League**, the **National Collegiate Athletic Association (NCAA)** football conferences, or traditionally all-male high school football teams.

The NFL is divided into two *conferences*, and the top teams in each conference compete in single-elimination postseason playoffs until the two conference champions meet in the **Super Bowl**. The regular season lasts from early September through mid-December, and the playoffs are in January. The college football season, also in the fall, ends with invitational **bowl games** on New Year's Day and the first weekend of the year.

NATIONAL FOOTBALL LEAGUE

American Football Conference (16 teams)
- Baltimore Ravens
- Buffalo Bills
- Cincinnati Bengals
- Cleveland Browns
- Denver Broncos
- Indianapolis Colts
- Jacksonville Jaguars
- Kansas City Chiefs
- Miami Dolphins
- New England Patriots
- New York Jets
- Oakland Raiders
- Pittsburgh Steelers
- San Diego Chargers
- Seattle Seahawks
- Tennessee Titans

National Football Conference (15 teams)
- Arizona Cardinals
- Atlanta Falcons
- Carolina Panthers
- Chicago Bears
- Dallas Cowboys
- Detroit Lions
- Green Bay Packers
- Minnesota Vikings
- New Orleans Saints
- New York Giants
- Philadelphia Eagles
- St. Louis Rams
- San Francisco 49ers
- Tampa Bay Buccaneers
- Washington Redskins

WATCHING FOOTBALL

The football field is 100 yards long with lines marking off every yard. (A yard is 90 cm.) The center line is the 50-yard line and the yards are numbered from 50 down to zero in each direction. If the home team is defending the goal to your left and the visiting team is defending the goal to your right, the 30-yard line to your left is identified as the home team's 30-yard line and the one to your right is identified as the visitors' 30-yard line.

Two teams of 11 take turns keeping possession of the ball and trying to carry or throw it across the *goal line* at the opponents' end of the field. The teams will line up in formation facing each other across the *line of scrimmage,* the position of the ball at the end of the previous play. The *quarterback*, protected by *offensive linemen* (collectively the *offensive line*), will throw the ball to a *wide receiver* or hand it to a *running back,* either of whom will run as far as possible with the ball before being tackled—physically forced to the ground—by the *defensive line* near the line of scrimmage or *defensive backs* downfield.

The offense has four chances, called *downs,* to advance the ball; every time the ball is moved at least 10 yards forward, the offense earns another set of four downs. If the offense succeeds in moving the ball across the goal line, it scores a *touchdown*—six points, plus the opportunity to score an *extra point* by kicking the ball through the goalpost. (The team may elect to score two extra points by moving the ball across the goal line a second time, a rare and difficult play attempted only when a single point could alter the outcome of the game.) If the offense does not succeed in scoring a touchdown and does not expect to gain another set of downs, it may instead attempt to kick the ball from the line of scrimmage through the goalpost for a *field goal,* worth three points. And if the line of scrimmage is too far from the goalpost (as judged by the coach and the kicker), the team may elect to surrender possession of the ball by *punting* (kicking) it ball as far as possible, hoping to stick the opposing team with unfavorable *field position*. The offense will also surrender possession after scoring, and will kick the ball to the other team. Then the kicking team's defense players and the receiving team's offense players take the field.

A game lasts for one hour of actual action, with the clock stopping whenever the ball goes out of bounds, a pass is not caught, a player is injured, a penalty is imposed for misconduct, or either team takes one of its allotted opportunities to call *time out*. The teams change ends after each 15-minute quarter and there is an intermission at *halftime*. In real time, a game usually takes three hours or more. For more details about rules, schedules, and teams, visit **www.nfl.com**.

BASEBALL

Known for generations as "the national pastime," baseball indeed occupies a special place in U.S. culture and has produced more legendary sports figures whose names are household words than any other U.S. sport—in part because it has been popular since the mid-19th century, whereas football and basketball came into their own after World War I.

Major League Baseball consists of the **American League** and the **National League** (each of which, despite the names, has included a team from Canada). The top teams from each league meet in the annual **World Series**—another questionable name, as it involves only teams from the United States and sometimes Canada. The league champions are determined by postseason playoffs—best-of-five tournaments at the quarterfinal level and best-of-seven tournaments in the semifinals.

Minor league baseball is professional baseball at a less polished level—played mostly in smaller cities and towns, at smaller stadiums. Most minor-league teams are *farm clubs*—training teams affiliated with a major-league team. Many baseball enthusiasts prefer minor-league games because you

• • • • • • • • • • • • • • •

MAJOR LEAGUE BASEBALL

American League (14 teams)
  Anaheim Angels
  Baltimore Orioles
  Boston Red Sox
  Chicago White Sox
  Cleveland Indians
  Detroit Tigers
  Kansas City Royals
  Minnesota Twins
  New York Yankees
  Oakland Athletics
  Seattle Mariners
  Tampa Bay Devil Rays
  Texas Rangers
  Toronto Blue Jays

National League (16 teams)
  Arizona Diamondbacks
  Atlanta Braves
  Chicago Cubs
  Cincinnati Reds
  Colorado Rockies
  Florida Marlins
  Houston Astros
  Los Angeles Dodgers
  Milwaukee Brewers
  Montreal Expos*
  New York Mets
  Philadelphia Phillies
  Pittsburgh Pirates
  San Diego Padres
  San Francisco Giants
  St. Louis Cardinals

* At press time, the Expos were moving to Washington, D.C.

• • • • • • • • • • • • • • •

can sit much closer to the action and see promising young players being groomed for the majors.

There is currently no women's professional baseball (there was a women's league in the 1940s), and at the college level, women generally play **softball**—essentially the same game, but with a larger, softer ball that is thrown at a slower speed. (Amateur men and women play softball together, and many workplaces have company softball teams that play against rival companies.)

The season starts in early April and regular play ends in September. The playoffs continue for several weeks until the World Series in October.

WATCHING BASEBALL

The game is played on a diamond-shaped field, with one base at each corner of the diamond. Counterclockwise from the rear point of the field, these are known as *home plate, first base, second base* and *third base.* One player defends each base, and the *shortstop* stands between the second baseman and third baseman where a right-handed *batter* is most likely to hit the ball. *Outfielders* catch balls hit into the right, left and center sections of the outer diamond. With the pitcher standing on a small mound in the center of the infield diamond and the catcher defending home plate, there are nine players on each team.

The batter stands behind home plate, and the *pitcher* throws the ball across home plate at speeds approaching 100 mph (160 kph). The batter is supposed to hit the ball—about the size of an orange—as far as possible and then run to a base before the ball is thrown there; in other words, after hitting the ball, the batter will run to first base and the defending team will try to catch the ball and throw it to the first baseman. If the batter reaches the base first, he or she is *safe* there; if the first baseman, with the ball, touches the base first, the batter is *out.* If the next batter runs to first base, the runner at first has a chance to advance to second base. The batting team scores a *run* each time a runner rounds all the bases. So, if the batter hits the ball over the outfield wall and it cannot be recovered by the defending (fielding) team, every runner on base is guaranteed to score; the play is called a *home run,* and a home run hit with the bases *loaded* (all three bases occupied by runners) is a *grand slam.*

The batter gets more than one chance to hit the ball. The pitcher is supposed to be sporting, to throw the ball directly across the plate and not so high or so low that it cannot be hit. If the pitch meets those criteria and the batter fails to hit it, the pitch is recorded as a *strike*—hence the expression "three strikes, you're out." But if the pitch is off-center or unreasonably hard to hit, it is counted as a *ball* (from the archaic phrase *unfair ball*), and if the pitcher throws four balls to the same batter, the batter may walk to first base unimpeded. And if the batter hits the ball straight up, or backward, or generally not into the field, it is a *foul ball* and does not count as either a strike or a ball. (Some fans bring a catcher's mitt, a scoop-like padded glove, to the ballpark to try to catch foul balls hit into the stands. Especially if later autographed by the player who hit them, these make prized souvenirs.)

If the ball is hit into the field and caught by a fielding player before it touches the ground, it is called a *fly ball* and the runner is out. A foul ball caught before it hits the ground is also "an out." The batting team continues to send batters to the plate until it accumulates three outs—whether by striking out, hitting fly balls, or being tagged out at a base—and then the teams switch: the fielding team takes its turn at bat and the batting team takes the field. Each rotation in which both teams take a turn at bat is called an *inning*, and regular play lasts for nine innings; extra innings are added if the score is tied.

Umpires (referees) watch the action closely and make rulings as to the fairness of a pitch or whether a runner is safe on base or out. Players who argue with an umpire can be ejected from the game. For more details about rules, schedules, and teams, visit **www.mlb.com**.

BASKETBALL

Basketball was invented in the 1890s by a Canadian doctor, James Naismith, who thought American football was too violent. Naismith, living in Massachusetts, introduced his game at a local gymnasium. The game caught on quickly and was played professionally throughout the United States by 1920. The **National Basketball Association** was founded in 1949, and today draws 20 million people a year to its games; almost twice as many people attend **NCAA** college basketball games. Women's professional basketball—the **WNBA**—is a recent innovation, founded in 1997, but it already attracts large audiences and loyal fans.

The season begins in October and the college playoffs leading to the Final Four tournament are in March; the NBA championship is in June. Women's professional basketball season is May through September.

• • • • • • • • • • • • •

NATIONAL BASKETBALL ASSOCIATION

Eastern Conference (15 teams)
Atlanta Hawks
Boston Celtics*
Charlotte Hornets
Chicago Bulls
Cleveland Cavaliers
Detroit Pistons
Indiana Pacers
Miami Heat
Milwaukee Bucks
New Jersey Nets
New York Knicks
Orlando Magic
Philadelphia 76ers
Toronto Raptors
Washington Wizards

Western Conference (14 teams)
Dallas Mavericks
Denver Nuggets
Golden State Warriors
Houston Rockets
Los Angeles Clippers
Los Angeles Lakers
Memphis Grizzlies
Minnesota Timberwolves
Phoenix Suns
Portland Trail Blazers
Sacramento Kings
San Antonio Spurs
Seattle Supersonics
Utah Jazz

* The name of the basketball team is pronounced SELL-tiks—no offense intended to persons of Celtic (KELL-tik) ancestry.

• • • • • • • • • • • • •

WATCHING BASKETBALL

Competitive basketball is played on a 50' x 94' indoor court with a wooden floor. The goal is an 18" hoop (traditionally a peach-picker's basket with the bottom cut out) mounted 10' above the floor. Recreational basketball is often played outdoors on an asphalt court—or half-court, with both teams shooting into the same hoop.

Teams of five *pass* and *dribble* the ball, as in soccer, into shooting position and aim for the basket either directly or by bouncing the ball off a backboard behind the hoop. (Dribbling, in basketball, is bouncing the ball off the floor.) In normal play, a *basket* (goal) is worth two points if the shot is taken close to the hoop and three points if shot from beyond the *3-point line,* an arc roughly 23' from the basket. A basket scored on a *free throw*—an unimpeded shot awarded after a foul, such as tripping or shoving—is worth one point. Free throws are taken from a line 15' from the basket, usually by the player who was fouled.

A player who commits five fouls in a game—or two *technical fouls,* such as arguing or unsportsmanlike conduct—is ejected. However, players *talk trash*—taunt and tease opposing players—in an attempt to distract their attention from the ball.

A professional basketball game is 48 minutes of play divided into 12-minute periods, with an intermission at halftime. Five-minute overtime periods are added to break a tie. The clock stops after a foul or when a team calls for a *time out* (allowed six times per game, but no more than three in the fourth period). The team with possession must take at least one shot every 24 seconds or forfeit the ball to the other team.

It's a fairly simple game. For more details about rules, schedules, and teams, visit **www.nba.com**.

SOCCER (FOOTBALL)

The world's most popular sport is steadily gaining popularity in the United States, but here it is less popular as a spectator sport than as an afterschool pastime for children and teens. There is men's professional **Major League Soccer**, but in general, U.S. women are better at soccer than U.S. men. (The men's national team has never competed in World Cup semifinals or an Olympic medal match; the women's national team has won several Olympic and World Cup titles.) The men's season is April through late October, with playoffs in November; for more information, visit www.MLSnet.com.

Indoor soccer, played on a court the size and shape of a hockey rink, has a small but loyal following. It's a fast-paced game with smaller teams and generally more scoring than field soccer, and it's played during the winter. Most indoor soccer is played at the *semi-pro* level—by part-time professional athletes who have other jobs. Visit www.usindoor.com or www.misl.com.

HOCKEY

Ice hockey has a smaller following than the three major spectator sports, but it's a loyal audience. The **National Hockey League**, which actually includes teams from the United States and Canada, plays from October through April, with the regular season followed by the **Stanley Cup** tournament extending into June. Women's hockey is a relatively

WOMEN'S NATIONAL BASKETBALL ASSOCIATION

Eastern Conference (6 teams)
- Charlotte Sting
- Connecticut Sun
- Detroit Shock
- Indiana Fever
- New York Liberty
- Washington Mystics

Western Conference (7 teams)
- Houston Comets
- Los Angeles Sparks
- Minnesota Lynx
- Phoenix Mercury
- Sacramento Monarchs
- San Antonio Silver Stars
- Seattle Storm

• • • • • • • • • • • • • •

AMERICA'S FAVORITE LIVE SPECTATOR SPORT

Although football, baseball, and basketball command larger TV audiences, the sport that draws the biggest crowds in the United States is **auto racing**. An average NFL game draws 63,000 fans; a big-league baseball game, 31,000; an NBA game, 21,000. An average **NASCAR** (National Association of Stock Car Auto Racing) event on the Winston Cup trophy circuit draws 191,000 fans, and a race on the NASCAR Busch Grand National circuit draws an average of 69,000. In late February, 200,000 fans in Florida and millions on TV watch the **Daytona 500**, the signature event in the Winston Cup series. Check out www.nascar.com. Another major race is the **Indianapolis 500** in late May—with even louder, faster cars designed for racing. Visit www.indy500.com.

• • • • • • • • • • • • • •

new sport in the United States and is not played professionally, though the United States won the first Olympic gold medal ever awarded in women's hockey (1998). For information about pro hockey, visit www.nhl.com.

O beautiful for spacious skies, for amber waves of grain,
For purple mountains' majesty above the fruited plain...
America, America, God shed His grace on thee
And crown thy good with brotherhood from sea to shining sea

— "America the Beautiful" by Katharine
Lee Bates

The United States is the fourth-largest country in the world—9.4 million square kilometers. It includes three mountain ranges each bigger than Japan and a desert almost as big as Saudi Arabia. On any given day, a national weather map might show temperatures of 0°F and 100°F and many in between; there are places where it has never snowed and places where the snow never melts. And each region of the country has its own distinctive cultural traits and reputations—stereotypes, of course, but most with a kernel of truth at the heart. Once you know your way around your new city, you'll probably want to start exploring on a larger scale. If you stay long enough, you might even move to another city someday—Americans move around a lot. Between 1995 and 2000, 46% of the U.S. population over the age of 5 had moved to a new home. Grab a good map or an atlas and start to get your bearings.

REGIONS & STATES

As in any vast country, the predominant language is spoken with many different accents and in slightly different dialects. With practice, you can listen to the way Americans talk and guess what part of the country they come from—and be right most of the time. There are many different ways to group the states into unofficial regions. For example, the **continental United States**—the area between Canada and Mexico, excluding the states of Alaska and Hawaii and the offshore

Western, Mountain, Central, and Eastern Time Zones

235

territories—cover four time zones: **Eastern, Central, Mountain,** and **Pacific**. Some people think of the areas east and west of the **Mississippi River** as distinct regions—or, likewise, the areas east and west of the **Continental Divide**, the line where rivers to the east flow into the Atlantic Ocean and rivers to the west flow into the Pacific. In the East, etched in people's consciousness is the **Mason-Dixon Line** that once divided the states that allowed slavery from those that did not; with just a few exceptions, the states to the south of this line were members of the Confederacy that seceded from the nation in 1861, resulting in four years of civil war.

Still other regions are defined by industry, such as the steel-producing **Rust Belt** along the Ohio River and the Great Lakes, or by cultural attributes, such as the conservative **Bible Belt** through the central and southeastern states. Mountain ranges, deserts, and other **physical features** can be used to distinguish one interstate area from another. And a few groups of states enter into regional interstate **compacts**, or agreements, such as the interstate plans for stewardship of the Chesapeake Bay, the Great Lakes, or the Colorado River.

NATIONAL PARKS

Many of the nation's most beautiful places, or places of special cultural significance, are designated **National Parks** and protected by the U.S. Department of the Interior for the common enjoyment of the public and future generations. The National Parks system includes, just for a few examples, 1.4 million acres of Florida wetlands; a forest of California redwood trees 350 feet tall; a North Atlantic fjord; natural stone arches carved by the winds of the Utah desert; hundreds of miles of caves beneath New Mexico and Kentucky; wild bison (American buffalo) habitats on the North Dakota prairie; a Pacific Northwest rainforest in Washington state; and Utah canyons, Virginia mountains, lush islands in the Great Lakes, and cliff dwellings of ancient peoples of Colorado. The great monuments of Washington, D.C. and the historic sites of the Revolution and the Civil War are also maintained by the National Park Service.

Bookstores and travel outfitters sell a number of guides to the National Parks system and detailed guides to specific parks, but you can also get free information from the National Park Service at 202-619-7275 or www.nps.gov. Most parks charge an entrance fee for each carload of visitors; if you want to explore several parks, it's a good idea to get an **annual pass** from the **National Parks Foundation**. Special lifetime passes are available for seniors (age 65 or over) and people with disabilities. Call 800-467-2757 or visit www.nationalparks.org.

The regions described below are based on all of those factors, and on American custom and habit. Each of these regions has a distinct culture that reflects its history, patterns of ethnic settlement, sources of livelihood, terrain, climate, and—as always—some broad generalizations that will certainly be wrong some of the time, but will be right often enough to make them worth knowing.

ABOUT THIS INFORMATION

- **Nickname**: Most states have a widely recognized nickname that lends itself to the names of businesses, newspapers, sports teams, and school mascots throughout the state.
- **Capital**: The capital city of a state is not necessarily the largest city.
- **Cities**: Every city with a population of 100,000 or more (by the 2000 Census) is listed here.* For states with no cities of 100,000, the two largest cities other than the capital are listed.
- **Economy**: These are the industries and crops for which the state is most renowned or which are found most commonly throughout the state—not necessarily the industries or crops that bring the most revenue to the state.
- **Landmarks**: These are the natural or cultural sites most commonly associated with the state.
- **Statehood**: For the first 13 states, this is the date the U.S. Constitution was ratified by the state legislature. For states that joined the Union after the original 13, this is the year the state's delegation was admitted to Congress.

NEW ENGLAND

The Northeast is a land of rugged mountains, rugged rocky shores, and rugged people—the true and original Yankees (an indigenous word for English folk). New England is one of the few places where most people still live in small towns that govern their affairs through town hall meetings where everyone can have a chance to speak out. North of Boston, there are few metropolitan areas and relatively few

---

*   Except in California, where there are 59. For California, only cities with a population of 150,000 or more are listed.

outposts of trendy nationwide retail chains; instead, you'll find small businesses run by local families in picturesque old mill towns or former whaling villages. But today, the whaling boats shoot photos instead of harpoons.

NEW ENGLAND RECOMMENDED READING:

- The poetry of Robert Frost
- *A Week on the Concord and Merrimack Rivers* by Henry David Thoreau
- *John Adams* by David McCullough

CONNECTICUT

An affluent state just northeast of New York City, Connecticut is home to the nation's principal naval shipbuilding facility and its economy prospers from military contracts as well as a high concentration of corporate headquarters and factories.

- Nickname: Nutmeg State
- Capital: Hartford
- Cities: Bridgeport, New Haven, Stamford, Waterbury
- Economy: insurance, finance, manufacturing
- Landmarks: Mystic Seaport, Yale University, Dinosaur State Park
- Statehood: 5th state (1788)

MAINE

The rocky coast of Maine, with picture-perfect lighthouses and wooden lobster boats in every cove, draws lots of tourists in the summer—but the hardy locals like to say, "If you can't handle the winter, you don't deserve the summer." Most of the population lives *down east,* as they say—near the coast. The interior, the northeastern corner of the country, is a vast woodland populated mainly by timber workers. Paper mills line the Androscoggin and Kennebec Rivers, which have started to recover from decades of uncontrolled pollution. If you drive inland, through the countless lakes and ponds of the northern Appalachian Mountains, watch out for moose.

- Nickname: Pine Tree State
- Capital: Augusta
- Cities: Portland, Lewiston-Auburn, Bangor
- Economy: timber, paper, seafood, potatoes, tourism
- Landmarks: Acadia NP, Mt. Katahdin, Allagash Wilderness Waterway, historic lighthouses
- Statehood: 23rd state (1820)

MASSACHUSETTS

 Home of Harvard University, MIT, U-Mass Amherst, Boston College, Boston University, Brandeis, Smith, and Hampshire, among other respected colleges and universities, Massachusetts is one of the strongholds of higher education in the United States. It's also the cradle of the American Revolution, which broke out with skirmishes at Lexington and Concord in 1775. Cape Cod and the islands of Martha's Vineyard and Nantucket are fashionable sailing resorts.

- Nickname: Bay State
- Capital: Boston
- Cities: Worcester, Springfield, Cambridge, Lowell
- Economy: technology, finance, tourism
- Landmarks: Boston Common, Cape Cod National Seashore, Old North Church
- Statehood: 6th state (1788)

NEW HAMPSHIRE

 New Hampshire holds its primary elections earlier than any other state, so presidential hopefuls come here early and often as they seek their respective parties' nominations to run in the general election. The state's most celebrated landmark, the Old Man of the Mountains—a natural stone formation resembling a human face—collapsed in an avalanche in 2003; it is immortalized, however, in the New Hampshire commemorative quarters issued by the U.S. Mint three years earlier.

- Nickname: Granite State
- Capital: Concord
- Cities: Manchester, Nashua
- Economy: quarrying, tourism

- Landmarks: Mt. Washington, Lake Winnepesaukee, Bretton Woods, Dartmouth College
- Statehood: 9th state (1788)

RHODE ISLAND

 The smallest state in land area, Rhode Island, has almost twice the population of the largest (Alaska). It also has the longest name: officially, Rhode Island and Providence Plantations. The state is not, in fact, an island, but the Narragansett Bay island that shares its name is the venue of the America's Cup international sailboat race held every four years. The state has a long history as a haven of religious freedom—founded by religious outcasts from colonial Massachusetts, it is home to the continent's first Quaker meetinghouse and oldest surviving Jewish synagogue.

- Nickname: Ocean State
- Capital: Providence
- Cities: Warwick, Newport
- Economy: manufacturing (notably toys), finance
- Landmarks: Narragansett Bay, Block Island
- Statehood: 13th state (1790)

VERMONT

 Best known for maple syrup, a sweet and costly condiment made from the sap of maple trees, Vermont is also a notable dairy producer whose biggest corporation is Ben & Jerry's ice cream company. The state is also famous for left-leaning politics: it's the only state to send a self-declared socialist to Congress and was the first to recognize a form of same-sex marriage.

- Nickname: Green Mountain State
- Capital: Montpelier
- Cities: Burlington, Rutland, Bennington
- Economy: dairy, apples, quarrying
- Landmarks: Lake Champlain, Green Mountain National Forest, Stowe ski resort
- Statehood: 14th state (1791)—first new state to join the Union after the founding colonies

THE MID-ATLANTIC

From colonial days, the region from New York Harbor to the mouth of the Chesapeake Bay has been busy with shipping and industry. The Appalachian Mountains made the region rich with coal and steel; the coastal plains made it rich with tobacco. The Civil War between Northern loyalists and Southern separatists raged across this central region for four bloody years, and almost every town and county here has its share of little monuments and markers to that grim history.

MID-ATLANTIC RECOMMENDED READING:

* *The Killer Angels* by Michael Shaara
* *Beautiful Swimmers* by William Warner
* *Narrative of the Life, My Bondage and My Freedom* by Frederick Douglass

DELAWARE

The state of Delaware is dominated by the chemical industry in general and DuPont in particular. Its low taxes and business-friendly state laws also attract many corporations from all over the country; they maintain official headquarters here just to have a Delaware address. The tiny state has several beach resorts in the south and legal gambling resorts in the north.

* Nickname: The First State
* Capital: Dover
* Cities: Wilmington, Rehoboth Beach
* Economy: chemicals, corporate administration, shipping
* Landmarks: Delaware Memorial Bridge, Cape Henlopen, Chesapeake & Delaware Canal
* Statehood: 1st state (1787)

DISTRICT OF COLUMBIA

The nation's capital is not only the seat of government, but a living city with nearly 600,000 residents. The city has been allowed limited self-government since 1973, but is still officially governed as a colony by the U.S. Congress. The federal government is the District's main industry—not only is the government the nation's largest employer, but it creates jobs for vast ranks of messengers, janitors, bus drivers, sandwich makers, journalists, lobbyists, and lawyers. Tourism is also a huge industry in the hometown of the nation's most famous monuments, the Kennedy Center for the Performing Arts, most of the Smithsonian Institution museums, and—on display under special glass designed to withstand an explosion—the Constitution itself.

District residents voted in 1980 to apply for statehood, but Congress refused; the Constitution requires the seat of the federal government to be on federal land outside the influence of any state government. Statehooders want to redraw the boundaries of the District to separate the seat of government from the residential city.

MARYLAND

The Chesapeake Bay carries modern cargo ships to the busy Port of Baltimore; destroyers to the U.S. Naval Academy; and old-fashioned wooden skipjacks to the choice coves for harvesting oysters, clams, and the state's signature delicacy, the blue crab. And the twin spans of the Chesapeake Bay Bridge carry city dwellers to the bustling beaches of Ocean City and the quiet, rustic beaches of Assateague Island National Seashore.

- Nickname: The Free State
- Capital: Annapolis
- Cities: Baltimore, Rockville
- Economy: seafood, poultry, tobacco, biotech, coal, shipping
- Landmarks: Chesapeake Bay, Ft. McHenry, Mason-Dixon Line
- Statehood: 7th state (1788)

NEW JERSEY

Between the shipyards of Newark and the bridges and tunnels crossing the Hudson River into New York City, "Joisey" can seem like a chemical wasteland. But the state also has farms that produce prized cranberry, blueberry, and tomato crops, and the vast forest of the Pine Barrens region is still largely unspoiled.

Endangered birds find sanctuary at Cape May, and up the coast is Atlantic City, the nation's biggest gambling resort outside Nevada.

- Nickname: Garden State
- Capital: Trenton
- Cities: Newark, Jersey City, Paterson, Elizabeth
- Economy: manufacturing, chemicals, pharmaceuticals, shipping, gambling, tourism
- Landmarks: Delaware Water Gap, Princeton University, New Jersey Turnpike
- Statehood: 3rd state (1787)

NEW YORK

 No few words can do justice to the busy, bewildering, diverse vastness of New York City—which may be why so many songs have been written about the place, from Woody Guthrie to Frank Sinatra to Simon & Garfunkel. The state (of which New York City is just the southeast corner) was once the homeland of the Iroquois nation, whose government—a federal structure with separation of powers—was studied carefully by the founders of the United States. New York boasts many prestigious colleges and universities, including Columbia, Cornell, New York University, Syracuse, Rensselaer, Vassar, and the U.S. Military Academy, and important cultural institutions such as the Guggenheim Museum, the Metropolitan Museum of Art, the Museum of Modern Art, the Cooper-Hewitt Museum, Carnegie Hall, and Lincoln Center for the Performing Arts. Oh, and the United Nations.

- Nickname: Empire State
- Capital: Albany
- Cities: New York City, Buffalo, Rochester, Syracuse, Yonkers
- Economy: finance, advertising, media, tourism, manufacturing, shipping
- Landmarks: Statue of Liberty, Niagara Falls, Broadway theater district, Wall Street, Empire State Building, Central Park, Ground Zero (World Trade Center site)
- Statehood: 11th state (1788)

PENNSYLVANIA

In 1776, the Liberty Bell in Philadelphia rang above Independence Hall to announce that the colonial delegates meeting there in 1776 had unanimously passed a resolution declaring their independence from England and creating the United States of America. Ironically, the state founded by pacifist Quakers, the first state to abolish slavery, the state that today is still home to peaceful Amish sects that shun most modern technology, was also the site of the bloodiest battle in U.S. history. At Gettysburg, in 1863, an estimated 5,600 Americans were killed and 27,000 wounded—all at the hands of other Americans, in the Civil War. Abraham Lincoln's speech at the dedication of the Army cemetery there is perhaps the most celebrated piece of American oratory—read it in Appendix C.

- Nicknames: Keystone State, Quaker State
- Capital: Harrisburg
- Cities: Philadelphia, Pittsburgh, Erie, Allentown
- Economy: coal, steel, snack foods
- Landmarks: Independence Hall and the Liberty Bell, Gettysburg National Battlefield Park, Philadelphia Navy Yard
- Statehood: 2nd state (1787)

THE SOUTH

Also known as Dixie, this is the region that seceded from the United States in 1861 when the federal government sought to abolish slavery. Almost a century later, federal troops came here again to end racial segregation in schools. Even after generations of progress and healing, the South is still a conservative place, and many Southerners still assert the doctrine of *states' rights*—freedom from excessive federal involvement in state affairs.

DIXIE RECOMMENDED READING:

- *The Color Purple* by Alice Walker

- *To Kill a Mockingbird* by Harper Lee
- *Gone with the Wind* by Margaret Mitchell

ALABAMA

Montgomery, Alabama was the birthplace of the civil rights movement of the 1950s and '60s. There Rosa Parks defied the segregation policy on city buses, and young Rev. Martin Luther King Jr. led a successful boycott to end legal segregation on the buses. Over the next 12 years, Dr. King led protests in Selma and Birmingham as well, facing violent repression and death threats; in Montgomery, he founded the influential Southern Christian Leadership Conference, putting the nonviolent resistance methods of Mohandas Gandhi to use in the struggle for racial justice in the United States.

- Nickname: Heart of Dixie
- Capital: Montgomery
- Cities: Birmingham, Huntsville, Mobile
- Economy: cotton, mining, manufacturing, aerospace
- Landmarks: Mobile Bay, Russell Cave National Monument
- Statehood: 22nd state (1819)

ARKANSAS

The stereotypical image of Arkansas is of rugged hill folk living in remote homesteads, but actually, the state is home to industrial poultry farms, mineral quarries, and even some diamond deposits—as well as the headquarters of the world's biggest retail company, Wal-Mart. In 1957, the state resisted new federal laws that ended racial segregation of public schools; federal troops were sent to escort African-American children to school. Today, however, Arkansas is best known as the birthplace of President Bill Clinton. It was also the first state to elect a female U.S. Senator: Hattie Caraway, in 1932.

- Nickname: Land of Opportunity
- Capital: Little Rock
- Cities: Ft. Smith, Pine Bluff
- Economy: poultry, mining, rice
- Landmarks: Hot Springs NP
- Statehood: 25th state (1836)

FLORIDA

A low-lying peninsula between the Atlantic Ocean and the Gulf of Mexico, Florida grows most of the nation's oranges and grapefruit, and its warm climate attracts many retirees who settle here or spend the winter here. The vast Everglades wetlands in the south are the main habitat of the endangered manatee, and the state is also home to alligators and rare birds. The nation's first spaceport is here—until the 1980s, almost all U.S. spacecraft were launched from the Kennedy Space Center at Cape Canaveral.*

- Nickname: Sunshine State
- Capital: Tallahassee
- Cities: Miami, Tampa, St. Petersburg, Hialeah, Jacksonville, Orlando, Ft. Lauderdale, Hollywood, Clearwater, Coral Springs, Pembroke Pines, Cape Coral
- Economy: tourism, citrus, aerospace, retirement living
- Landmarks: Kennedy Space Center, Everglades NP, Walt Disney World
- Statehood: 27th state (1845)

GEORGIA

Atlanta, where the Coca-Cola Company is based, established itself as a major world city when it hosted the 1996 Olympics, and Hartsfield-Jackson International Airport there is one of the world's busiest. But most of the state—the biggest state east of the Mississippi River—is still rural and conservative. There are still traces of resentment lingering from the Civil War: Union troops left a 200-mile swath of destruction and looting from Atlanta to the coast, burning civilian farms and houses. Only in the 1990s did Georgia remove the old emblem of the Confederacy from the state flag.

- Nickname: Peachtree State
- Capital: Atlanta
- Cities: Columbus, Augusta, Athens, Savannah
- Economy: cotton, peanuts, peaches, media, finance, technology

---

* Spacecraft are also launched at Vandenberg Air Force Base in California and Wallops Island in Virginia.

- Landmarks: Okefenokee Swamp, Stone Mtn., Ft. Benning, Centennial Olympic Park
- Statehood: 4th state (1788)

LOUISIANA

Home of Cajun culture—descendants of French-Canadian settlers who migrated down the Mississippi River—Louisiana is famous for spicy creole cuisine and lively zydeco music, as well as New Orleans jazz and the annual Mardi Gras festival. Some residents speak a local Cajun dialect blending English and French. In Louisiana, the local unit of government is called a *parish* instead of a county.

- Nickname: Pelican State
- Capital: Baton Rouge
- Cities: New Orleans, Shreveport, Lafayette
- Economy: oil refining, seafood, tourism, agriculture
- Landmarks: Mississippi Delta, Bourbon Street
- Statehood: 18th state (1812)

MISSISSIPPI

A state with a diverse agricultural and industrial economy, Mississippi is unfortunately known also as the scene of violent resistance to the civil rights revolution of the 1960s. Volunteers called "Freedom Riders" came here from the Northeast in 1964 to help African-American citizens register to vote, and several volunteers were assassinated. A state and its people change with the times, but reputations linger, and this history is still the subject of movies and songs.

- Nickname: Magnolia State
- Capital: Jackson
- Cities: Biloxi, Gulfport, Tupelo
- Economy: cotton, soybeans, oil, poultry, cattle
- Landmarks: Vicksburg battlefield, Mississippi Sandhill Crane National Wildlife Refuge
- Statehood: 20th state (1817)

NORTH CAROLINA

 Best known as a producer of cigarettes and furniture, North Carolina also has a large and growing sector devoted to scientific research. The cities of Raleigh, Durham, and Chapel Hill are collectively known as the "Research Triangle," and the central part of the state has a high concentration of colleges and universities—Duke, the University of North Carolina (Chapel Hill, Greensboro, Charlotte, and Asheville), Wake Forest, Guilford, and Elon, among others. On the beach at Kitty Hawk, in 1903, Wilbur & Orville Wright conducted the first successful airplane flight. North Carolina also draws beach crowds to the east and rock climbers to the west, and is famously fanatical about college basketball.

- Nickname: Tarheel State
- Capital: Raleigh
- Cities: Charlotte, Greensboro, Winston-Salem, Fayetteville, Durham
- Economy: tobacco, furniture, insurance, banking, research
- Landmarks: Kitty Hawk, Outer Banks, Great Smoky Mountains NP, Ft. Bragg
- Statehood: 12th state (1789)

SOUTH CAROLINA

 This is the climate boundary between the temperate zone of the mid-Atlantic region and the northern reaches of the tropics. Palm trees and fruit orchards are found here, and some beaches are nesting grounds for giant sea turtles. The state's distinctive place in history is the outbreak of the Civil War—it was the first of 12½ states to secede from the nation, in 1860; the following spring, war broke out when federal troops refused to leave Ft. Sumter, a fortified island in Charleston Harbor.

- Nickname: Palmetto State
- Capital: Columbia
- Cities: Charleston, Greenville, Spartanburg
- Economy: peaches, tobacco, tourism
- Landmarks: Hilton Head and Myrtle Beach resorts, Ft. Sumter, Parris Island
- Statehood: 8th state (1788)

TENNESSEE

American music owes a lot to Tennessee. Nashville is the capital of the recording industry, especially (but not only) for *country* music, a modernized form of the 19th-century folk music of the Appalachian region. And Elvis Presley moved to Memphis at age 13; his estate, Graceland, is a shrine that draws thousands of pilgrims every year. Tennessee also—like Texas and North Carolina—claims to produce the country's best barbecue. (Ask any barbecue enthusiast. Many Americans have strong opinions on the subject.) Despite a lingering image of early 19th-century pioneers Daniel Boone and Davy Crockett in their coonskin hats (made from a whole raccoon pelt, complete with tail), the state is home to advanced physics research at the government's Oak Ridge laboratory.

- Nickname: Volunteer State
- Capital: Nashville
- Cities: Memphis, Knoxville, Chattanooga, Clarksville
- Economy: music production, cotton, coal
- Landmarks: Grand Ole Opry, Graceland, Great Smoky Mountains NP
- Statehood: 16th state (1796)

VIRGINIA

Virginia calls itself the "Birthplace of Presidents" and, more recently, the birthplace of the internet. Fair enough—nearly 20% of the nation's Presidents have been born in Virginia, including four of the first five. And the Virginia suburbs of Washington, D.C. are home to Network Solutions Inc., the first company to register internet domains, and the nation's largest internet service provider, America Online. Outside the cluster of high-tech businesses in the north, however, Virginia remains an agricultural state producing ham and tobacco. One of the nation's biggest naval bases is at Norfolk, near the site of the first battle ever fought between armored ships (during the Civil War). A state with a strong sense of history, Virginia features the first permanent European settlement in North America (Jamestown); also, the Civil War ended here when, in 1865, General Robert E. Lee surrendered the rebel army to General Ulysses S. Grant in the village of Appomattox.

- Nickname: Old Dominion
- Capital: Richmond
- Cities: Virginia Beach, Norfolk, Chesapeake, Arlington, Newport News, Hampton, Alexandria
- Economy: technology, tobacco, pork, shipping, aerospace
- Landmarks: Mt. Vernon, Jamestown, Williamsburg, Shenandoah NP, the Pentagon
- Statehood: 10th state (1788)

THE MIDWEST

The industrial "Rust Belt" winds through the region just west of the Appalachian coal country, making cars and steel and manufactured goods to be shipped across the Great Lakes and out to sea. Midwesterners have a reputation for being wholesome, no-nonsense folk with a strong work ethic; outside the industrial areas, the Midwest is a land of small towns and big county fairs.

MIDWEST RECOMMENDED READING:

- *Life on the Mississippi* by Mark Twain
- *The Gift of Good Land* by Wendell Berry
- *The Road to Wellville* by T. Coraghessan Boyle

ILLINOIS

Chicago, one of the world's biggest inland ports, stands near the southern tip of Lake Michigan; cargo ships can reach the North Atlantic through the Great Lakes and St. Lawrence River, and canal barges can reach the Mississippi River. The city is known for blues music and Polish-American cuisine, busy O'Hare Airport, and the green Chicago River. (Locals dye it green every St. Patrick's Day and it keeps a greenish tint all year.) The rest of the state is largely agricultural, especially producing corn for both humans and farm animals.

- Nickname: Prairie State
- Capital: Springfield

- Cities: Chicago, Rockford, Naperville, Aurora, Peoria, Joliet
- Economy: food processing, corn, shipping, finance
- Landmarks: Art Institute of Chicago, Sears Tower
- Statehood: 21st state (1818)

INDIANA

 The first U.S. automobile was made here, in 1894, and Indiana was the center of the nation's auto industry well into the 20th century. The car manufacturers moved north to Michigan, but Indiana still provides much of the steel. Aside from motor sports, the state's main hobby is basketball. South of the Great Lakes industrial region, it's a largely agricultural state; a few Amish and Bruderhof communities—agrarian religious groups that reject many modern conveniences—find haven here.

- Nickname: Hoosier State
- Capital: Indianapolis
- Cities: Ft. Wayne, Evansville, South Bend, Gary
- Economy: turkeys, soybeans, steel, manufacturing, pharmaceuticals
- Landmarks: Indianapolis Motor Speedway, southern reach of the Great Lakes
- Statehood: 19th state (1816)

IOWA

 Almost synonymous with corn, and not too different from the stereotypes portrayed in musical plays such as *State Fair* and *The Music Man,* Iowa also features a river culture of small towns along the Mississippi. Iowans are quick to point out that the state's signature crop is *feed* corn, not for human consumption but for livestock. The town of Ames is a center of agronomy research.

- Nickname: Hawkeye State
- Capital: Des Moines
- Cities: Cedar Rapids, Davenport
- Economy: corn, pork
- Landmarks: Effigy Mounds National Monument, Riverboat Museum
- Statehood: 29th state (1846)

KENTUCKY

 Birthplace of bluegrass, a uniquely American style of fiddle and banjo music, Kentucky is also renowned for bourbon whiskey and thoroughbred horse racing. The biggest event in U.S. horse racing is the Kentucky Derby in Louisville every May. There are also finance businesses in Kentucky cities that would like to leave these stereotypical images behind.

- Nickname: Bluegrass State
- Capital: Frankfort
- Cities: Louisville, Lexington-Fayette
- Economy: horses, tobacco, coal, whiskey, finance
- Landmarks: Mammoth Cave NP, Ft. Knox, Churchill Downs racetrack
- Statehood: 15th state (1792)

MICHIGAN

 Detroit is the capital of the U.S. auto industry, with the "Big Three" auto manufacturers—Ford, General Motors, and Chrysler—based here. Nicknamed the Motor City, Detroit is also the birthplace of Motown music, an upbeat style exemplified by Aretha Franklin, the Temptations, and Diana Ross and the Supremes. Michigan also produces most of the nation's breakfast cereal. The state is divided by the Mackinac Straits between Lake Michigan and Lake Huron; until a five-mile suspension bridge was completed in 1957, you had to travel through Wisconsin (or by boat) to go from the Lower Peninsula to the isolated Upper Peninsula.

- Nickname: Wolverine State
- Capital: Lansing
- Cities: Detroit, Grand Rapids, Warren, Flint, Sterling Heights, Ann Arbor, Livonia
- Economy: autos, steel, food processing, chemicals, appliances
- Landmarks: Mackinac Straits Bridge, Isle Royale NP
- Statehood: 26th state (1837)

MINNESOTA

Peppered with more than 10,000 lakes created by ancient glaciers, Minnesota is a popular place for camping and fishing. The "Twin

Cities" of Minneapolis and St. Paul straddle the Mississippi River, which has its source in the woods around Lake Itasca. The Minnesota Vikings football team takes its name from the fact that the first Europeans here were Scandinavian trappers and traders. This was the first state to elect a governor from the Reform Party—former wrestler Jesse Ventura, in 1998.

- Nickname: Gopher State
- Capital: Minneapolis
- Cities: St. Paul, Duluth
- Economy: iron, food processing, technology, dairy
- Landmarks: source of the Mississippi River
- Statehood: 32nd state (1858)

MISSOURI

The city of St. Louis calls itself the "Gateway to the West," as it was here that the Army Corps of Discovery, led by Meriwether Lewis and William Clark, set out in 1803 to survey the 800,000 square miles that President Thomas Jefferson had purchased from Napoleon for $15 million—the Louisiana Purchase. Missouri also gave the literary world Mark Twain, one of the nation's most influential writers. Though its image is defined by Twain's riverboat culture, Missouri is the home of biotechnology giant Monsanto and several major aerospace companies—as well as the nation's biggest beer producer, Anheuser-Busch.

- Nickname: Show Me State
- Capital: Jefferson City
- Cities: Kansas City, St. Louis, Springfield, Independence
- Economy: brewing, biotech, chemicals, agriculture, aerospace
- Landmarks: Gateway Arch, Branson resort
- Statehood: 24th state (1821)

OHIO

The Ohio River and the shores of Lake Erie are lined with steel mills and heavy industry, and some parts of Ohio are dangerously polluted; in 1969, the Cuyahoga River in Cleveland actually caught on fire, and the world's biggest toxic waste incinerator is just south of Youngstown. But the state provides most of the world's tires and significant amounts of steel and manufactured goods. In the early 19th century, the legendary Johnny Appleseed—a Pennsylvania-born planter named John Chapman—wandered Ohio planting apple trees.

- Nickname: Buckeye State
- Capital: Columbus
- Cities: Cleveland, Cincinnati, Toledo, Akron, Dayton
- Economy: rubber, steel, manufacturing, chemicals, pork, corn, soybeans
- Landmarks: ancient burial mounds near Chillicothe
- Statehood: 17th state (1803)

WEST VIRGINIA

 You can make a rough map of West Virginia by looking at the palm of your right hand and curling the last three fingers toward yourself. The subject of many mean jokes about rustic or "redneck" families, mountainous West Virginia is indeed a state of small towns that depend on coal mining and the steel industry. It's the only state that has *no* major flatlands, and it attracts many rock climbers and whitewater boating enthusiasts. In 1859, a band of abolitionists (anti-slavery partisans) led by John Brown seized a small military depot in the town of Harper's Ferry, hoping to arm themselves for a violent revolt against the government that still allowed slavery. The subsequent execution of John Brown set a series of political events in motion that led to the Civil War.

- Nickname: Mountain State
- Capital: Charleston
- Cities: Huntington, Wheeling, Parkersburg
- Economy: coal, steel, oil
- Landmarks: Harper's Ferry, New River Gorge, National Radio Astronomy Observatory
- Statehood: 35th state (1863)

WISCONSIN

"America's Dairyland," Wisconsin is famous for its butter and cheese. It's also a stronghold of liberal politics, with more Greens elected to office than any state except California; the first openly lesbian member of the U.S. House of Representatives (Tammy Baldwin); and the

nation's only community-owned professional sports team, the Green Bay Packers. Dotted by many lakes, Wisconsin is nestled between Lake Superior and Lake Michigan.
   • Nickname: Badger State
   • Capital: Madison
- Cities: Milwaukee, Green Bay
- Economy: dairy, shipping, textiles, brewing, insurance
- Landmarks: Apostle Island, Ice Age National Scientific Reserve
- Statehood: 30th state (1848)

GREAT PLAINS

Also called the Heartland, this region is often described as the "breadbasket of the world"— a vast, fertile area the size of India that produces most of the nation's grain and live-stock. Many of the people here are descendants of the pioneer families that settled here a century and a half ago. Though it sprawls more than a thousand miles north and west of the modern state of Louisiana, this region was the bulk of the Louisiana Territory purchased from France for $15 million—about 3¢ an acre—in 1803.

GREAT PLAINS RECOMMENDED READING:

- *The Grapes of Wrath* by John Steinbeck
- *Little House on the Prairie* by Laura Ingalls Wilder
- *Woody Guthrie: A Life* by Joe Klein

KANSAS

Once a state of wheatfields and cattle pastures, Kansas also has pockets of industry near the Missouri River, producing farm machines and aircraft parts. Kansas City, KS and Kansas City, MO face each other across the Missouri River. The book and movie *The Wizard of Oz* gave Kansas a reputation for tornadoes; this is indeed tornado country, but it extends south to Texas and east to Ohio. Small oil rigs dot the land-scape, too, here at the northern fringe of the same oil deposits that made Texas rich.

- Nickname: Sunflower State
- Capital: Topeka
- Cities: Wichita, Kansas City, Overland Park
- Economy: wheat, cattle, oil, food processing, aerospace
- Landmarks: Ft. Leavenworth
- Statehood: 34 (1861)

NEBRASKA

 Many U.S. cities and farms occupy land that the nation once recognized as the territory of the indigenous people, but Nebraska is an extreme example: the whole state was once recognized as Oglala Sioux land in which white people were not allowed to settle. By the middle of the 19th century, Congress changed its mind, and some of the U.S. migrants crossing the plains after the California gold rush of 1849 settled along the wagon routes. This agrarian state is the only one with a one-chamber legislature, and the state constitution protects family farms from being taken over by big farming conglomerates.

- Nickname: Cornhusker State
- Capital: Lincoln
- Cities: Omaha, Bellevue
- Economy: cattle, corn, wheat, food processing
- Landmarks: Chimney Rock, Offutt Air Force Base
- Statehood: 37th state (1867)

NORTH DAKOTA

 This is where the Lewis & Clark expedition spent the winter, at Ft. Mandan, and met Sacagawea, who became their interpreter among the indigenous people of the Northwest and only the second female historical figure depicted on American money. A vast agrarian land of grains and feedgrasses, North Dakota also boasts scenic lakes and canyons. Some residents want to rename the state simply Dakota, to avoid the misleading image of a chilly arctic "North."

- Nickname: Sioux State
- Capital: Bismarck

- Cities: Fargo, Grand Forks
- Economy: flax, hay, barley, wheat, beet sugar
- Landmarks: Ft. Mandan, Theodore Roosevelt National Memorial Park
- Statehood: 39th state (1889)

OKLAHOMA

Mention this state to Americans from "back East" and there's a good chance they will burst into song: "Ooooh-klahoma, where the wind comes sweeping down the plain," the opening lines from a musical play about everyday life on the frontier on the eve of the Industrial Revolution. Even with its oil deposits, Oklahoma has had a rough history. As novelist John Steinbeck recalls in *The Grapes of Wrath* and folksinger Woody Guthrie recalls in dozens of songs, dust storms in the 1930s drove many struggling Oklahoma farmers off their land to become migrant workers in California fruit orchards. And in 1995, American terrorists led by Timothy McVeigh set off a crude but devastating truck bomb at a federal office building in Oklahoma City, killing 168 people.

- Nickname: Sooner State
- Capital: Oklahoma City
- Cities: Tulsa, Lawton
- Economy: wheat, corn, cattle, oil
- Landmarks: Oklahoma City National Memorial
- Statehood: 46th state (1907)

SOUTH DAKOTA

The Sioux nation held out against U.S. settlement of South Dakota until 1890, when the U.S. Army massacred the Sioux at Wounded Knee Creek. Today Wounded Knee and the neighboring village of Pine Ridge are part of a Sioux reservation that is one of the poorest areas in the country. In the 1970s, Native American activists occupied a federal courthouse and ended up in a gunfight with FBI agents; activist Leonard Peltier was sent to prison, and he is considered a political prisoner by Amnesty International and many Americans who believe he did not have a fair trial. The state is most famous, however, for giant statues: on the cliffs of Mt. Rushmore, the faces of Presidents George Washington, Thomas Jefferson, Abraham Lincoln, and Theodore (Teddy) Roosevelt are carved in granite, each 60 feet tall, and a 560-foot-tall likeness of Sioux leader Crazy Horse is taking shape on the cliffs of Thunderhead Mountain.

- Nickname: Coyote State
- Capital: Pierre
- Cities: Sioux Falls, Rapid City
- Economy: food processing, cattle, mining
- Landmarks: Badlands NP, Mt. Rushmore, Crazy Horse monument, Wounded Knee
- Statehood: 40th state (1889)

THE WEST

Glorified in hundreds of old movies about gun-toting cowboys, the West is indeed suited to people of a self-reliant spirit. Distances are great between small towns here, and outside the cities of east Texas oil country and the vast retirement towns of Arizona, the deserts and canyons of this region are among the last remaining places where Americans have not built a burger joint and souvenir shop in the foreground of every magnificent landscape.

RECOMMENDED READING OF THE WEST:

- *Desert Solitaire* by Edward Abbey
- *Ceremony* by Leslie Marmon Silko
- *A Story that Stands Like a Dam* by Russell Martin

ARIZONA

Arizona's warm, dry climate has attracted older and retired Americans for more than a century. The Grand Canyon of the Colorado River is a vast landscape cut a mile deep into the red rock of the desert, and no words can prepare you for your first glimpse of it. Elsewhere, the desert state features saguaro cactus plants

70 feet tall and hundreds of years old, among many other plant and animal species not found anywhere else in the world.
- Nickname: Grand Canyon State
- Capital: Phoenix
- Cities: Tucson, Mesa, Glendale, Scottsdale, Chandler, Tempe, Gilbert, Peoria
- Economy: copper, precious metals, retirement living, tourism
- Landmarks: Grand Canyon NP, Lake Havasu, Petrified Forest NP, Painted Desert, Glen Canyon Dam
- Statehood: 48th state (1912)

COLORADO

From east to west, Colorado slopes up from the Great Plains until, abruptly, the Rocky Mountains rise to snowy peaks; draping over the Continental Divide, the state stretches into the canyons of the Southwestern desert. "There's gold in them there hills," as some hopeful pioneer always says in movies about the Old West, and there's silver and industrial metals too—but mostly Colorado is a paradise for skiers and other outdoor enthusiasts, who flock to mountain resorts such as Aspen and Vail.
- Nickname: Centennial State
- Capital: Denver
- Cities: Colorado Springs, Aurora, Lakewood, Ft. Collins, Arvada, Pueblo, Westminster
- Economy: precious metals, tourism, brewing
- Landmarks: Pike's Peak, Rocky Mountains NP, Mesa Verde NP, Dinosaur National Monument
- Statehood: 38th state (1876)

IDAHO

Mountain lions and bighorn sheep stride around like they own the place, in a sense, they do. The Bitterroot Mountains north of the Salmon River are the largest region of the continental United States not traversed by roads. To the west, boaters and rafters love to "run" Hell's Canyon on the Snake River. The timber industry takes a busy saw to Idaho's forests, and a lot of gems and precious metals come from

Idaho's mines, but the state is best known as the leading producer of potatoes in a nation whose motto, it sometimes seems, is "Would you like fries with that?"

- Nickname: Gem State
- Capital: Boise
- Cities: Pocatello, Idaho Falls
- Economy: potatoes, lumber, paper, mining
- Landmarks: Hell's Canyon
- Statehood: 43rd state (1890)

MONTANA

This is one of the few places where Native Americans defeated the U.S. Army in the territorial wars of the 19th century. The Dakota nation stopped General George Custer's cavalry at Little Big Horn in 1876, and a year later, the Nez Perce nation stopped the federal troops at Big Hole. But U.S. mining companies made their way into the Rocky Mountains anyway, and metals—especially copper—dominate the state's economy. Perhaps the most famous image of Montana is photojournalist Margaret Bourke-White's classic photo of the massive Ft. Peck Dam under construction in 1936.

- Nickname: Big Sky Country
- Capital: Helena
- Cities: Billings, Great Falls
- Economy: copper and precious metals, timber, oil
- Landmarks: Little Big Horn battlefield, Waterton-Glacier International Peace Park
- Statehood: 41st state (1889)

NEVADA

The resort city of Las Vegas, where gambling is legal and a huge industry, is a favorite venue for conventions and trade shows. The state has a reputation for speedy processing of marriage licenses and divorce decrees, and for legal prostitution, opulent hotels, and nightly performances by big-name entertainers. But that's all concentrated in resort areas—Reno and Lake Tahoe as well as Las Vegas. Elsewhere, the state is desert and mesas (flat-topped mountains), with some boating and fishing made possible by Hoover Dam on the Colorado River.

The Nevada Test Site is a Department of Energy reservation where the government tested nuclear weapons throughout the Cold War.

- Nickname: Silver State
- Capital: Carson City
- Cities: Las Vegas, Reno, Henderson
- Economy: gambling, tourism, convention services, precious metals
- Landmarks: Hoover Dam, Nevada Test Site
- Statehood: 36th state (1864)

NEW MEXICO

Parts of this desert state are white sands, high in gypsum, and parts are redrock mesas where ancient peoples left carvings and dug out apartments in the cliffs. The atomic bomb was developed here, in Los Alamos, and first tested here, near Tularosa. Some of the earliest signs of human activity in North America have been found near Clovis—distinctive spearheads carved with stone tools. And UFO buffs—people who believe our planet has been visited by inhabitants of other planets—make pilgrimages to Roswell, where a mysterious accident occurred in 1957. Some Americans believe it was a secret military plane that crashed; others insist that it was an extraterrestrial spaceship and that the government has been concealing information about it all along. Either way, the story has been good for business and tourism in the little town.

- Nickname: Land of Enchantment
- Capital: Santa Fe
- Cities: Albuquerque, Las Cruces
- Economy: uranium, natural gas, oil
- Landmarks: Clovis, Roswell, Carlsbad Caverns NP, Los Alamos National Laboratory
- Statehood: 47th state (1912)

TEXAS

American expatriates in a province of Mexico seceded in 1836 and founded their own country, the Lone Star Republic, which joined the United States nine years later as the state of Texas. As depicted in movies, it was a land of cowboys and outlaws and open spaces—until 1901, when oil was discovered there. Now the state ranks second by population (behind California) as it does by size (behind Alaska). Texas has given the nation many political leaders in modern times, including George W. Bush, Lyndon Johnson, Lloyd Bentsen, Dick Cheney, Barbara Jordan, H. Ross Perot, and Sam Rayburn—and witty political critics, too, such as Molly Ivins and Jim Hightower.

- Nickname: Lone Star State
- Capital: Austin
- Cities: Houston, Dallas, San Antonio, El Paso, Ft. Worth, Arlington, Corpus Christi, Plano, Garland, Lubbock, Irving, Laredo, Amarillo, Brownsville, Grand Prairie, Pasadena, Mesquite, Abilene, Beaumont, Waco, Carrollton, McAllen, Wichita Falls
- Economy: oil, cattle, technology
- Landmarks: The Alamo, Big Bend NP, Guadalupe Mountains NP, Johnson Space Center
- Statehood: 28th state (1845)

UTAH

Adherents of the Mormon religious sect migrated here in the 1840s to escape persecution in the Midwest, and here in the desert and canyonlands, they practiced polygamy in freedom; however, Utah was not admitted to the Union as a state until the sect renounced polygamy. The population is still predominantly Mormon—the collective term for members of the Church of Jesus Christ of Latter-Day Saints—and generally quite conservative. Utah's colorful canyons and natural stone arches are protected in half a dozen big National Parks. And the state's good reputation for skiing and winter sports was magnified when Salt Lake City hosted the 2002 Winter Olympics.

- Nickname: Beehive State
- Capital: Salt Lake City
- Cities: West Valley, Provo
- Economy: copper, uranium, tourism, poultry
- Landmarks: Great Salt Lake, Arches NP, Bryce Canyon NP, Capitol Reef NP, Canyonlands NP, Zion NP, Mormon Tabernacle
- Statehood: 45th state (1896)

WYOMING

There are two dozen U.S. cities that each have a bigger population than Wyoming, the ninth largest state (almost 98,000 square miles). But population isn't everything. Wyoming was the first state to give women the right to vote, and the first to have a female governor—Nellie Ross, in the 1920s. The country's first (and still largest) National Park, Yellowstone, is mostly in Wyoming; it's a place of bubbling hot springs, geysers, geothermal vents, and indeed yellow stone stained by minerals in the water. It's a place where the crust of the Earth hasn't finished baking yet. The most famous landmark here is Old Faithful, a large geyser that erupts 18 times a day. To the south, high in the Grand Teton mountains, is the fashionable ski resort of Jackson Hole.

- Nickname: Equality State
- Capital: Cheyenne
- Cities: Casper, Laramie
- Economy: uranium, tourism, cattle, oil, quarrying
- Landmarks: Yellowstone NP, Grand Teton NP, Devil's Tower
- Statehood: 44th state (1890)

THE WEST COAST

People on the West Coast tend to be more relaxed, or *laid back,* than their perpetually hurried counterparts on the East Coast. The West Coast has a greater diversity of lifestyles, ideologies, and ethnicities than you're likely to find anywhere else in the country except New York City, Chicago, or Washington, D.C.—and it also has more varied climates and terrain. Just within 100 miles of Los Angeles, you can stand in a desert, a lime orchard, on a wooded mountaintop, or in a grove of the world's largest trees. Up the coast, there are rainforests and snow-capped volcanoes, too.

WEST COAST RECOMMENDED READING:

- *Nature Writings* by John Muir
- *On Good Land* by Michael Ableman
- *The River Why* by David James Duncan

CALIFORNIA

Los Angeles (population 3.7 million) and San Francisco (almost another million) each have their own *Newcomer's Handbooks*® and their own rich history and culture—and they're a tiny chip of this vast state. L.A. is best known as the capital of the entertainment industry—the home of most of the nation's film and TV studios, actors, directors, and writers. The San Francisco Bay area is home to prominent universities such as Stanford and Berkeley, major naval bases, and the state's most cherished landmark, the Golden Gate Bridge; also, it was the first area to gain a reputation for being hospitable to its gay and lesbian residents. Nearby is Silicon Valley—not a real valley, but the nickname of the region where most of the world's computer hardware is invented and produced—and the real Napa and Sonoma valleys, the wine capital of North America. The mountainous forests of Northern California are a battleground between timber companies and environmentalists, while in Southern California, the deserts are famous for military flight testing and the beaches are almost synonymous with surfing.

- Nickname: Golden State
- Capital: Sacramento
- Cities: Los Angeles, San Diego, San Jose, San Francisco, Long Beach, Fresno, Oakland, Santa Ana, Anaheim, Riverside, Bakersfield, Stockton, Fremont, Glendale, Huntington Beach, Modesto, San Bernardino, Chula Vista, Oxnard, Garden Grove, Oceanside, Ontario, Santa Clarita, Salinas
- Economy: technology, filmmaking, fruit and nuts, vegetables, wine, timber, aerospace
- Landmarks: Golden Gate Bridge; Hollywood studios; Yosemite NP; Redwoods NP; Sequoia-King's Canyon NP; Death Valley (hottest place in North America); Disneyland
- Statehood: 31st state (1850)

OREGON

The mighty Columbia River carries young salmon to the sea, and they swim back upstream as mature fish to spawn—or to get caught and eaten. Oregon is a leading producer of salmon, hops (a key ingredient in beer), cultivated Christmas trees, and nickel.

Parallel to the coast, about 100 miles inland, the 10,000-foot peaks of the Cascade Range attract hikers and skiers; one Cascades mountain, an extinct volcano, is filled with water nearly 2,000 feet deep—Crater Lake.

- Nickname: Beaver State
- Capital: Salem
- Cities: Portland, Eugene
- Economy: technology, salmon, hops, timber, paper, fruit, shipping
- Landmarks: Crater Lake NP, Mt. Hood, Multnomah Falls, Bonneville Dam
- Statehood: 33rd state (1859)

WASHINGTON

The Puget Sound area, the inlet at the northwest corner of the continental United States, is home to Microsoft and other technology companies. But there's nothing high-tech about the Olympic Peninsula to the west and the Cascade Range to the east—rugged, green areas whose beauty was best expressed by the jurist William O. Douglas in his hiking memoir, *Of Men and Mountains*. The gigantic Grand Coulee Dam impounds the Columbia River for 150 miles. Mount St. Helens, a volcano in the Cascades, erupted in 1980, sending storms of hot ash across thousands of square miles.

- Nickname: Evergreen State
- Capital: Olympia
- Cities: Seattle, Spokane, Tacoma, Vancouver, Bellevue
- Economy: technology, aerospace, fruit, salmon, timber, shipping
- Landmarks: Mt. Rainier NP, Mount St. Helens, Olympic NP, Grand Coulee Dam
- Statehood: 42nd state (1889)

ALASKA, HAWAII, AND OFFSHORE TERRITORIES

Though physically isolated from the continental United States, Alaska (the northwest corner of North America) and Hawaii (a group of islands in the Pacific Ocean) are states just like the 48 profiled above. The territories are a different story. These are, strictly speaking, colonies subject to U.S. law made by the U.S. Congress in which their inhabitants do not have any voting representatives. They govern their own internal affairs, but their laws are applied by U.S. courts and their native residents are U.S. citizens. In modern times, their affiliation with the United States is voluntary and mutually beneficial—in fact, Puerto Rico put the question of statehood to its voters in 1998 and chose to maintain its current status. Like the District of Columbia, each territory (except the Northern Marianas, which has a more autonomous arrangement than the others) sends a nonvoting *delegate,* or observer, to the U.S. House of Representatives. These delegates may serve on House committees and introduce bills of legislation, but cannot vote to adopt or reject a bill on the floor.

ALASKA

Russian colonists settled here in the late 18th century—after all, Russia is just 70 miles away across the Bering Strait—and stayed until 1867, when the United States purchased the territory of "Russian America" for about 2¢ an acre. Now an 800-mile pipeline brings oil from the North Coast to the port of Valdez, famous for the 1989 oil spill there by an Exxon tanker of the same name. As compensation for the land rights for the pipeline and the oilfields—and for the high cost of living in this remote state—every legal resident of Alaska is paid an annual dividend from a fund endowed by the oil industry. Roughly a third of the state lies within the Arctic Circle, where the Sun never sets at the summer solstice and never rises at the winter solstice. To the south, Denali (Mt. McKinley) rises 20,320 feet above sea level, nearly 6,200 meters—the highest peak in North America. The coast draws cruise ships full of tourists on the lookout for whales and giant Kodiak bears.

- Nickname: Yukon State
- Capital: Juneau
- Cities: Anchorage, Fairbanks
- Economy: oil, salmon, tourism
- Landmarks: Mt. McKinley NP, Glacier Bay, Arctic National Wildlife Refuge
- Statehood: 49th state (1959)

HAWAII

Aloha means both hello and goodbye in the indigenous language of Hawaii, a group of seven populated islands (and many smaller, uninhabited ones) about 3,000 miles west-southwest of Los Angeles. The United States supported indigenous rebels in the late 19th century and, in 1893, stepped in and said *aloha* to the native queen. Today there is a small Hawaiian nationalist movement, but the U.S. flag isn't likely to leave these islands anytime soon. Most of the population lives on Oahu Island, home of the historic U.S. naval base at Pearl Harbor; touristy Waikiki Beach; and the ancient volcanic crater of Diamond Head. Volcanoes Kilauea and Mauna Loa still erupt on Hawai'i Island.

- Nickname: Aloha State
- Capital: Honolulu
- Cities: Hilo, Kailua
- Economy: fruit and nuts, sugar, tourism, coffee
- Landmarks: Hawaii Volcanoes NP, Haleakala NP, Pearl Harbor, Diamond Head
- Statehood: 50th state (1959)

AMERICAN SAMOA

The Samoan Islands were colonized by the United Kingdom, Germany, and the United States in the late 19th century; by 1900, the British abandoned the islands and the United States and Germany divided the territory.

- Location: South Pacific Ocean
- Capital: Pago Pago
- Economy: tuna and canning, fruit

- Government: elected governor and legislature serve with oversight from U.S. Department of the Interior; judges appointed by Secretary of the Interior
- Web site: www.samoanet.com

GUAM

The island of Guam was colonized by Spain in the 17th century and was ceded to the United States in 1899 as spoils of war. It was conquered by Japan during World War II and recaptured by the United States after three years of occupation.

- Location: western Pacific Ocean (between Japan and Papua-New Guinea)
- Capital: Agana
- Economy: tourism, refining, military base
- Government: home rule authorized by Congress
- Web site: www.gov.gu

NORTHERN MARIANAS

The first European to visit the Northern Mariana Islands was Ferdinand Magellan, in 1521, on his mission to circle the globe. The islands were colonized by Spain within 50 years and remained under Spanish rule until 1898, when they were ceded to Germany. After World War I they were transferred to Japan, and after World War II to the United States. Today, the U.S. government recognizes the commonwealth's own constitution, which generally binds the commonwealth to U.S. law; wage and tax policies, however, are autonomous.

- Location: western Pacific Ocean (north of Guam)
- Capital: Saipan
- Economy: coffee, fruit, livestock
- Government: elected governor and legislature; U.S. courts
- Web site: www.mariana-islands.gov.mp

PUERTO RICO

A Spanish colony from the early 16th century to the end of the 19th, Puerto Rico was taken by the United States as spoils of war and administered by the U.S. government until 1952. The island has had an independent government since then, but its people are U.S. citizens—and about 40% of the 6.6 million ethnic Puerto Ricans live on the U.S. mainland. A growing number of retired Americans spend the winter on the tropical island.

- Location: Caribbean Sea (east of the Dominican Republic)
- Capital: San Juan
- Cities: Bayamón, Ponce, Carolina, Caguas
- Economy: sugar, coffee, chemicals, refining, tourism
- Government: autonomous
- Web site: http://www.gobierno.pr

U.S. VIRGIN ISLANDS

Colonized by Denmark in the 17th century, the islands of St. Croix, St. John, and St. Thomas were purchased by the United States in 1917 and administered by the U.S. government until 1970.

- Location: Caribbean Sea (east of Puerto Rico)
- Capital: Charlotte Amalie
- Economy: refining, tourism, finance
- Government: elected governor and legislature; U.S. courts
- Web site: www.usvi.org

U.S. POSSESSIONS

The United States owns or controls a number of islands in the Pacific Ocean, most acquired as a result of World War II or the Spanish-American War of 1898. These islands are generally populated with indigenous people and U.S. military personnel, in small numbers, and are administered by the U.S. Department of the Interior or the Navy: Baker Island, Howland Island, Jarvis Island, Johnston Atoll, Kingman Reef, Midway Island, Palmyra Island, Peale Island, Wake Island, and Wilkes Island. The United States also controls Navassa Island in the Caribbean Sea.

POPULATION & DEMOGRAPHICS

In general, the coastal areas are more densely populated, more cosmopolitan, more liberal, and more socially diverse than the interior, and most new immigrants reside in coastal cities. According to the Center for Immigration Studies, 53% of the nation's immigrants live in or near one of these cities:

METROPOLITAN AREA	IMMIGRANTS	% IMMIGRANT
Los Angeles	4.71 million	30
New York	4.69 million	23
San Francisco	2.01 million	28
Miami	1.65 million	43
Chicago	1.07 million	12
Baltimore/Washington	.86 million	12

STATES RANKED BY POPULATION

State population figures here are rounded from figures in the *World Almanac & Book of Facts*. The second figure, also rounded from World Almanac data, is the population density—the average number of people per square mile. This figure is not to be taken literally; rather, it provides a rough idea of the level of urbanization. A high figure (compared to the national population density, 80) means a state is largely urban or suburban; a low figure represents lots of agricultural or open land.

	POPULATION in millions	DENSITY per square mile
CALIFORNIA	34.5	221
TEXAS	21.3	82
NEW YORK	19.0	402
FLORIDA	16.4	304
ILLINOIS	12.5	225
PENNSYLVANIA	12.3	274
OHIO	11.4	278
MICHIGAN	10.0	176
NEW JERSEY	8.5	1,144
GEORGIA	8.4	145
NORTH CAROLINA	8.2	168
VIRGINIA	7.2	182
MASSACHUSETTS	6.4	814
INDIANA	6.1	170
WASHINGTON	6.0	90
TENNESSEE	5.7	139
MISSOURI	5.6	82
WISCONSIN	5.4	100
MARYLAND	5.3	550
ARIZONA	5.3	47
MINNESOTA	5.0	63
LOUISIANA	4.5	103
ALABAMA	4.5	88
COLORADO	4.4	43

	POPULATION in millions	DENSITY per square mile
KENTUCKY	4.1	102
SOUTH CAROLINA	4.1	135
OREGON	3.5	36
OKLAHOMA	3.5	50
CONNECTICUT	3.4	707
IOWA	2.9	52
MISSISSIPPI	2.9	61
KANSAS	2.7	33
ARKANSAS	2.7	52
UTAH	2.3	28
NEVADA	2.1	19
NEW MEXICO	1.8	15
WEST VIRGINIA	1.8	75
NEBRASKA	1.7	22
IDAHO	1.3	16
MAINE	1.3	42
NEW HAMPSHIRE	1.3	137
HAWAII	1.2	191
RHODE ISLAND	1.1	1,013
MONTANA	0.9	6
DELAWARE	0.8	408
SOUTH DAKOTA	0.8	10
ALASKA	0.6	1
NORTH DAKOTA	0.6	9
VERMONT	0.6	7
WYOMING	0.5	5

	POPULATION in millions (M) in thousands (K)	DENSITY per square mile
PUERTO RICO	4 M	1,156
DISTRICT OF COLUMBIA	572 K	9,374
GUAM	161 K	766
U.S. VIRGIN ISLANDS	124 K	922
NORTHERN MARIANAS	77 K	432
AMERICAN SAMOA	69 K	892

WEATHER & CLIMATE

The continental United States is situated in a prevailing westerly weather pattern—weather fronts generally move from west to east. Some winter storms on the East Coast move north from the Gulf of Mexico, and hurricanes move west or north from the tropical Atlantic, but most other weather systems ride arctic winds from western Canada across the Great Plains and out to the Atlantic.

Weather forecasts on TV and radio news broadcasts are usually fairly dependable up to 48 hours in advance (though Americans love to complain when the forecasters get it wrong). Many weather reports on TV and in daily newspapers also provide a five-day forecast, but those are naturally less accurate. Newspapers list temperatures and weather conditions in dozens of major cities around the country and world, and if you're traveling, you can always use an internet search engine to find a local forecast for your destination.

You can also listen to a free **recorded weather forecast** for your city by phone—check the consumer information section of the local phone book—and most cable TV systems offer **The Weather Channel** with its round-the-clock weather reports. A free service available from www.weather.com sends you a message announcing any storm warnings or watches affecting your area. You can also get detailed weather information, including a huge library of current satellite images, from the **National Weather Service** at www.nws.noaa.gov.

THUNDERSTORMS & TORNADOES

Lightning and wind can damage power lines and, in an urban area, cut off electricity to tens of thousands of households at a time. If you come from an area where severe thunderstorms are uncommon, visit the "Extreme Weather Conditions" page at the **National Center for Environmental Health** web site, www.cdc.gov/nceh/hsb, for tips about storm safety. Thunderstorms can pop up anywhere. Though the most violent storms, **tornadoes** (twisters), are most common in the sparsely populated Plains region, they do occur in the Midwest, the South, and the Mid-Atlantic regions too. Tornadoes are far more common in the United States than anywhere else in the world, but fortunately, they tend to be small, localized storms—the chances of any given spot being hit by a tornado are quite low. That is, of course, no comfort to the people whose homes *do* get blown apart by winds that, according to survivors, roar like a freight train. **A severe storm watch** means conditions are right for the formation of storms marked by strong winds, cloud-to-ground lightning, hail (falling ice), and heavy rains. **A severe storm warning** means such storms have been detected by satellite or eyewitness reports and are moving toward the area specified. Likewise, a **tornado watch** means conditions are right for the formation of tornadoes; a **tornado warning** means a funnel cloud has actually been spotted and you should take cover immediately. A thunderstorm or rainstorm can also be accompanied by **flash floods**—sudden flooding of rivers, streams, or low-lying areas.

HURRICANES

Several of these huge windstorms strike the eastern United States each year, causing extensive damage from wind and flooding. Most hurricanes occur in late August or September, but they can form as early as June or as late as November. If you live near the Gulf of Mexico or the Atlantic Ocean, find out how local officials will notify and direct the public if the area must be evacuated due to severe weather. Fortunately, these storms form out at sea and move slowly enough to be detected several days before they reach land. Florida, Georgia, and the Carolinas can expect to be hit by one or two hurricanes a year; any coastal area from the Gulf Coast of Texas to the Delaware Bay will get hit occasionally.

Hurricanes are rated in intensity on a scale of 1 to 5, with a very rare Category 5 hurricane the most severe. A rotating storm that could develop into a hurricane is called a *tropical storm*. It is customary to **name** each tropical storm, for tracking purposes, and the **National Hurricane Center** in Florida issues a list of names in advance for each year's hurricane season. The first name on the list will begin with A, the second with B, and so on. For general information about hurricanes, visit www.nhc.coaa.gov.

EARTHQUAKES & LANDSLIDES

Geologists believe that a large part of California will eventually break away from North America and become an island. The **San Andreas Fault** runs from the Gulf of California (in Mexico) north to San Francisco, and cities along the fault line, including Los Angeles, are sometimes rattled by serious quakes; so are parts of Oregon, Washington, and Alaska. (Smaller quakes occur throughout the country, but they seldom cause much damage.) If you plan to live in California, ask a local real estate agent or insurance agent how to choose an earthquake-safe home—and study the safety pages in the **Newcomer's Handbook®** for San Francisco or Los Angeles. Low-lying areas near the coast of California, and near the great volcanoes in Washington and Oregon, are also vulnerable to **mudslides** and **avalanches** of rock and debris. In California, mudslides are caused by heavy rains after soil has been loosened by natural wildfires in the mountains, and by seismic activity; in the Northwest, volcanoes occasionally belch out a river of mud. Volcanic eruptions are rare in North America, but there are some cities and towns near active volcanoes.

FLOODING

Most homeowner's and renter's insurance plans do not cover damage due to floods. The federal government provides flood insurance through the National Flood Insurance Program to people who live near rivers and streams or in coastal areas where hurricanes or storm surges can cause flooding. For information about flood insurance and precautions, contact the **Federal Emergency Management Agency** at 800-480-2520 or www.fema.gov/nfip, or ask your insurance agent.

HEAT & COLD

If you are moving to a much warmer or colder climate than you're accustomed to, you will need to learn how to avoid **heat-related illness** (heatstroke) and **hypothermia**, both of which can be very dangerous. In extremely hot or cold weather, it's important to stay hydrated—drink lots of water and avoid alcohol and caffeine, which have a dehydrating effect. For more information, contact the National Center for Environmental Health at 888-232-6789 or visit the agency's "Extreme Weather Conditions" page at www.cdc.gov/nceh/hsb. Additional tips are available from SafeUSA at 888-252-7751 or http://safeusa.org. Also, ask your insurance agent how to prepare your home for the winter—in cold climates, you may need to take precautions to prevent plumbing lines from cracking.

TRAVEL

Even with tight security at the nation's airports, train stations, and bus terminals, it's easy to travel around the United States. Aside from showing ID when you purchase tickets (or pick up tickets that you purchase by phone or internet using a credit card), you don't need permission or travel papers. But remember, it's a big place—distances are great, and so is the cost of travel if you don't shop around carefully. Most travel arrangements cost less if you buy tickets at least a few weeks in advance, and it is often cheaper to travel in the middle of the week than on a weekend. Sometimes you can get a *companion fare*—a discount on a second ticket if you buy one ticket at full price—and there are usually **discounts** for children, seniors (age 65 or over), and students with a school ID.

Travel agents (listed in the Yellow Pages) help you find low fares and hotel rooms at no cost for their services—they earn a commission on the travel services they sell. However, as more people rely on the internet to find low airfares, airlines have been reducing or eliminating the commissions they pay travel agents; as a result, some agents won't handle just airfares, but will be happy to help you arrange a complete travel package that includes hotel accommodations, tours, and tickets to attractions in your destination city.

SECURITY

The federal Transportation Security Administration was created after the September 11 attacks to standardize and improve airport security. Many natural-born citizens as well as immigrants and tourists are asked a lot of personal questions at security checkpoints; all bags may be searched, and travelers may be asked to step into a privacy booth with an agent of the same gender and remove most of their clothing. This is not considered a violation of your constitutional right to freedom from unreasonable searches and seizures, because nobody is forced to

THREAT LEVELS

The Department of Homeland Security uses the following color-coded scale to describe its current assessment of the likelihood of a terrorist attack against the United States or U.S. citizens abroad:

- **Green.** There is a **low** risk of terrorist attack.
- **Blue.** Federal and local agencies are on **guarded** alert.
- **Yellow.** Federal and local agencies are on **elevated** alert due to a significant risk of terrorist attack. Critical sites may be under increased surveillance.
- **Orange.** Federal and local agencies are on **high** alert, usually due to specific and credible threats against U.S. assets or citizens. Some public events may be canceled. Access to some government facilities and other critical sites may be restricted. Transportation security measures are at maximum and may cause significant delays.
- **Red.** Federal and local agencies take **severe** protective measures due to actual or attempted terrorist activity. Public facilities, government offices, and transportation systems may be closed.

Changes in the threat level are reported in most news broadcasts and daily newspapers, and most government web sites indicate the current threat level. For more information, visit www.dhs.gov or the Department of Homeland Security's public information site for preparedness advice, www.ready.gov.

travel by air; by purchasing an airline ticket, you give consent to airport security measures. If your visa is in order and you are not trying to bring any dangerous items aboard, the inspection and interview should be just a formality. But allow plenty of time—try to arrive at the airport at least 1½ hours before a domestic flight and three hours before an international flight. **Warning**: at an airport, do not make any jokes about hijacking, explosives, weapons, or any other threats. Even before September 11, such behavior was taken very seriously.

Security is not as heavy at train and bus stations, but you still might have your bags searched and be asked to show your ID. Also, at least at big-city train stations, it is no longer permissible for friends and family to go onto a train platform to say hello or goodbye to passengers—there are gates beyond which only people with tickets are allowed.

AIRLINES

Domestic airfares vary by season, day of the week, fluctuating fuel costs, and the authorities' current assessment of the terrorist threat level. Prices even vary from one airport to another within a city—for example, flights to Chicago's Midway Airport might be cheaper than flights to Chicago's O'Hare—and a nonstop flight is usually more expensive than a flight where you land to take on passengers or even change planes. Most airlines have **frequent-flier** programs that allow you to earn points (called "miles") every time you buy a ticket or when you use certain credit cards or stay at certain hotels; when you save up enough miles, you can trade them in for a free plane ticket.

Web sites that claim to find you the best airfares—as well as hotel rooms, car rentals, and other travel services—include:

- **Expedia**, www.expedia.com
- **Orbitz**, www.orbitz.com
- **www.lowestfare.com**
- **www.hotwire.com**

You can also bid for airline tickets through **Priceline**, www.priceline.com—name your price, and within a few hours, you'll get an e-mail message telling you whether any airlines are willing to sell you a ticket at that price.

If you must travel unexpectedly to the funeral of a close relative, most airlines offer **bereavement fares** (discounts). These are not advertised—you have to ask—and the airline will, after a few weeks, check official records to verify that the person you name really died.

Most airlines sell tickets in three **classes**: *coach* (standard), *business class* (with more comfortable seating), and *first class* (with luxury seating and special services). On short flights to smaller towns, you might be flying on a small aircraft (a "puddle-jumper") with only one class of seating. After September 11, due to the decline in air travel, several major airlines went bankrupt and many others took drastic measures to cut costs—so, for example, some airlines no longer include meals in the price of a ticket on domestic flights.

RAIL

Newcomers from Europe will probably find the national passenger railway, **Amtrak**, to be expensive and slow. It is, however, a great way to see the country if you're not in a hurry, and it's a popular choice for business travel along the East Coast. The high-speed **Acela** trains between Washington, D.C. and Boston reach speeds of 150 miles per hour where track conditions permit, and the **Metroliner** trains provide express (limited stop) service between D.C. and New York City. For schedules, tickets, and other information, call 800-USA-RAIL (800-872-7245) or visit www.amtrak.com.

BUS

Intercity buses are the slowest way to get around the country, but by far the least expensive. The bus lines that run scheduled coaches nationwide are **Greyhound**, 800-231-2222 or www.greyhound.com, and **Peter Pan Trailways**, 800-343-9999 or www.peterpanbus.com. There are also many tour companies that offer bus trips to popular tourist destinations, sometimes as part of a guided tour package and sometimes just for transportation purposes. Ask a travel agent or look in the Yellow Pages under BUSES.

CAR

These national chains rent cars, minivans, and pickup trucks on a daily or weekly basis, one-way or round-trip. Of these, only Alamo and National will rent cars to drivers under 25 years old, and if you don't have a major credit card, forget it.*

---

* Before you pay extra for collision insurance from a rental company, find out whether you're automatically insured through your credit card institution or your existing auto insurance policy.

- **Alamo**, 800-327-9633, www.alamo.com
- **Avis**, 800-831-2847, www.avis.com
- **Budget**, 800-527-0700, www.budgetdc.com
- **Dollar**, 800-800-4000, www.dollar.com
- **Enterprise**, 800-736-8222, www.enterprise.com
- **Hertz**, 800-654-3131, www.hertz.com
- **National**, 800-227-7368, www.nationalcar.com
- **Thrifty**, 800-847-4389, www.thrifty.com

AUTO CLUBS AND BREAKDOWNS

If you're traveling a long distance in your own car, it's a good idea to join an auto club that provides emergency assistance if you have a mechanical problem or run out of gas in a remote area. The **American Automobile Association (AAA)**, usually called *Triple A,* offers these services plus general and personalized travel advice for motorists. It also rates repair shops, hotels, and other roadside amenities nationwide, and members are given discounts at many hotels and motels. To find the regional chapter nearest you, visit www.aaa.com or call directory assistance.* The **Auto Club of America** provides emergency road services (but fewer extra perks) and—unlike AAA—doesn't spend any membership dues on political lobbying. Call 800-411-2007 or visit www.autoclubofamerica.com. Also, many nationwide chains of **gas stations** (service stations) and some **insurance companies** offer their own road service plans.

HELP!

If you have a problem while traveling and you need help, most major airports and train stations have a **Travelers Aid** desk. For information, call 202-546-1127 or visit www.travelersaid.org. And before you go anywhere, register for free with the **International Association for Medical Assistance to Travelers**; as a member, if you have a medical problem while traveling, you can get low-cost treatment from any of the association's affiliated medical professionals worldwide. Call 716-754-4883 or visit www.iamat.org.

---

* If you look up AAA in the business White Pages, make sure you are dealing with the American Automobile Association. Many unrelated businesses choose names that begin with AAA—such as AAA Plumbing or AAA Lawn Care—in order to be listed first in alphabetical directories.

MOVING & STORAGE

If you're here for longer than a year or two, you might end up moving around within a metropolitan area or between different parts of the country. For local moves, you can often round up a few friends to help load and unload a rented **moving van**. For long-distance relocation, though, or if you have a lot of heavy furniture, you might need to hire professional **movers**—chosen carefully on the basis of reputation.

TRUCK RENTALS

If you plan to move your own belongings with the help of a few friends, you can simply rent a vehicle and head for the open road. Look in the Yellow Pages under TRUCK RENTAL or online at www.vanlines.com or www.unitedrentals.com, and then call around for quotes. (AAA members usually get a discount—see AUTO CLUBS above.) Even if you're dealing with a nationwide company, call the location nearest you. If you need a truck between May and September—peak moving season—be sure to reserve one at least a month in advance, especially for one-way rentals. In fact, if you make arrangements during the winter to move in the summer, you may be able to pay the cheaper winter rate.

Once you're on the road, keep in mind that your rental truck may be a tempting target for thieves. If you must park it overnight or for more than a couple of hours, try to find a well-lit place where you can keep an eye on it, and don't leave anything valuable in the cab.

Here are the major national van lines:

- **Budget**, 800-527-0700, www.budgetdc.com
- **Hertz**, 888-999-5500, www.hertztrucks.com
- **National**, 888-628-5826, www.nationalvanlines.com
- **Penske**, 800-222-0277, www.pensketruckleasing.com
- **Ryder**, 800-297-9337, www.ryder.com
- **U-Haul**, 800-468-4285, www.uhaul.com

If you just need a minivan or a small trailer, get quotes from a regular **car rental** company. If you don't want to hire movers *or* drive a truck, there's a third option: you can hire a commercial freight carrier to bring a truck or trailer to your house and then drive it to your destination after you load it. Contact **CF Moves U** at 800-419-7395, www.cfmovesu.com, or **ABF U-Pack Moving** at 800-355-1696, www.upack.com.

MOVERS

Start with the Yellow Pages and get references. For long-distance moves, the **American Moving & Storage Association** web site, www.moving.org, features a good directory; also check out the most recent *Consumer Reports* index at a public library or www.consumerreports.org to find any helpful articles or surveys.

Interstate movers are licensed by the **Federal Motor Carrier Safety Administration** (FMCSA). As the agency's safety chief testi-fied to Congress in 2001, "Consumers are well served by registered, legitimate, safe, and efficient household goods carriers. However, we receive letters and complaints from distraught consumers who have their household possessions held hostage for exorbitant, unexpected fees. ... [One] company's practice was to accept shipments under non-binding estimates and then, after the furniture and possessions were loaded on a truck and driven away, call customers and tell them the cost of delivery had increased, sometimes as much as 400%." If you check a company's record before you sign a contract, you can make sure you're among the customers "well served."

First, look for the federal motor carrier (MC) number on the company's advertising and promotional literature. Contact the FMCSA at 202-358-7028 or www.fmcsa.dot.gov to make sure the number matches the company's name, the license is current, and the com-pany is properly insured. As with any other big transaction, remem-ber the consumer protection resources listed in Chapter 7. Also, keep these tips in mind:

- Keep a record of the names of everyone you deal with at the moving company—the sales representative, the estimator, the driver, and the movers. And be nice to them. Tip the movers if they do a good job, and offer to buy them lunch while they load or unload.
- Before you move, take inventory of all of your posses-sions. Even though the movers will put numbered labels on everything, you should also make your own list of every item and the contents of every box. Take photos of anything valuable. *Don't sign anything* after the move until you've checked everything off the list at your desti-nation, and even then, keep the list until you're abso-lutely sure nothing was damaged. (A household inven-tory is a good thing to have anyway, for insurance purposes.)

- When you ask for an estimate, give accurate and thorough information. Mention any stairs, driveways, vegetation, long paths or sidewalks, or any other obstacles the movers will have to contend with. And be wary of any company that wants you to pay for an estimate. Ask for a "not to exceed" price—a guaranteed maximum. Some movers give *fixed price* quotes, but even a "fixed" price can be adjusted if the estimated weight is significantly wrong.

- Be ready for the truck on both ends of the trip—don't make the movers wait. It will cost you goodwill and money. On the other hand, understand your shipment can be delayed for reasons beyond the mover's control, such as bad weather or heavy traffic.

- Ask about insurance. The standard policy covers 60¢ per pound—not enough to replace most household goods. If you have homeowner's or renter's insurance, check to see whether it covers your belongings during transit. If not, you might want to buy *full replacement* or *full value* coverage from the moving company. If it's expensive, ask about a plan with a deductible of a few hundred dollars (a minimum amount of damages beneath which smaller damages aren't covered).

- Be prepared to pay the bill in cash upon delivery. This is an exception to the American preference for credit cards. You may be *required* to pay the movers in cash or with a cashier's check, money order, or traveler's checks in order to get your stuff off the truck.

Above all, ask questions; if you're concerned about something, ask for an explanation and get it in writing. And *listen* to your movers—they're professionals and can give you expert advice to make the job easier for everybody.

PACKING & ORGANIZING

Don't wait until the last minute to think about packing. You'll need plenty of boxes, tape, and packing material. Moving companies sell boxes, but most grocery stores or liquor stores will let you take some empty boxes. For foam "peanuts," bubble wrap, and other materials to protect fragile items, look in the Yellow Pages under PACKAGING

MATERIALS; if you have some especially fragile and valuable items, you might also want to look under PACKAGING SERVICE.

If you have a lot of stuff and don't know where to begin, call a moving consultant. These experts help you sort your belongings, get rid of unwanted items, unpack, arrange the furniture, and handle change-of-address paperwork. The **National Association of Professional Organizers** makes referrals at 202-362-6276 or www.napo.net.

STORAGE

Most communities have commercial storage facilities where you can rent a secure, climate-controlled *self-storage* locker—your own little warehouse—to keep items that don't fit in your home or that you only use occasionally. These can also be convenient places to store your belongings temporarily while you find a new home. Find a storage facility through **Storage Locator** at 800-301-8655 or www.storagelocator.com, or in the Yellow Pages under STORAGE - HOUSE-HOLD & COMMERCIAL. If you would like to arrange in advance for storage in your destination city, you can find most cities' Yellow Pages at a public library or online at www.bigyellow.com.

If you plan to open your storage locker only twice—the day you fill it and the day you empty it—then consider choosing a remote suburban location that will be cheaper than facilities closer to the heart of a city. If you need more frequent access to your locker, location will matter, and so will access fees. Also note that some storage facilities only allow daytime access. Others have gates that only open when a car or truck triggers a weight-sensitive lock, which can be a problem if you don't own a car. Ask about billing and security deposits, too, and don't be late with payments: if you fall behind, the storage company will *not* dump your stuff on your doorstep—they'll auction it off.

More convenient, and more expensive, than self-storage is *mobile* or *modular* storage. The company delivers a large container to your door, you load it, and the company hauls it away until you call for it. This can save you a lot of time and effort (it's one less round of unpacking and re-packing), but it's not good for easy access.

TAX DEDUCTIONS

If you move for work-related reasons, some or all of your moving expenses may be tax-deductible—so keep the receipts for those expenses.

Generally, you can deduct the cost of moving if your new job is at least 50 miles away from your current U.S. home and you work at the new site for at least 39 weeks during the first 12 months after you relocate. If you take the deduction and then fail to meet the requirements, you will have to pay the IRS back, unless you were laid off through no fault of your own or transferred again by your employer. You'll need to file IRS Form 3903 (available at www.irs.gov or a public library), and it's a good idea to consult a tax expert.

RELOCATION RESOURCES

These web sites feature moving tips and links to movers, real estate leads, and other relocation resources:

- **American Moving & Storage Association**, www.moving.org: referrals to interstate movers, local movers, storage companies, and packing and moving consultants
- **Employee benefits**, www.erc.org: If your employer is a member of this professional organization, you may have access to special services. Nonmembers can use the online database of real estate agents and related services.
- **First Books**, www.firstbooks.com: relocation resources and information on moving to dozens of cities, including detailed **Newcomer's Handbook®** guides (see pages 114 & 341).
- **HomeFair**, www.homefair.com: realty listings, moving tips, cost-of-living calculators, and more
- **www.moverquotes.com**: comparison shopping site for movers' fees
- **www.moving.com**: packing tips, movers' estimates, and more
- **U.S. Postal Service Relocation Guide**, www.usps.com/moversnet: includes a detailed checklist and tips to help you avoid common mistakes that can delay your mail after you move.

CHAPTER SIXTEEN

HEART & SOUL

> When you're weary and feeling small, when tears are in your eyes
> I'll dry them all; I'm on your side.
> When times get rough, and friends just can't be found,
> Like a bridge over troubled water I will lay me down.
>
> — *Simon & Garfunkel*

In a nation founded as a haven of religious freedom, a nation hospitable to atheists and fundamentalists and everyone in between, a nation whose name around the world is synonymous with wealth and greed, it is striking that a majority—perhaps most—of the American people freely give some of their time, their labor, and their money to the common good. We come from countless inspirations: the online magazine *Adherents.com* reports, quite simply, "the United States has a greater number of religious groups than any other country in the world." But whether the spirit that moves us is religious or secular, and whether we come from a background of wealth and privilege or one of work and struggle, most of us take time to do some volunteer work to benefit the community, the nation, or the world, and most of us give money—in proportion to our own—to help those less fortunate or to support the causes that stir our hearts.

RELIGION IN AMERICA

The Constitution sets forth a clear separation of church and state—there can never be an official national religion or any government favoritism toward one religion or another, and no person can be forced to practice any particular religion or, indeed, any religion at all. Many of the first European settlers came to North America to escape religious persecution—or, as colonial leader Roger Williams put it, "to proclaim a true and absolute soul freedom to all the people of the land impartially so that no person be forced to pray, nor pray otherwise than as his soul believeth and consenteth." We're serious about that.

Nevertheless, most of the nation's founders were people of faith. The motto "In God We Trust" appears on U.S. currency and coins; the President and other public officials take an oath of office ending with the words "So help me, God"; sessions of Congress open with a prayer; the federal government and the states recognize Christmas as a holiday; and in some parts of the country, religious leaders wield tremendous political power and cultural influence. In one of the most famous court cases in U.S. history, in 1925, Tennessee schoolteacher John Scopes was punished for teaching Darwin's theory of evolution, which the state had outlawed—but his trial was the beginning of the end of theocratic control of the public schools.

Faith is not always a conservative force in U.S. politics. It was Quaker pacifists who led the movement to abolish slavery, and Roman Catholics today lead the movement to abolish capital punishment. Theologian Matthew Fox makes a Christian argument for environmental protection, and Rabbi David Shneyer makes a Jewish one. Every list of social justice leaders in U.S. history starts with Martin Luther King Jr., the Baptist minister who led the civil rights movement, and in many urban neighborhoods today, the shelters and soup kitchens that comfort the poor are run by local congregations.

WORSHIP

According to a poll taken by CNN in 2000, 42% of American adults say they attend religious services at least once a week—and the same number say they seldom or never attend services. A poll taken six months later by the Gallup research firm found that roughly 60% of the American people claim to be members of a religious congregation and that more than half say religion is a "very important" part of their lives. These findings might seem to contradict each other, or to suggest that a lot of people simply skip their own religious observances, but the numbers also reflect the fact that Americans are often self-reliant about their faith. Many of us leave our hometowns to attend college and never live there again; many of us live far away from extended family, or even close relatives, and take an independent approach to all sorts of matters—including worship. Still, on the other hand, a sense of community and fellowship is one of the factors most often cited by those who do attend services regularly.

In general, people in the South and the Plains are more likely to go to church regularly—and, for that matter, to profess a Christian faith—than people in big cities. There are, however, plenty of devout Christians in the most cosmopolitan cities, and there's plenty of religious diversity too. Almost every religious and spiritual tradition found anywhere in the world is practiced in the United States. Most religious congregations welcome newcomers even if they are just curious and not committed to a particular faith—and attending a religious service or activity can be a good way to meet people in your new community.

FINDING A PLACE OF WORSHIP

If you belong to a congregation already, your religious leader might be able to refer you to a kindred congregation in your new city. And faith communities are no exception to the general principle of using the Yellow Pages to find local services: look under CHURCHES and SYNAGOGUES. (Mosques and other temples are usually listed under "churches.") The phone book listings are arranged by denomination and include sections for nondenominational, interdenominational, and independent churches, as well as metaphysical and spiritual science centers.

The **National Council of Churches**, 212-870-2227, www.nccusa.org, publishes the *Yearbook of American & Canadian Churches*, a directory listing thousands of Christian churches. Order one for $35 at 888-870-3325 or browse the directory links at www.electronicchurch.org. Other online directories of churches—generally limited to Christian denominations—include www.netministries.org, www.churches.net, and www.forministry.com. Synagogues serving all branches of Judaism are listed at www.jewish.com. And practically every religious group in the world can be contacted through links at **www.adherents.com**.

VOLUNTEERING

Unpaid volunteer work—secular and faith-based charity work and community service—is a common and important activity in the United States, and volunteering is perhaps the best way to meet friendly people in your new community. Most Americans do some kind of volunteer work at some point in their lives, and it is increasingly common for public schools to require some community service experience before a student graduates—in the hope that young people who do volunteer work will continue to do voluntary service throughout their lives. Some people volunteer just once a year; some do a day or an evening of volunteer work every week; some people, especially students and recent graduates, take a summer or a semester to do full-time community service; and some retired people have permanent unpaid jobs with agencies that benefit the community.

The U.S. government officially encourages volunteerism, and has done so ever since President John F. Kennedy created the Peace Corps. In 1988, George H.W. Bush made community service a major theme of his successful campaign for the presidency, describing the nation's volunteer corps as "a thousand points of light"; his successor, Bill Clinton, promoted federal volunteer programs such as AmeriCorps and VISTA (Volunteers In Service To America). It might be the only thing that practically all Americans agree on: Not only is the nation enriched and improved by volunteers, but so are the lives of the people who do volunteer work.

Most states and many local jurisdictions have a **volunteer bureau** that keeps a list of nonprofit organizations that need people to help, and many **places of worship** operate their own charitable programs and services. Also, these web sites help individuals find volunteer opportunities throughout the country:

- **Action Without Borders**, www.idealist.org
- **Points of Light Foundation/Volunteer Center National Network**, www.pointsoflight.org
- **United Way of America**, www.volunteersolutions.org
- **VolunteerMatch**, www.volunteermatch.org

You can also contact any nonprofit organization whose work interests you—most are eager to welcome new volunteers, and many have specific programs or projects that are almost entirely staffed by volunteers. Some organizations offer structured volunteer programs with training sessions and schedules; others are grateful when you walk in off the street and help sort donated books or clothing for an hour.

Here's just a sample of the kinds of organizations that welcome, and attract, volunteers:

- **Animal shelters** that need people to take care of abandoned pets
- **Arts organizations** such as symphonies and theater companies that rely on volunteers to raise money and sell tickets
- **Athletic and recreational programs**, especially for young people, that need coaches and officials
- **Blood banks** that collect donations of blood for surgical use

- **Children's programs** such as afterschool recreational centers, tutoring services, and day care
- **Civic associations** that organize neighborhood festivals, cleanup and beautification projects, and other neighborhood improvement efforts
- **Crime prevention** organizations such as neighborhood watch groups
- **Services for the disabled** such as volunteers who read to the blind or help with chores and errands
- **Disaster relief agencies** such as the American Red Cross that aid victims of storms, earthquakes, and floods
- **Disease foundations** that raise money for medical research (such as the American Cancer Society and the American Heart Association)
- **Environmental groups** that protect and monitor streams, plant trees, and educate the public about waste reduction and pollution
- **Fire departments**, rescue squads, and ambulance agencies that provide free services to the community
- **Food co-ops** that rely on donated labor to sell "food for people, not for profit"
- **Geriatric services** such as nursing homes and seniors' centers, where volunteers provide companionship and organize group activities
- **GLBT organizations** that help gay, lesbian, bisexual, and transgender people deal with bigotry and discrimination
- **Hospices** that provide care and counseling to the terminally ill and their families
- **Hospitals** that need help with administrative tasks
- **Housing organizations** such as Habitat for Humanity that build or repair homes for low-income families
- **Hunger & homelessness services** such as emergency shelters and relief kitchens
- **International services** that help immigrants get settled in the United States! (Contact USCIS for a list of agencies in your area: 800-870-3676 or www.uscis.gov.)
- **Job training programs** that teach useful skills to people who wish to enter or re-enter the job market

- **Literacy programs** to help illiterate or semi-literate adults learn functional reading skills
- **Meals on Wheels** services that deliver food to sick or injured people who cannot leave their homes
- **Medical and pharmaceutical research** trials that need volunteers with certain medical histories to be treated with experimental new drugs
- **Mentoring programs** in which a young person is paired with a working adult who serves as a role model and counselor
- **Museums**, nature centers, zoos, and historic sites that train volunteers to give tours
- **Parks** that need to be cleaned up and maintained
- **Peace organizations** that promote conflict resolution and international understanding
- **Public radio and TV stations** that need people to answer phones during fundraising campaigns
- **Political parties and advocacy groups** representing your beliefs, even if you can't vote
- **Schools** where parents and retired persons help out in the library, provide tutoring services, or raise money for extracurricular programs
- **Thrift stores** that sell used goods to raise money for charity
- **Women's services** that provide assistance to victims of domestic violence, rape, or unwanted pregnancy

In many communities, certain days of the year are set aside as community service days when local schools, parks, shelters for the homeless, and other nonprofit institutions get a hand from groups of volunteers who spend the day doing major work projects. For example:

- **Martin Luther King Jr. Day of Service.** The Corporation for National Service encourages people to observe the birthday of Dr. Martin Luther King Jr. (celebrated on the third Monday in January) by doing volunteer work in their communities. Call 202-606-5000 or visit www.mlkday.org.
- **National Rebuilding Day.** Formerly called Christmas in April, this is a day when volunteers make home

repairs for senior citizens and low-income households. Call 800-473-4229 or visit www.rebuildingtogether.org.

- **Earth Day.** There are volunteer environmental restoration projects in most communities on or around April 22. Visit www.earthday.net.
- **Make a Difference Day.** *USA Weekend* magazine and the Points of Light Foundation sponsor this nationwide mobilization of thousands of volunteers in hundreds of cities on the fourth Saturday in October. Call 800-416-3824 or visit http://usaweekend.com/diffday.

CHARITABLE GIVING

By some estimates, U.S. taxpayers give nearly $160 billion every year to charitable organizations—any of a wide variety of nonprofit organizations that provide social, civic, or educational services for the common good. While it's true that a lot of money is given to charity by wealthy philanthropists, the sort of people who can afford to build a new wing of a hospital or museum, most ordinary middle-class households make some contribution every year to a favorite cause or institution.

Donations to recognized charities are *tax deductible*, meaning the amount you donate (minus the value of any souvenirs you get in return) may be subtracted from your income tax obligation. A charity's tax-exempt status is a good indication of its legitimacy. (There are plenty of fraudulent charities that collect money and never really serve the community.)

You can get information about specific charities from:

- **Council of Better Business Bureaus Philanthropic Advisory Service**, 703-276-0100 or www.bbb.org/about/pas
- **The Foundation Center**, 202-331-1400, www.foundationcenter.org
- **National Center for Charitable Statistics**, 202-261-5801, http://nccs.urban.org
- **National Committee for Responsive Philanthropy**, 202-387-9177, www.ncrp.org

Some employers have a policy of supporting the same charities their employees support—if you donate money to a charitable organization, your employer might make a **matching** donation in the same amount. And some companies give employees paid time off to do volunteer work in the community. Also, during the annual **United Way Campaign** in the fall, employers invite employees to enroll in a voluntary program of automatic payroll deductions; if you join, you designate a certain amount of your pay to be given every month to a charity you specify. Or you can specify a *federation* of charities devoted to a particular group of people, a particular set of issues, or a geographic area.

One easy way to give is to choose a credit card or long distance phone service that gives a percentage of its receipts to charity—many large charities have their own **affinity cards** issued in partnership with financial institutions, and **Working Assets** provides credit cards, long distance service, and investment services that pay annual dividends to nonprofits selected each year by account holders. For details, contact Working Assets at 800-537-3777 (for credit cards) or 800-788-0898 (for long distance), or visit www.workingforchange.com.

Some charities organize *pledge events* such as footraces or cross-country bike rides. Participants ask their friends and co-workers to sponsor their entry by making a donation to the charity. These events are a major source of funding for medical research and programs to help people living with cancer, HIV, and degenerative (neurological) diseases. If you see ads for a local *AIDS Ride* or a *Race for the Cure* (to benefit breast cancer research), those are examples—and such events need administrative volunteers as well as participants and sponsors.

APPENDICES

USEFUL PHONE NUMBERS & WEB SITES

These are just a few of the most important agencies and services you might need soon after you arrive in the United States. Remember, phone numbers that begin with 800, 866, 877 or 888 are **toll-free** numbers that you can call from any phone without paying long distance charges. Also remember that when you are calling another area code, you need to dial a 1 before it. (If you use a wireless phone, you will be charged for airtime as usual under your service plan.) Phone numbers with other three-digit area codes may be subject to long distance charges. Remember, too, that phone numbers containing letters (such as 598-KIDS) refer to the letters grouped with each number on the telephone keypad: ABC = 2, DEF = 3, GHI = 4, JKL = 5, MNO = 6, PRS = 7, TUV = 8, WXY = 9.

EMERGENCY

Police, Fire, Ambulance, 911 in most places
Poison Control Center, 800-222-1222
Federal Emergency Management Agency, 800-525-0321,
www.fema.gov

CHILDREN & YOUTH - CRISIS COUNSELING

Child safety seat, 800-422-4453
Child Quest International Hotline, 800-248-8020
Covenant House Nineline, 800-999-9999, www.
covenanthouse.org
Focus Adolescent Services (referrals), 877-362-8727,
www.focusas.com
Girls & Boys Town Hotline, 800-448-3000, www.
boystown.org
National Center for Missing & Exploited Children, 800-
843-5678

CONSUMER PROTECTION

Better Business Bureau directory, www.bbb.org

Consumer Product Safety Commission, 800-638-2772,
www.cpsc.gov

Federal Communications Commission, 888-225-5322,
www.fcc.gov

Federal Consumer information Center, 800-688-9889,
www.pueblo.gsa.gov

Federal Trade Commission, 202-382-4357, www.ftc.gov

ScamBusters, www.scambusters.org

GOVERNMENT

Local: http://officialcitysites.org; www.citysearch.com

State: www.state. __ .us (insert state postal abbreviation—
see page 59)

Federal: www.firstgov.gov (agencies); www.findlaw.com (laws);
www.loc.gov/thomas (records)

U.S. House of Representatives, 202-224-3121,
www.house.gov

U.S. Senate, 202-224-3121, www.senate.gov

White House, 202-456-1111 (comment line); 202-456-1414
(general information), www.whitehouse.gov

HEALTH & MEDICAL CARE

U.S. Department of Health and Human Services, 800-
336-4797, www.hhs.gov

Medical referrals: general practitioners, 800-DOCTORS;
specialists, 800-776-2378; dentists, 800-DENTIST

HUMAN RIGHTS, DISCRIMINATION, AND FAIR LABOR STANDARDS

U.S. Department of Justice, Civil Rights Division, 202-
514-2000; 800-514-0301 (disability matters); 800-896-7743
(housing); www.doj.gov

Equal Employment Opportunities Commission, 202-663-
4900, www.eeoc.gov

Occupational Safety & Health Administration, 202-219-
8148, www.osha.gov

U.S. Department of Housing & Urban Development,
800-669-9777 (discrimination complaints); 800-569-4287
(field offices); www.hud.gov

U.S. Department of Labor, Wage & Hour Division, 888-
487-9243, www.wagehour.dol.gov

IMMIGRATION

U.S. Citizenship & Immigration Services (formerly INS), 800-870-3676, www.uscis.gov

Bureau of Customs & Border Protection at 202-354-1000 or www.cbp.gov

POLICE & HOMELAND SECURITY

Emergency, 911 (in most areas)

Non-emergency, 311 (in most areas)

Bureau of Alcohol, Tobacco, Firearms & Explosives, 202-927-7777 or 800-283-4867

Federal Bureau of Investigation, 202-324-3000, www.fbi.gov

Transportation Security Administraion, 866-289-9673, www.tsa.dot.gov

U.S. Coast Guard Search & Rescue, 800-418-7314

U.S. Department of Homeland Security, 800-237-3239, www.dhs.gov (general information), www.ready.gov (safety advice)

U.S. Marshals Service, 202-353-0600

U.S. Park Police, 202-619-7310

U.S. Secret Service Uniformed Division, 202-395-2020

POST OFFICE

U.S. Postal Service, 800-275-8777, www.usps.com

RELOCATION

Storage Locator, 800-301-8655 or www.storagelocator.com

American Moving & Storage Association, www.moving.org

Employee benefits, www.erc.org

First Books, 503-968-6777, www.firstbooks.com

U.S. Postal Service Relocation Guide, www.usps.com/moversnet

TAXES

Internal Revenue Service, 800-829-1040 (help) or 800-829-4477 (recorded information), www.irs.gov

TELEPHONE NUMBERS (DIRECTORY ASSISTANCE)

Local and long-distance numbers, 411
Toll-free numbers, 800-555-1212

TIME

Time of Day recording, 844-2525 (in most areas)
U.S. Naval Observatory Atomic Clock, 202-762-1401

TRAVEL

International Association for Medical Assistance to Travelers, 716-754-4883
Travelers Aid, 202-546-1127; www.travelersaid.org/ta/dc
MapQuest maps and traffic reports, www.mapquest.com
Federal Highway Administration, 202-366-4000, www.fhwa.dot.gov
National Highway Traffic Safety Administration, 888-327-4236, www.nhtsa.dot.gov

WEATHER

Local weather report, 936-1212 (in most areas)
National Weather Service online, www.nws.noaa.gov
National Center for Environmental Health (weather safety information), 888-232-6789, www.cdc.gov/nceh/hsb

ABBREVIATIONS

Americans love to abbreviate things. We're always in a hurry. You will read and hear many more abbreviations and acronyms than just these—including some that are specific to your city and region, and to your job or industry. These are just some of the abbreviations and acronyms that many Americans use in everyday speech and writing, without further explanation, expecting to be understood.

In addition, refer back to the topical lists of abbreviations in the preceding chapters:

ACADEMIC DEGREES	page 176
ADDRESSES & GEOGRAPHY	pages 59–61
CLOTHING SIZES	page 24
COMPUTER GAME RATINGS	page 73
COURTESY TITLES	page 200
EDUCATIONAL TESTING	pages 180–181
EMPLOYMENT LISTINGS	page 196
MEASUREMENTS	page 22
MOVIE/TV RATINGS	pages 72–73
REAL ESTATE LISTINGS	page 129
STATES & TERRITORIES	pages 59–60

A

A&E	Arts & Entertainment (cable TV channel)
A&M	agricultural and mechanical (education), a type of state-funded university
AA	Alcoholics Anonymous
AAA	American Automobile Association—also called "Triple A"
AARP	American Association of Retired Persons
AAUW	American Association of University Women
ABA	American Bar Association (legal profession)

ABC	American Broadcasting Company (network)
ABC	Alcoholic Beverage Control (common name for state agencies that regulate liquor stores and restaurant liquor licenses)
AC	alternating current
ACL	anterior cruciate ligament (anatomy)
ACLU	American Civil Liberties Union
ADA	Americans with Disabilities Act
A.D.	*anno Domini* (Latin)—*in the year of our Lord,* referring to the Gregorian calendar
ADD	Attention Deficit Disorder (a type of learning disability)
ADHD	Attention Deficit Hyperactivity Disorder (a type of learning disability)
ADR	alternative dispute resolution (law)
AED	automated external defibrillator (medicine)—first aid device for heart attacks; sometimes posted in airports, shopping malls, and other crowded facilities
AFB	Air Force Base
AFC	American Football Conference
AFGE	American Federation of Government Employees (union)
AFL-CIO	American Federation of Labor & Congress of Industrial Organizations (union)
AFSCME	American Federation of State, County & Municipal Employees (union)
AIDS	Acquired Immune Deficiency Syndrome (disease)
AM	amplitude modulation (radio frequencies)
AMA	American Medical Association
AMC	American Movie Classics (cable TV channel)
Amex	American Express (personal finance)
AMEX	American Stock Exchange (finance)
AP	Associated Press (media)

APR	annual percentage rate (interest on debts or deposits)
ASAP	as soon as possible
ASCAP	American Society of Composers, Artists & Performers
ASPCA	American Society for Prevention of Cruelty to Animals
assn.	association
assoc.	associates
AT&T	American Telephone & Telegraph (company)
ATA	Air Transport Association
ATF	Bureau of Alcohol, Tobacco, Firearms & Explosives
ATM	automated teller machine

B

B&B	bed & breakfast inn
b-to-b:	business-to-business—describes transactions that do not involve end users (consumers); also written "B2B"
BAC	blood alcohol content (a measure of intoxication)
BB	ball bearing
BBB	Better Business Bureau
BBQ	barbecue (type of cuisine)
B.C.	before Christ—meaning prior to the year 1 of the Gregorian calendar
bcc:	blind carbon copy (see *cc:*)
B.C.E.	before the common era (a culturally inclusive alternative to *B.C.*)
BCIS	Bureau of Citizenship & Immigration Services (archaic)—old U.S. immigration agency whose functions are now handled by U.S. Citizenship & Immigration Services
BGH	Bovine Growth Hormone (agriculture)
BID	Business Improvement District (tax jurisdiction)

BLM	Bureau of Land Management
BLS	Bureau of Labor Statistics
BLT	bacon, lettuce and tomato sandwich
BS	bullshit (slang, considered vulgar)—meaning *nonsense*
BSE	Bovine Spongiform Encephalopathy ("mad cow" disease)
BTW	by the way (internet shorthand)
BVD	a brand of undergarments; slang for men's undergarments

C

©	copyright
CB	citizens band (radio frequencies)
CBO	Congressional Budget Office
CBP	Bureau of Customs & Border Protection
CBS	Columbia Broadcasting System (network)
CC	closed captioned
cc:	carbon copy (correspondence)—archaic phrase meaning *send a copy to*
CD	certificate of deposit (banking)
CD	compact disc (technology)
CDC	Centers for Disease Control & Prevention
CD-ROM	compact disc, read-only memory (technology)
CDT	Central Daylight Time (time zone)
CEO	chief executive officer (corporate title)
CFO	chief financial officer (corporate title)
CIA	Central Intelligence Agency
CIA	Culinary Institute of America
CIO	chief information officer (corporate title)
CNN	Cable News Network (media)
Co.	company

Co.	county
COD	collect on delivery
COO	chief operating officer (corporate title)
cond.	condition (in classified ads)
CPA	certified public accountant (professional credential)
CPI	consumer price index
CPR	cardiopulmonary resuscitation (medicine)
CPU	central processing unit (technology)
CRT	cathode ray tube (technology)—archaic name for a computer monitor
C-SPAN	Cable-Satellite Public Affairs Network (TV/radio network)—broadcasts the proceedings of Congress and government press conferences
CST	Central Standard Time (time zone)
CYA	cover your ass (slang)—meaning *take measures to avoid being held solely responsible*
CYO	Catholic Youth Organization

D

DAR	Daughters of the American Revolution (club)
DAT	digital audiotape
DC	direct current
DDT	dichlorodiphenyltrichloroethane, a pesticide banned for use in the United States
DEA	Drug Enforcement Agency
Del.	Delegate (title of legislators in some states and of elected observers in Congress)
DEP	Department of Environmental Protection (common name for state agencies responsible for controlling pollution)
dept.	department
DHS	Department of Homeland Security

DMV	Department of Motor Vehicles (common name of state agencies that issue driver's licenses and vehicle registration papers)
DNA	deoxyribonucleic acid (biology), genetic material
DNC	Democratic National Committee (representative body of Democratic political party)
DNR	Department of Natural Resources (common name for state agencies responsible for parks and conservation)
DOD	Department of Defense
DOE	Department of Energy
DOJ	Department of Justice
DOL	Department of Labor
DOS	disk operating system (technology)
DOT	Department of Transportation
DPW	Department of Public Works (common name of local agencies that build and maintain civil infrastructure)
DSL	digital subscriber line (technology)
DVD	digital versatile disc (technology)

E

ed.	edition (after a book title), editor (after a person's name)
EDT	Eastern Daylight Time (time zone)
EEOC	Equal Employment Opportunity Commission
e.g.	*exempli gratia* (Latin phrase), meaning *for example*
El.	elevation (geography)
EMS	Eastern Mountain Sports (company)
EMS	emergency medical services
EMT	emergency medical technician (professional designation)
EOE	equal opportunity employer

EPA	Environmental Protection Agency
ER	emergency room (medicine)
ERA	earned run average (sports)—baseball statistic rating the pitcher
ERA	Equal Rights Amendment (history)—a proposed constitutional amendment to ban discrimination against women
ERISA	Employee Retirement Income Security Act, federal law regulating pension funds
ESL	English as a Second Language (educational program)
ESOL	English for Speakers of Other Languages (variation of ESL)
ESPN	sports TV network
EST	Eastern Standard Time (time zone)
est.	estimated
est.	established
ETA	estimated time of arrival
etc.	*et cetera* (Latin), meaning *and so on*
ex.	example
ex.	excellent (in classified ads)
ext.	extension (to a phone number)

F

FAA	Federal Aviation Administration
FAQ	frequently asked questions
FBI	Federal Bureau of Investigation (law enforcement)
FCC	Federal Communications Commission
FDA	Food & Drug Administration
FDIC	Federal Deposit Insurance Corporation (finance)
FEC	Federal Election Commission
FEMA	Federal Emergency Management Agency

FHA	Federal Housing Administration
FICA	Federal Insurance Contribution Act, federal law establishing Social Security program
FM	frequency modulation (radio frequencies)
FOB	free on board (shipping)
FTAA	Free Trade Agreement of the Americas
FTC	Federal Trade Commission
FTD	Florists Transworld Delivery (company)

G

G	grand, meaning thousand (slang)
GAO	General Accounting Office (government)
GATT	General Agreement on Tariffs & Trade
GB	gigabyte (technology)—in writing; *gig* in spoken slang
GDP	gross domestic product
GED	General Educational Development certificate (formerly General Equivalency Diploma)
GEICO	Government Employees Insurance Company
G.I.	government issue (slang, military) meaning a soldier
GI	gastrointestinal (medicine)
GIS	geographic information systems (technology)
GLBT	gay, lesbian, bisexual, transgender
GM	general manager (corporate title)
GM	General Motors (company name)
GMO	genetically modified organism
GMT	Greenwich Mean Time (geography, travel)
GNP	gross national product
GOP	Grand Old Party (political affiliation; alternate name of the Republican Party)
Gov.	Governor (title)
GP	general practitioner

GPA	grade point average (education)
GPO	Government Printing Office—official publisher of federal laws and reports
GPS	global positioning system (navigation)
GSA	General Services Administration (government)—federal agency in charge of government property

H

HBO	Home Box Office (TV network)
HDTV	high-definition television
HERE	Hotel & Restaurant Employees Union
HHS	Department of Health & Human Services
HI	Hostelling International
HIPAA	Health Insurance Portability and Accountability Act (legislation, health care)
HIV	Human Immunodeficiency Virus
HMO	health maintenance organization (health insurance)
Hon.	The Honorable (government title)
HPV	Human Papilloma Virus
HR	human resources
HTS	Home Team Sports (TV network)
HUD	Department of Housing & Urban Development
HVAC	heating, ventilation, air conditioning

I

I	interstate highway (I-95, I-70)
I-9	immigration status documents used to show eligibility to work
i.e.	*id est* (Latin), meaning *that is* or *in other words*
IADB	Inter-American Development Bank

IAFF	International Association of Firefighters (union)
IBM	International Business Machines (company)
IBO	International Baccalaureate Organization (education)
IBT	International Brotherhood of Teamsters (truck drivers' union)
ILGWU	International Ladies' Garment Workers Union
Inc.	incorporated
INS	Immigration & Naturalization Service (archaic)—old U.S. immigration agency whose functions are now handled by U.S. Citizenship & Immigration Services
IPO	initial public offering (finance)
IRA	individual retirement account (finance)
IRS	Internal Revenue Service
ISBN	International Standard Book Number
ISDN	integrated services digital network (technology)
ISO	International Standards Organization
ISP	internet service provider
IUD	intrauterine device (medicine)

J

JCC	Jewish Community Center
JCT	junction
JHS	junior high school
JROTC	Junior Reserve Officers Training Corps (military)

K

K	thousand (slang); also, kilobytes (technology)
K-12	kindergarten through grade 12 (education)
KKK	Ku Klux Klan, a racist hate group

L

L	lobby (level of a building)
L.A.	Los Angeles
LA	legislative assistant
LCD	liquid crystal display (technology)
LED	light-emitting diode (technology)
LL	lower level (basement, in a high-rise building)
LLC	limited liability company
LLP	limited liability partnership
LPGA	Ladies Professional Golf Association
LSD	lysergic acid diethylamide, an illegal hallucinogenic drug commonly called *acid*
Ltd.	limited partnership

M

M&M	a candy product and the company that makes it
MD	medical doctor
MDA	Muscular Dystrophy Association
MDMA	methylenedioxy-n-methylamphetamine, an illegal drug commonly called *ecstasy*
MDT	Mountain Daylight Time (time zone)
mgmt.	management
mgr.	manager
MIS	management information systems (business)
MIT	Massachusetts Institute of Technology (university)
MLB	Major League Baseball (sports league)
MLS	Major League Soccer (sports league)
MLS	Multiple Listing Service (real estate)—agents' directory of homes for sale

M/M	Mr./Ms. (correspondence; sometimes used when gender is unknown)
MO	*modus operandi* (Latin), legal phrase—literally, *method of operations*
MOU	memorandum of understanding
MP	Military Police
mpg	miles per gallon (fuel efficiency)
mph	miles per hour
MS	multiple sclerosis (disease)
MS	Microsoft (company name), abbreviated when preceding a product name (MS Word, MS Office)
MSA	metropolitan statistical area
MSN	Microsoft Network (internet service provider)
MSNBC	(media) a joint venture of Microsoft and NBC
MSRP	manufacturer's suggested retail price
MST	Mountain Standard Time
MTA	Metropolitan Transit Authority (common name for city agencies that administer public transportation)
MTV	Music Television (TV network)

N

NAA	Newspaper Association of America
NAACP	National Association for the Advancement of Colored People*
NAFTA	North American Free Trade Agreement
NASA	National Aeronautics & Space Administration
NASDAQ	National Association of Securities Dealers Automated Quotations (stock exchange)
NATO	North Atlantic Treaty Organization

---

* This organization was founded in 1909. The term *colored* is no longer used to describe racial minorities.

NBA	National Basketball Association
NBC	National Broadcasting Company (network)
NCAA	National Collegiate Athletic Association
NFL	National Football League
NGO	nongovernmental organization
NHL	National Hockey League
NIH	National Institutes of Health
NIMH	National Institute of Mental Health
NIOSH	National Institute of Occupational Safety & Health
NIST	National Institute of Standards & Technology
NL	National League (baseball)
NLRB	National Labor Relations Board
no.	number
NOAA	National Oceanic & Atmospheric Administration
NOW	National Organization for Women
NP	nurse practitioner (professional credential)
NP	National Park
NPS	National Park Service
NRA	National Rifle Association
NRC	Nuclear Regulatory Commission
NWF	National Wildlife Federation
NWS	National Weather Service
NYC	New York City
NYSE	New York Stock Exchange

O

OAS	Organization of American States
OB/GYN	obstetrician/gynecologist (medicine)
OBO	or best offer (in classified ads—invitation to negotiate price)

O.J.	orange juice
OK	okay
OMB	Office of Management & Budget (federal agency)
OR	operating room (medicine)
OPEC	Organization of Petroleum Exporting Countries
OSHA	Occupational Safety & Health Administration

P

PAC	political action committee
PBJ	peanut butter and jelly sandwich
PBS	Public Broadcasting Service (media)
PD	police department
PDT	Pacific Daylight Time (time zone)
PETA	People for the Ethical Treatment of Animals
PGA	Professional Golfers' Association
PH	penthouse
PI	private investigator
pkg.	package
p.m.	*post meridiem* (Latin)—*after the meridian* (morning), referring to the position of the Sun after noon
PMS	premenstrual syndrome (medicine)
PO	post office
pop.	population
POS	point of sale, point of service
POV	point of view
pp.	pages
PPD	purified protein derivative (medicine), a type of test for tuberculosis
PPO	preferred provider organization (health insurance)
PPV	pay-per-view (type of cable TV service)

PR	public relations
PRI	Public Radio International (media)
PS	public school
p.s.:	postscript (correspondence)
PST	Pacific Standard Time (time zone)
PTA	parents & teachers association

Q

Q&A	questions and answers
QA	quality assurance (business)

R

®	registered trademark
R&B	rhythm & blues music (forerunner of rock 'n' roll)
R&D	research and development (business, science)
R&R	rest and relaxation—military (and civilian slang) term for vacation
RBI	runs batted in (sports)—baseball statistic rating the batter
re:	regarding (correspondence)
REIT	real estate investment trust (finance)
RFP	request for proposals (business)
RFQ	request for quotes (business)—meaning *price estimates*
Rep.	Representative (title of members of the lower house of Congress and of state legislators in some states)
rm.	room
R.N.	registered nurse (professional credential)
RNC	Republican National Committee (representative body of Republican political party)
ROTC	Reserve Officers Training Corps

rpm	revolutions per minute
RR	railroad
rsvp	*répondez s'il vous plait* (French), a phrase requesting a reply to an invitation; literally, *respond if you please*
RTK	right to know (consumer protection)
Rx	prescription, pharmacy

S

S&P	Standard & Poor's (company)
S&P 500	stock market index compiled by Standard & Poor's
SARS	Severe Acute Respiratory Syndrome (disease)
SBA	Small Business Administration
SDI	Strategic Defense Initiative (missile defense program commonly known as "Star Wars")
SEC	Securities & Exchange Commission
SIDS	Sudden Infant Death Syndrome (disease)
SOL	shit out o' luck (slang, considered vulgar)—meaning "trapped in an unpleasant situation"
SSA	Social Security Administration
SSN	Social Security number
STD	sexually transmitted disease
SUV	sport utility vehicle
SVP	senior vice president (corporate title)
SWP	Socialist Workers Party (political affiliation)

T

TB	tuberculosis (disease)
TBS	Turner Broadcasting Service (TV network)
TCM	Turner Classic Movies (TV network)

TIAA-CREF	Teachers Insurance & Annuity Association / College Retirement Equities Fund
TLC	tender loving care (slang)
TM	trademark
TNT	Turner Network Television (TV network)
TNT	trinitrotoluene, an explosive
TQM	total quality management (business)
TRW	former name of Experian (company); slang for *credit rating*
TSA	Transportation Security Administration

U

U	university
UAW	United Auto Workers (union)
UCLA	University of California, Los Angeles
UFCW	United Food & Commercial Workers
UFO	unidentified flying object
UHF	ultra-high frequency (TV frequencies associated with broadcast channels 14-82)
UL	Underwriters Laboratories (product safety testing agency)
ULLICO	Union Labor Life Insurance Company
UMW	United Mine Workers (union)
U.N.	United Nations
UNESCO	United Nations Educational, Cultural & Scientific Organization
UNICEF	United Nations Children's Fund
UPI	United Press International (media)
UPN	United Paramount Network (media)
UPS	United Parcel Service (company)
U.S., USA	Used interchangeably in casual speech, but in formal speech and in writing, the abbreviation *U.S.* is

	used only as an adjective; the noun is abbreviated *USA*.
USAF	U.S. Air Force
USCG	U.S. Coast Guard
USCIS	U.S. Citizenship & Immigration Service
USDA	U.S. Department of Agriculture
USFWS	U.S. Fish & Wildlife Service
USGS	U.S. Geological Survey
USMC	U.S. Marine Corps
USO	United Service Organizations (charity serving military personnel)
USOC	U.S. Olympic Committee
USPS	U.S. Postal Service
USS	U.S. Ship

V

v	version (technology), in reference to software
v.	*versus* (Latin), meaning *against*—variation used in reference to court cases
VA	Department of Veterans Affairs (formerly *Veterans Administration*)
VCR	videocassette recorder
VFD	volunteer fire department
VFW	Veterans of Foreign Wars
VHF	very high frequency (TV frequencies associated with broadcast channels 2-13)
VHS	a standard home videocassette format
VISTA	Volunteers In Service To America
VOA	Voice of America (media)
vs.	*versus* (Latin), meaning *against*—variation used in reference to sports and games
VP	Vice President

W

W-2	tax form reporting wages withheld to pay income taxes
WB	Warner Brothers (network, media)
WD-40	standard grade of machine oil
WIC	Women, Infants & Children (federal food program to assist needy families)
WNBA	Women's National Basketball Association
WNFA	Women's National Football Association
WWF	World Wildlife Foundation
WWF	World Wrestling Federation

X

Xing	crossing
XM	trade name of a satellite radio network
XO	hugs and kisses (correspondence)

Y

Y	"the Y"—slang for YMCA/YWCA
YMCA	Young Men's Christian Association, a community service organization/facility
YWCA	Young Women's Christian Association, a community service organization/facility

NUMBERS

10-4	OK, acknowledged (slang), based on CB radio code
1040	standard form of personal income tax return
10W40	standard grade of motor oil

24/7	24 hours a day, seven days a week
401(k)	type of retirement savings account (slang), based on the section of tax law authorizing it
411	information (slang), based on the phone number for directory assistance
5-O	police (slang), based on CB radio code
501(c)3	charity or educational tax-exempt nonprofit organization, based on the section of tax law authorizing it
990	tax form reporting fees paid to self-employed contractors

THE NATION IN ITS OWN WORDS

THE DECLARATION OF INDEPENDENCE
OF THE THIRTEEN COLONIES IN CONGRESS, JULY 4, 1776

The unanimous Declaration of the thirteen united States of America,

When in the Course of human events, it becomes necessary for one people to dissolve the political bands which have connected them with another, and to assume among the powers of the earth, the separate and equal station to which the Laws of Nature and of Nature's God entitle them, a decent respect to the opinions of mankind requires that they should declare the causes which impel them to the separation.

We hold these truths to be self-evident, that all men are created equal, that they are endowed by their Creator with certain unalienable Rights, that among these are Life, Liberty and the pursuit of Happiness. —That to secure these rights, Governments are instituted among Men, deriving their just powers from the consent of the governed, —That whenever any Form of Government becomes destructive of these ends, it is the Right of the People to alter or to abolish it, and to institute new Government, laying its foundation on such principles and organizing its powers in such form, as to them shall seem most likely to effect their Safety and Happiness. Prudence, indeed, will dictate that Governments long established should not be changed for light and transient causes; and accordingly all experience hath shewn, that mankind are more disposed to suffer, while

• • • • • • • • • • • • • •

**THE DECLARATION OF
INDEPENDENCE**

The North American colonies of Great Britain were the first colonies ever in history to win independence from their sovereign nation. Though the United States, ironically, suppressed a secessionist rebellion 85 years later and hasn't always lived up to its promises of equality, the Declaration of Independence is much more than an assertion of the people's right to overthrow an oppressive regime; it is a timeless statement of the very purpose of government. It was written mainly by Thomas Jefferson along with John Adams, Benjamin Franklin, Roger Sherman, and Robert Livingston.

• • • • • • • • • • • • • • • •

evils are sufferable, than to right themselves by abolishing the forms to which they are accustomed. But when a long train of abuses and usurpations, pursuing invariably the same Object evinces a design to reduce them under absolute Despotism, it is their right, it is their duty, to throw off such Government, and to provide new Guards for their future security. —Such has been the patient sufferance of these Colonies; and such is now the necessity which constrains them to alter their former Systems of Government. The history of the present King of Great Britain [George III] is a history of repeated injuries and usurpations, all having in direct object the establishment of an absolute Tyranny over these States. To prove this, let Facts be submitted to a candid world.

He has refused his Assent to Laws, the most wholesome and necessary for the public good.

He has forbidden his Governors to pass Laws of immediate and pressing importance, unless suspended in their operation till his Assent should be obtained; and when so suspended, he has utterly neglected to attend to them.

He has refused to pass other Laws for the accommodation of large districts of people, unless those people would relinquish the right of Representation in the Legislature, a right inestimable to them and formidable to tyrants only.

He has called together legislative bodies at places unusual, uncomfortable, and distant from the depository of their public Records, for the sole purpose of fatiguing them into compliance with his measures.

He has dissolved Representative Houses repeatedly, for opposing with manly firmness his invasions on the rights of the people.

He has refused for a long time, after such dissolutions, to cause others to be elected; whereby the Legislative powers, incapable of Annihilation, have returned to the People at large for their exercise; the State remaining in the mean time exposed to all the dangers of invasion from without, and convulsions within.

He has endeavoured to prevent the population of these States; for that purpose obstructing the Laws for Naturalization of Foreigners; refusing to pass others to encourage their migrations hither, and raising the conditions of new Appropriations of Lands.

He has obstructed the Administration of Justice, by refusing his Assent to Laws for establishing Judiciary powers.

He has made Judges dependent on his Will alone, for the tenure of their offices, and the amount and payment of their salaries.

He has erected a multitude of New Offices, and sent hither swarms of Officers to harass our people, and eat out their substance.

He has kept among us, in times of peace, Standing Armies without the consent of our legislatures.

He has affected to render the Military independent of and superior to the Civil power.

He has combined with others to subject us to a jurisdiction foreign to our constitution and unacknowledged by our laws; giving his Assent to their Acts of pretended Legislation:

For Quartering large bodies of armed troops among us:

For protecting them, by a mock Trial, from punishment for any Murders which they should commit on the Inhabitants of these States:

For cutting off our Trade with all parts of the world:

For imposing Taxes on us without our Consent:

For depriving us, in many cases, of the benefits of Trial by Jury:

For transporting us beyond Seas to be tried for pretended offences:

For abolishing the free System of English Laws in a neighbouring Province, establishing therein an Arbitrary government, and enlarging its Boundaries so as to render it at once an example and fit instrument for introducing the same absolute rule into these Colonies:

For taking away our Charters, abolishing our most valuable Laws, and altering fundamentally the Forms of our Governments:

For suspending our own Legislatures, and declaring themselves invested with power to legislate for us in all cases whatsoever.

He has abdicated Government here, by declaring us out of his Protection and waging War against us.

He has plundered our seas, ravaged our Coasts, burnt our towns, and destroyed the lives of our people.

He is at this time transporting large Armies of foreign Mercenaries to compleat the works of death, desolation and tyranny, already begun with circumstances of Cruelty and perfidy scarcely paralleled in the most barbarous ages, and totally unworthy the Head of a civilized nation.

He has constrained our fellow Citizens taken Captive on the high Seas to bear Arms against their Country, to become the executioners of their friends and Brethren, or to fall themselves by their Hands.

He has excited domestic insurrections amongst us, and has endeavoured to bring on the inhabitants of our frontiers, the merciless Indian Savages, whose known rule of warfare, is an undistinguished destruction of all ages, sexes and conditions.

In every stage of these Oppressions We have Petitioned for Redress in the most humble terms: Our repeated Petitions have been answered only by repeated injury. A Prince whose character is thus marked by every act which may define a Tyrant, is unfit to be the ruler of a free people.

Nor have We been wanting in attentions to our British brethren. We have warned them from time to time of attempts by their legislature to extend an unwarrantable jurisdiction over us. We have reminded them of the circumstances of our emigration and settlement here. We have appealed to their native justice and magnanimity, and we have conjured them by the ties of our common kindred to disavow these usurpations, which, would inevitably interrupt our connections and correspondence. They too have been deaf to the voice of justice and of consanguinity. We must, therefore, acquiesce in the necessity, which denounces our Separation, and hold them, as we hold the rest of mankind, Enemies in War, in Peace Friends.

We, therefore, the Representatives of the united States of America, in General Congress, Assembled, appealing to the Supreme Judge of the world for the rectitude of our intentions, do, in the Name, and by the Authority of the good People of these Colonies, solemnly publish and declare, That these United Colonies are, and of Right ought to be Free and Independent States; that they are Absolved from all Allegiance to the British Crown, and that all political connection between them and the State of Great Britain, is and ought to be totally dissolved; and that as Free and Independent States, they have full Power to levy War, conclude Peace, contract Alliances, establish Commerce, and to do all other Acts and Things which Independent States may of right do. And for the support of this Declaration, with a firm reliance on the protection of divine Providence, we mutually pledge to each other our Lives, our Fortunes and our sacred Honor.

THE BILL OF RIGHTS

AMENDMENT I

Congress shall make no law respecting an establishment of religion, or prohibiting the free exercise thereof; or abridging the freedom of speech, or of the press; or the right of the people peaceably to assemble, and to petition the Government for a redress of grievances.

AMENDMENT II

A well regulated Militia, being necessary to the security of a free State, the right of the people to keep and bear Arms, shall not be infringed.

AMENDMENT III

No Soldier shall, in time of peace be quartered in any house, without the consent of the Owner, nor in time of war, but in a manner to be prescribed by law.

AMENDMENT IV

The right of the people to be secure in their persons, houses, papers, and effects, against unreasonable searches and seizures, shall not be violated, and no Warrants shall issue, but upon probable cause, supported by Oath or affirmation, and particularly describing the place to be searched, and the persons or things to be seized.

AMENDMENT V

No person shall be held to answer for a capital, or otherwise infamous crime, unless on a presentment or indictment of a Grand jury, except in cases arising in the land or naval forces, or in the Militia, when in actual service in time of War or public danger; nor shall any person be

THE BILL OF RIGHTS

The U.S. Constitution provides the structure of the national government and lists the powers and duties of the President, the legislature, and the courts. The Constitution can be amended with the approval of 3/4 of the states, and indeed it has been amended 26 times. Ratified December 15, 1791, the first 10 amendments are collectively known as the Bill of Rights, the most fundamental expression of civil liberties guaranteed to every person in the United States—citizens, resident aliens, and visitors alike. The group of early U.S. leaders who created the Bill of Rights was led by George Mason of Virginia.

subject for the same offence to be twice put in jeopardy of life or limb; nor shall be compelled in any criminal case to be a witness against himself, nor be deprived of life, liberty, or property, without due process of law; nor shall private property be taken for public use, without just compensation.

AMENDMENT VI

In all criminal prosecutions, the accused shall enjoy the right to a speedy and public trial, by an impartial jury of the State and district wherein the crime shall have been committed, which district shall have been previously ascertained by law, and to be informed of the nature and cause of the accusation; to be confronted with the witnesses against him; to have compulsory process for obtaining witnesses in his favor, and to have the Assistance of Counsel for his defence.

AMENDMENT VII

In Suits at common law, where the value in controversy shall exceed twenty dollars, the right of trial by jury shall be preserved, and no fact tried by a jury, shall be otherwise re-examined in any Court of the United States, than according to the rules of the common law.

AMENDMENT VIII

Excessive bail shall not be required, nor excessive fines imposed, nor cruel and unusual punishments inflicted.

AMENDMENT IX

The enumeration in the Constitution, of certain rights, shall not be construed to deny or disparage others retained by the people.

AMENDMENT X

The powers not delegated to the United States by the Constitution, nor prohibited by it to the States, are reserved to the States respectively, or to the people.

THE NATIONAL ANTHEM

O say, can you see, by the dawn's early light
What so proudly we hailed at the twilight's last gleaming —
Whose broad stripes and bright stars, through the perilous fight,
O'er the ramparts we watched, were so gallantly streaming?
And the rockets' red glare, the bombs bursting in air,
Gave proof through the night that our flag was still there...
O say does that star-spangled banner yet wave
O'er the land of the free and the home of the brave?

• •

THE NATIONAL ANTHEM

The first verse of "The Star-Spangled Banner," a poem by Francis Scott Key set to the tune of an old British drinking song, is often sung before sporting events and played when a TV station signs off the air at night. It recalls events witnessed by Key during a British naval attack on Baltimore in 1812.

• •

THE PLEDGE OF ALLEGIANCE

I pledge allegiance to the flag of the United States of America and to the republic for which it stands—one nation under God, indivisible, with liberty and justice for all.

THE PLEDGE OF ALLEGIANCE

These words are recited by U.S. citizens when saluting the national flag—for example, at the beginning of a school day.

THE GETTYSBURG ADDRESS

GETTYSBURG, PENNSYLVANIA
NOVEMBER 19, 1863

Four score and seven years ago our fathers brought forth on this continent, a new nation, conceived in Liberty, and dedicated to the proposition that all men are created equal.

• • • • • • • • • • • • • • • •

THE GETTYSBURG ADDRESS

President Abraham Lincoln was mistaken when he said "the world will little note nor long remember" his brief remarks at the dedication of the military cemetery at Gettysburg, Pennsylvania, after the pivotal battle of the American Civil War. His speech was not only to consecrate the resting place of the fallen soldiers, but to express and reaffirm the *purpose* of the United States.

• • • • • • • • • • • • • • • •

Now we are engaged in a great civil war, testing whether that nation, or any nation so conceived and so dedicated, can long endure. We are met on a great battle-field of that war. We have come to dedicate a portion of that field, as a final resting place for those who here gave their lives that that nation might live. It is altogether fitting and proper that we should do this.

But, in a larger sense, we can not dedicate — we can not consecrate — we can not hallow — this ground. The brave men, living and dead, who struggled here, have consecrated it, far above our poor power to add or detract. The world will little note, nor long remember what we say here, but it can never forget what they did here. It is for us the living, rather, to be dedicated here to the unfinished work which they who fought here have thus far so nobly advanced. It is rather for us to be here dedicated to the great task remaining before us — that from these honored dead we take increased devotion to that cause for which they gave the last full measure of devotion — that we here highly resolve that these dead shall not have died in vain — that this nation, under God, shall have a new birth of freedom — and that government of the people, by the people, for the people, shall not perish from the earth.

Price 27, 45, 55, 57, 70, 75, 85-87, 94-101, 104, 107, 111, 113, 117, 118, 136, 141-143, 145, 186, 202, 208, 226, 274, 276, 277, 281, 303, 310, 311, 313,
Primary school 161, 162, 168, 169, 172
Prison 9, 19, 71, 82, 88, 90, 257
Privacy 197, 198, 275
Private school 3, 160, 163-165, 167-169, 173, 175, 179
Probation 90, 185, 196
Property 3, 12, 37, 46, 70, 75, 81, 86, 88, 92, 115, 125, 127-129, 134-137, 140-143, 145, 146, 168, 171, 182, 307, 324
Prosecution 90, 324
Prosecutor 89, 90
Prostitution 72, 260
PTA 132, 167, 313
Public radio 63, 289, 313
Public school 3, 12, 46, 65, 160-164, 168, 170, 172, 173, 175, 221, 245, 285, 286, 313
Public service commission 50, 145
Public transportation 2, 4, 29, 70, 113, 118, 121, 123, 128, 130, 175, 186, 310

R

Radio 47, 62-64, 72, 79, 133, 254, 272, 289, 300, 302, 303, 306, 313, 317, 318
Radon 108, 130, 131
Ramadan 221
Rape see also Sexual assault 81, 82, 198, 289
Rating 38, 40, 41, 43, 72, 73, 103, 109, 122, 299, 305, 313, 315
Real estate 20, 93, 100, 115, 116, 125, 127-129, 135, 137, 142-144, 163, 273, 283, 299, 309, 313
Realtor 125, 128
Recall 87, 104, 109, 112
Recreation department 116, 175
Recycling 3, 46, 83, 109, 136, 146
Red Cross 153, 159, 288
Reference books 4, 209
References 24, 86, 134, 186, 196, 280
Refugees 14, 152, 188
Region 47, 100, 101, 126, 165, 174, 197, 235-237, 241, 242, 244, 248-251, 255, 258, 259, 264, 272, 299
Registration 14, 74, 75, 79, 104, 304
Regulation 17, 19, 74, 107, 119, 120, 137, 189

Religion 1, 4, 9, 10, 12, 135, 152, 173, 188, 197, 211, 284, 285, 323
Religious 7, 9, 14, 43, 69, 74, 99, 119, 120, 160, 168, 173, 175, 179, 198, 201, 204-206, 210, 211, 213-215, 218, 225, 240, 251, 262, 284-286
Religious school 164
Relocation 40, 44, 125, 128, 144, 187, 279, 283, 297
Rent 31, 40, 62, 65, 72, 84, 118, 125-127, 129, 131, 135-142, 277, 279, 282
Rental application 134, 139
Renter's insurance 136, 140, 141, 274, 281
Repair(s) 4, 42, 43, 51, 75, 86, 87, 94, 95, 103, 104, 112, 118, 126, 136, 137, 142, 288, 290
Representative 15, 36, 50, 177, 181, 189, 196, 208, 266, 280, 304, 313, 320, 322
Republican Party 17, 306
Research 108, 120, 125, 148, 149, 155, 170, 172, 177-179, 183, 191, 200, 248, 249, 251, 285, 288, 289, 291, 313
Restaurant 10, 34, 40, 42, 45, 47, 49, 54, 62, 67, 68, 70, 71, 91, 94, 97, 98, 104, 106, 107, 114, 115, 121, 122, 187, 190, 198, 201, 202, 211, 212, 217, 300, 307
Restroom 68, 69, 167
Résumé 186, 196
Retirement 4, 35, 36, 38, 186, 187, 246, 258, 259, 305, 315, 318
Ride-sharing see Carpooling
Rights 12, 15, 18, 31, 39, 74, 82, 88, 89, 93, 139, 140, 153, 188, 192, 214, 219, 244, 245, 247, 266, 285, 296, 305, 319, 320, 323, 324
Rites of passage 205, 206
Roads 46, 58, 60, 61, 74, 76, 78-80, 113, 127, 259, 278, 279
Robbery 81-83, 191
Rowhouses see Townhouses
Rush hour 26

S

Safe deposit box 84
Safety 17, 70, 75-80, 83, 87, 102, 104, 105, 107, 109-112, 118, 119, 131, 133, 137, 175, 191, 192, 272, 273, 280, 296-298, 311, 312, 315, 319
Salary 27, 28, 43, 100, 150, 185, 187, 192, 196, 320

ABOUT THE AUTHOR

MIKE LIVINGSTON is a freelance editor and writer whose clients include the Citizen Policies Institute, Conservation International, *Legal Times,* Nonprofit Watch, the Points of Light Foundation, *Roll Call,* and the *Washington Business Journal.* He was born in Washington, D.C. and currently lives in Takoma Park, Maryland. He is the lead author of the *Newcomer's Handbook® for Washington, D.C.,* 3rd edition, published by First Books in 2002. Mike was the Green Party candidate for D.C.'s "shadow" seat in Congress in 1998. He remains active in Green politics and is also an emergency medical technician and CPR instructor with the Takoma Park Volunteer Fire Department. He graduated from Guilford College in 1993 with a B.A. in political science and peace studies.

The author gratefully acknowledges the insights, research, and perspectives shared by: Luanne Arangio, Matt Bivens, Dave Bosserman, Olivia Cadaval, Kathy Caisse, Tara Campbell, Max Carter, Michèle Colburn, Tile von Damm, Vernie Davis, Susan Doran, Wendy Dunham, Bernadette Duperron, Calluna Euving, JoAnn Giovannoni, Annie Goeke, Francisco Gónima, Jose Gonzalez, Rob Greenway, Nika Greger, Peter Hollin, Tom Horne, Victoria Kao, Lorin Kleinman, Gabriela Kohout, Virginia Linnman, Heather Pankl, Monika Puglielli, Felipe Ramirez, Pat Shen, Tes Slominski, Louis Solomon, Deborah Stadtler, the Fourth World Movement USA, Heinrich Böll Foundation, Hostelling International, Portal World Travel, Volunteers for Peace International, and especially the late George LaRoche.

We would appreciate your comments regarding the *Newcomer's Handbook for Moving to and Living in the USA*. If you've found any mistakes or omissions, or if you would just like to express your opinion about the guide, please let us know. We will consider any suggestions for possible inclusion in our next edition and if we use your comments, we'll send you a free copy of our next edition. Please send this response form to:

> First Books
> 6750 SW Franklin St.
> Portland, OR 97223-2542
> USA
> Fax: (503) 968-6779

Comments:

_____

_____

_____

_____

_____

_____

Name _____

Address _____

_____

_____

Telephone _____

E-mail _____

6750 SW Franklin St
Suite A
Portland, OR 97223-2542
USA
503-968-6777
www.firstbooks.com

FIRST BOOKS

THE ORIGINAL, ALWAYS UPDATED, ABSOLUTELY INVALUABLE GUIDES FOR PEOPLE MOVING TO A CITY!

Find out about neighborhoods, apartment and house hunting, money matters, deposits/leases, getting settled, helpful services, shopping for the home, places of worship, cultural life, sports/recreation, volunteering, green space, schools and education, transportation, temporary lodgings, and useful telephone numbers!

	# COPIES	TOTAL
The Immigration Handbook	_____ x $21.95	$_____
Newcomer's Handbook® for Atlanta	_____ x $17.95	$_____
Newcomer's Handbook® for Boston	_____ x $23.95	$_____
Newcomer's Handbook® for Chicago	_____ x $21.95	$_____
Newcomer's Handbook® for London	_____ x $20.95	$_____
Newcomer's Handbook® for Los Angeles	_____ x $17.95	$_____
Newcomer's Handbook® for Minneapolis-St. Paul	_____ x $20.95	$_____
Newcomer's Handbook® for New York City	_____ x $22.95	$_____
Newcomer's Handbook® for San Francisco	_____ x $20.95	$_____
Newcomer's Handbook® for Seattle	_____ x $21.95	$_____
Newcomer's Handbook® for Washington D.C.	_____ x $21.95	$_____
Newcomer's Handbook® for the USA	_____ x $23.95	$_____

SUBTOTAL $_____

US POSTAGE AND HANDLING *($7.00 first book, $1.00 each add'l.)* $_____

TOTAL $_____

SHIP TO:

Name _____

Title _____

Company _____

Address _____

City _____ State _____ Zip/Postal Code _____

Country _____

Phone _____

Send this order form and a check or money order payable to:
First Books
6750 SW Franklin St., Suite A
Portland, OR 97223-2542
USA
P: 503.968.6777   F: 503.968.6779
Allow 1-2 weeks for delivery